AUBREY DE VERE

VICTORIAN OBSERVER

Aubrey de Vere at Twenty

Aubrey de Vere : Victorian

Observer

S. M. Paraclita Reilly, C.S.J.

UNIVERSITY OF NEBRASKA PRESS

TO

M.J.F.

_____

CONTENTS

(continued)

(contents continued)

ACKNOWLEDGMENTS

For permission to reprint, acknowledgment is made to the following publishers:

George Allen & Unwin, Ltd., London, England, for 12 lines from E. T. Cook's *Life of Ruskin;*

The Bruce Publishing Company, Milwaukee, Wis., for short quotation from Calvert Alexander, S.J.'s *The Catholic Revival;*

Cambridge University Press, New York, N.Y., for various short passages from Hugh Walker's *The Literature of the Victorian Era;*

The Clarendon Press, Oxford, England, for a few lines from Garrod's *Wordsworth: Lectures and Essays;*

Cornell University Press, Ithaca, N.Y., for material from *Sara Coleridge and Henry Reed* (ed. Leslie Nathan Broughton), and *Wordsworth and Reed* (ed. Broughton) ;

Doubleday & Company, New York, N.Y., for 160 words from *The Great Victorians,* by H. J. & Hugh Massingham;

E. P. Dutton, New York, N.Y., for approximately 34 lines from *Letters of Edward Dowden and His Correspondents;*

Harcourt, Brace and Company, New York, N.Y., for short passages from George Edward Woodberry's *Studies of a Litterateur;*

Houghton Mifflin Company, Boston, Mass., for material requested from Longfellow's *Random Memories, Letters of Richard Watson Gilder, Letters of Charles Eliot Norton;*

Longmans Green & Co., Inc., New York, N.Y., for seven and one-half lines from *Letters of William Allingham,* edited by Allingham & Williams;

Longmans Green & Co., Ltd. London, England, for permission to quote from Wilfrid Ward's *Aubrey de Vere: A Memoir;*

The Macmillan Company, New York, N.Y., for specified material from *Tennyson and His Friends*, by Hallam Lord Tennyson, from Charles Tennyson's *Alfred Tennyson*, Legouis & Cazamian's *History of English Literature*, Garnett & Gosse's *Illustrated History of English Literature;*

John Murray, Ltd., London, England, for a short extract from *Jane Welsh Carlyle, Letters to Her Family* (ed. Leonard Huxley);

Oxford University Press, London, England, for certain passages from Griggs' *Coleridge Fille*, Una Taylor's *Guests and Memories*, and *Letters of Gerard Manley Hopkins to Robert Bridges* (ed. Abbott);

Derek Patmore, and Harper Brothers, New York, N.Y., for about 65 lines from *Portrait of My Family;*

Routledge and Kegan Paul, Ltd., London, England, for eight and one-half lines from *Protrait of My Family;*

Charles Scribner's Sons, New York, N.Y., for brief quotation from one of *The Letters of Henry James* (Edited by Percy Lubbock) and brief quotations from Viola Meynell's *Alice Meynell: A Memoir,* Edmund Gosse's *Coventry Patmore,* Alice Meynell's *Early Poems* and *Later Poems;*

Sheed and Ward, New York, N.Y., for two lines from *The Wilfrid Wards and the Transition,* by Maisie Ward;

Trustees of the Pierpont Morgan Library, for permission to quote from de Vere's letters to William Knight;

University of London Press, London, England, for a short extract from Grigg's *Hartley Coleridge: His Life and Work.*

INTRODUCTION

The Victorian age, as much as we sometimes suppose we have outgrown it, keeps reminding us that it will not be laid to rest so easily. The reaction of successive periods was to be expected—the revolt of children. But as children often take more kindly to grandparents than to parents, the attitude of patronizing condescension has definitely receded, and there are signs that it is now undergoing a kind of transformation into an interested, though detached, scrutiny.

Like any period of cultural history with definite characteristics and boundaries, the Victorian era drew its vitality, its breath of life, from the men and women—and not merely the major figures—who in their preoccupation with the characteristic problems and interests of the time gave the period its historical expression. This is not the commonplace it may at first appear. It is precisely this interrelationship in which the nineteenth century was so rich—in contrast to the marked and often debilitating isolation of the modern writer and artist. In the last century there was a realization of the idea of community in which poet and statesman, philosopher and priest, shared their gifts and intellectual enthusiasms. Perhaps it would not be an overstatement to say that artistic creation, though finally a most personal experience, was in a measure *cooperative*. Friendships were not so accidental as they appear to be now; they

were, to a degree, purposefully formed. Genuine and deep as they
might be, they were motivated by consciousness and direction.

In a remarkable position to participate in the cultural movements of his time was a man with a great capacity for friendships:
Aubrey de Vere, the Irish poet and critic. Historically, his life
(1814-1902) spanned the century—from the Battle of Waterloo
to the death of Queen Victoria. Personally, it was the life of a
gentleman of leisure and culture, but it was lived out in a period
of political and religious ferment. There was scarcely a movement
in nineteenth-century England or Ireland in which de Vere was
not in some way involved. Though he was a loyal member of the
Church of England at the time, he celebrated the passing of Daniel
O'Connell's Catholic Emancipation Bill in 1821. While still a
youth, he considered himself a disciple of Edmund Burke and remained throughout his life essentially true to the wisdom of that
enlightened conservative. With the Corn Laws and the later Reform
Bills he was much concerned. When the Irish peasants turned
against their landlords, he realized that democracy was on its way
to Ireland, that "the great democratic battle had begun." He believed fervently in personal (and spiritual) liberty, but true to
Burke, he knew the creative value of a properly understood tradi-
tion and rejected radical or violent means. He feared that the
peasants were not yet ready to take charge of affairs themselves.

The coming of the Industrial Revolution did not have the effect
on de Vere that might be expected of a man of his social and political acumen. But this is not hard to understand: its full implications would not have been likely to impinge on the son of a noble
landed squire living in a country where peasants were "landless"
and mostly agricultural workers. During the Famine years he
worked from morning till night providing food and clothing for the
poor, and he helped his family to better the conditions of the
peasants by building up the lace-making and knitting industries—
though there was little market for their products. Throughout his
life he worked diligently in behalf of his countrymen, promoting
religious equality, lending his support to the Irish Land Act of
1881, to the earlier disestablishment of the Irish Church, and to
the cause of popular education. His concern for the working man

and his deep sense of justice aroused his sympathy for F. D. Maurice's experiment in Christian Socialism, though it appeared to him rather too visionary.

De Vere was just as sensitive to the religious trends and changes of his times as he was to the political developments. His *Recollections* contains the reactions of a sensitive and probing mind to the drama of the Oxford Movement and the less orthodox "Apostles" of Cambridge. No one could stand aloof from the Victorian re-appraisal of religion or, if he sensed that reason could not furnish the final answers, fail to experience in some way the religious doubts of the age. In de Vere's case these doubts were resolved by his conversion to the Roman Catholic Church. Throughout his life he felt, like Newman, the spiritual influence of Coleridge, reacting against the utilitarianism and determinism of Hartley and Bentham. As a friend of Manning, Newman, Pusey, and Sewell, he was acutely aware of their sometimes painful divergence of viewpoints. His writings show him concerned with the spiritual crises of his day: Tennyson's doubt and groping which finally led to belief, Wordsworth's restraint which held him from writing anything that might detrimentally affect the young, Matthew Arnold's disbelief in the divinity of Christ and his idea of God as "a stream of tendency." The life-and-death conflict between science and religion he regarded as only apparent and due to ignorance of the full potentials and the ultimate affinity of the two.

But of greater significance than de Vere's movements in the worlds of politics and religion are his remarkable and enduring friendships. Here emerges his real talent, one which remains largely unrecognized. He counted among his friends the most eminent literary and ecclesiastical figures of the last century. He promoted the prestige of writers who finally attained fame. And he exerted a definite, though unobtrusive, influence on the destinies of persons whose reputations loom large today.

De Vere lived through many literary movements, from the triumph of Romanticism to the Celtic revival, of which he was an unrecognized forerunner. He was an ideal critic of poetry, for, as several of his friends attest, he had to an extraordinary degree a poet's temperament and an instinctive understanding of the creative process. Though not a popular poet in his time, he does reflect the transition from the stately school of an earlier day to the impulsive and penetrating genius of modern times. This is his significance as a poet. His poetry is often interesting and occasionally impressive, but it is his literary criticism which in any time can be read with pleasure on its own merits. In an excellent position to exercise his gifts of critical penetration and judgment, he was early to recognize exceptional talent in the work of Alice Thompson Meynell and Coventry Patmore and was among the first to discover the true genius of Tennyson.

His real significance as a man of letters rests finally in such creative relationships as these. They are his contribution to the intellectual and spiritual life of the age. And it is this generous giving of self that is the present concern. This book is not a biography, though its center and point of departure is always Aubrey de Vere, a man of culture and rare capacities for human sympathies. Its purpose is to allow de Vere's life and work, but especially his fruitful relationships, to illuminate further the fascinating and complex intellectual movements of his time.

*   *   *

Valuable in the writing of this book were de Vere's *Recollections* and Wilfrid Ward's *Aubrey de Vere: a Memoir,* both now long out of print. A manuscript portion of de Vere's Diary, copied under the generous direction of Mrs. Isabel de Vere (Robert's widow), unpublished reminiscences of de Vere's friends and relatives, many in epistolary form, and letters and notes of de Vere himself, kindly supplied by the late Wilfrid Meynell, have furnished new and often most revealing insights into de Vere's friendships. In fact, since the number of these unpublished letters, most of them in the author's possession, is so great, they are not listed in the Bibliography, though they are cited specifically in the appropriate places in the Notes. In addition to these literary materials, the author's visit to Curragh Chase, de Vere's ancestral home near Adare, and her conversations and correspondence with de Vere's niece, Lady Shaw, and other relatives and friends, have provided striking glimpses of Aubrey de Vere—one who could have lived only in the Victorian era.

*   *   *

The author owes a debt of sincere gratitude to Reverend Mother Charles Edward, for making possible the publishing of this work; to Professors L. V. Jacks and L. C. Wimberly, for criticism and review; and to Miss Emily Schossberger, for editorial counsel and for seeing the work through the press.

Her thanks go to Mrs. Robert Stephen de Vere, for information and for the invitation to Curragh Chase; to Commander and Mrs. Geoffrey Marescaux, for making that visit informative and memorable; to Mr. D. R. O'Brien and Mr. J. R. Monsell, for boyhood reminiscences of their relative; to the librarians of Fordham University, Columbia University, Harvard University, and the Morgan Library, for research facilities; and to Sister M. Prisca, the faithful traveling companion to the home and haunts of Aubrey de Vere.

The author gratefully remembers the late Dr. Joseph J. Reilly (who first interested her in de Vere), Lady Eleanor Shaw, Mrs. Prescott Decie (her sister), and Mrs. Vere O'Brien.

1

AUBREY DE VERE,

THE MAN

IN HIS AGE

The de Vere family was of Norman origin. As Earls of Oxford they date back to the England of the twelfth century and count among their ancestors Robert, the third Earl of Oxford, who was one of the twenty-five executors of the Magna Charta. Edward, the seventeenth Earl, a courtier and lyric poet of the time of Queen Elizabeth, has been claimed by the so-called Oxfordian scholars as the author of Shakespeare's dramas. Two valiant "fighting Veres," also of Elizabeth's reign, Francis and Horace, inspired the parents of Aubrey de Vere to name their youngest son Francis Horace.

The poet's grandfather, Sir Vere Hunt, was descended from a Cromwellian officer, Vere Hunt, who settled at Curragh in 1647. Sir Vere's son, Aubrey Hunt, later inherited the title from his father and in 1831 legally assumed the name de Vere. Born in 1788, Sir Aubrey became a poet and dramatist as well as a country-gentleman and proprietor-landlord. When he was a boy of ten, his mother sent him to be educated by a tutor, the Reverend John Dawes, at Ambleside, thus removing him from the adulation of servants and the enervating influence of home. Later, at Harrow, Sir Aubrey was a schoolmate of George Gordon Byron and Robert Peel. The environs of the Lake Country as well as the excellent

influence of tutor and mother had their beneficial effect on the young
man, who at eighteen married Mary Spring Rice, then seventeen
years old. She was a sister of Thomas Spring Rice, later Lord
Monteagle, who was at various times member of Parliament, Under
Secretary of State for the Home Department, and Chancellor of
the Exchequer in Lord Melbourne's administration. This marriage
was a most happy and successful one. Of the family, de Vere's
close friend of three decades, William Rowan Hamilton, wrote:

> The de Veres had for several generations resided at Cur-
> ragh Chase, a country-seat and desmesne of wildly pictur-
> esque beauty, not far from Adare. The father was the second
> baronet of a line descendant, through a granddaughter, from
> the nineteenth Earl of Oxford; the mother of Aubrey de Vere
> was sister of Mr. Spring Rice, afterwards Lord Monteagle of
> Brandon. Both parents were highly cultivated in intellect
> and taste.[1]

Sir Aubrey de Vere and his wife had eight children: Vere,
Ellen, Stephen, Aubrey (christened Aubrey Thomas), Mary,
Catherine, William, and Horace (called Horatio).[2]

Ellen remained through all her life Aubrey's most congenial
companion. Stephen, who became a great Latin scholar and poet,
distinguished himself as a philanthropist. At his own expense he
took Irish emigrants to Quebec, traveled with them in steerage,
hired a house for them, nursed them through infection and fever
and, when they were well, obtained employment for them. After a
year of such heroic work, he returned to Ireland and prepared a
report for Parliament on the lamentable conditions endured by
emigrants on English vessels. When this report was read in the
House of Lords, the lawmakers added to the Passage Act an
amendment which paved the way for respectable ship accommodations for emigrants. William and Horace, the younger sons of the
family, became respectively sailor and soldier; both fought in the
Crimean War. In 1835, Ellen married Robert O'Brien, fourth son
of Sir Edward O'Brien, a direct descendant of Brian the Great,
the King of Ireland—a Gael—who centuries ago destroyed the
power of the Danish invaders in Ireland.

Sir Aubrey, with Lady de Vere and his beautiful mother, who
lived at Curragh Chase, no doubt set the pattern for a peaceful

and happy life at the manor house. Sir Aubrey, whom Aubrey resembled somewhat in appearance and character, was tall. He had a musical voice and gray eyes — bright when he was glad, dark when "he heard anything unworthy."[3] He was generally considered a liberal or moderate Tory in politics, perhaps because of the combination of his love for liberty and his reverence for the authority of the past. But no party could claim his entire sympathy. He loved England as the land of his earlier ancestors, yet he was deeply devoted to Ireland and her people. For England he wrote such historical sonnets as "The House of Tudor" and "Queen Elizabeth." For Ireland, the country of his birth, he composed *Lamentations of Ireland* as he sat in her ruined monasteries. Though he despised tyranny and oppression, he also hated jacobinism and all forms of violent radicalism: like his son later, he believed that more could be accomplished by peaceable means. He sympathized with both Norman and Gaelic Irish and firmly believed in religious equality. In religion, he adhered to the Church of England and possessed a simple faith which increased as he grew older. Before his death in his fifty-eighth year, when Ireland was entering the throes of the great Famine, he did everything possible to alleviate the sufferings of the poor. One of his last remarks to his son Aubrey was that he must build cottages instead of stables that year. For him and his family, the poor always felt reverence and gratitude.

As an author, Sir Aubrey won the praise of his friend William Wordsworth, who proclaimed his sonnets the best of his age— with the understanding, of course, that they were not to be compared with William Wordsworth's.[4] As a dramatist, Sir Aubrey wrote *Julian the Apostate,* published in 1822; *The Duke of Marcia,* which came out the following year; and *Mary Tudor,* which he felt compelled to write from a sense of justice since he maintained that history had not been honest in dealing with Mary Tudor. This last play, published by his son Aubrey after his death, Gladstone and Manning ranked next to Shakespeare's play. Matthew Arnold claimed it was better than Tennyson's *Queen Mary.*

Aubrey de Vere was born on January 10, 1814, in the large stone house at Curragh Chase which had originally been the castle,

and from his childhood on he occupied a small room on the second
floor. From his window he could see the lake, which each spring
was fringed with sheets of daffodils and white narcissus. There
were islands in the lake, gay with rhododendrons, pink and violet.
Aubrey studied with tutors until he entered college at eighteen
and used a room on the first floor for his classroom. As a small boy
he would browse in the spacious library and wander around the
large entrance hall, a habit which stayed with him all through life.
He was fascinated by the works of sculpture collected by his
father, especially the colossal one, a copy of Michelangelo's
Moses. Later he would often recall how the "lower orders" (the
servants) stood aghast on first viewing this statue, which they
erroneously thought to be the likeness of a de Vere ancestor—a
joyant.

Aubrey never tired of the beautiful desmesne which formed
the background for his happy life at Curragh Chase. One of the
approaches to the house was three miles long. It passed three
lakes—one surrounded by meadows, pastures and groves, another
by woods never planted by man, though sometimes cut down and
successively renewed, a sort of "primeval forest." Through these
woods Sir Aubrey, the father, would continuously make new drives
and walks, not only to beautify the estate but also to provide employment for the poor, with whom the boys Aubrey and Stephen
had become well acquainted.

Aubrey de Vere's earliest recollections went back to the death
of King George III in 1820, on which occasion the family, as loyal-
ists, all wore mourning. However, little six-year-old Aubrey soon
forgot his grief, for the family spent the following summer at
Mount Trenchard on the River Shannon, the home of his maternal
grandmother. In a little boat with four sails he and the other children drifted along the Shannon and saw in the distance Knock
Patrick, the mountain from which, as their father told them,
St. Patrick had blessed all of Ireland. They loved to hear the roar
of the magnificent submarine caves of distant Ballybunion and
enjoyed their games and the freedom of the beautiful countryside.

The following year, 1821, the de Vere family set out for a
three years' visit to England. They traveled in an old family stage-

coach drawn by four horses and arrived at Dublin four days later. The remainder of the journey to London consumed eight days. During these years Aubrey lost his French governess, whose parting message to him was that he must never forget her since she had taught him to write. He then, like his two older brothers, came under the instruction of an excellent tutor, William Saint George Pelissier, who taught the boys not only Latin, English literature and other necessary subjects, but also kite-flying and cricket. Beautiful places—such as Hampton Court, Ruxley and Bushey Park—so impressed young Aubrey that in later life he visited them each year. Meanwhile, the older boys were advancing in Latin, but Aubrey found Latin grammar so difficult that Mr. Pelissier told him that he was an idiot, without any intellectual faculties, and had better give up the study of Latin for the cultivation of his moral faculties. Sir Aubrey, learning that ten-year-old Aubrey was spending his time tracing maps, in accordance with the tutor's suggestion, ordered that the study of Latin be resumed. Young Aubrey improved in the language, although he continued to find Latin distasteful; like his father, however, he always had a keen enthusiasm for Greek.

When the de Vere family returned to Curragh Chase in 1824, Mr. Pelissier accompanied them and continued to work with the boys for another year. Aubrey always regarded him as the best of the many tutors he had had, not only for his marked ability to teach and read Shakespeare, but also for his training in principles of character. Through a later tutor, Edward Johnstone, Aubrey developed an appreciation for Wordsworth; Mr. Johnstone's interpretation of "The Vernal Ode" awakened the boy's interest.

From his eleventh to his nineteenth year Aubrey de Vere followed a well-planned schedule of life at Curragh Chase. Study with the tutor, work in the garden, in which each boy had his own little domain to cultivate, long walks or rides through the woods, as well as chats with the workers on the estate, constituted the events of the day. Dinner at five—a very simple one in those days—left a long evening, perhaps the happiest period of the day for the entire family. Music—generally Mozart, played by Lady de Vere, accompanied on the flute by her brother, Lord Monteagle, and in

later years Beethoven, interpreted by Aubrey's eldest brother,
Vere, or a visitor—was a frequent entertainment at the family
gathering. Reading aloud a book of travel, a biography, a novel—
often one of Scott's — or speeches of such public figures as
Brougham[5] and Plunket,[6] Prime Minister Canning[7] or (at a later
period) Sir Robert Peel,[8] kept parents and children aware of what
was going on in the political world. Art and sculpture, too, played
a prominent part in evening recreation and interests.

A poetic expression of Sir Aubrey's keen enjoyment of this
happy home life appears here and there in his *Sonnets*.[9] "The
Portrait—T.S.R." mirrors Sir Aubrey's admiration for his wife's
brother, Lord Monteagle (Thomas Spring Rice), who was a frequent visitor to Curragh Chase:

> My brother!—For to me, indeed, thou art
> What nature hath denied me—in my heart
> I treasure thy dear lineaments, and dwell
> Long-lingering over each, and loth to part.
> Thou look'st upon me with a silent spell
> Imagining her fair face we love so well.[10]

Devotion to wife and children is revealed in "The Family Picture,"
written when there were only four children:

> . . . One rosy boy struggling to mount her lap,
> The eldest studious with a book or map;
> Her timid girl beside, with a faint bloom,
> Conning some tale: while with no gentle tap
> Yon chubby urchin beats his mimic drum,
> Nor heeds the doubtful frown her eyes assume.
> So sits the Mother! with her fondest smile
> Regarding her sweet little ones the while:
> And he, the happy man! to whom belong
> These treasures, feels their living charm beguile
> All mortal care . . .[11]

(The children are, no doubt, Aubrey, Vere, Ellen, and Stephen.)
Sir Aubrey's love for social life as well as for solitary enjoyment
of nature—a love which he passed on to his namesake—is evident

in his "Solitude and Society." The octet suggests the joy of wandering unaccompanied in the wood, and the sextet runs:

> Yet do I love thee well, Society!
> When on my hearth the wintry faggots blaze,
> And jest, and friendly laugh ring cheerily:
> Or some dear voice recounts heroic lays:
> Or gentle maid, blushing at whispered praise,
> Sings some pathetic strain of antique harmony.[12]

The last three lines imply also Sir Aubrey's and his children's interest in Ireland's heroic past. Dr. James Henthorne Todd of Trinity College, their friend and an authority on literature and history, translated the most important ancient Irish documents, and Stephen de Vere, Aubrey's elder brother, collected from the country people old Irish airs, to which Aubrey wrote many of the poems found in his *Inisfail*.

In 1829, when Aubrey was fifteen years old, there was rejoicing in the de Vere family because of Catholic Emancipation, gained by Daniel O'Connell. Sir Aubrey and his family, although members of the Church of England, had long wished for religious equality. All at Curragh Chase admired the Emancipator for his love of justice and his dislike of violence. To express his joy on the occasion, Aubrey climbed a high hill opposite the house, and mounting a column, he stood and waved a torch, as bonfires of celebration burned on the surrounding hills.[13]

Some variation from routine life occurred each year when the boys spent Christmas holidays at Adare Manor, in the nearby village of Adare. Lord Adare, son of Lord Dunraven, and his guests spent the days following the clear River Maique as it wound its way through the estate; they climbed and re-climbed the ruins of Kildare Castle, and reconstructing in their imagination the Franciscan Monastery, suppressed by Henry VIII in 1539, they listened to the mellow tones of the old bell, once in the monastery but now in the manor-house. In the evening they entertained with theatricals, games and dances; and at odd moments Aubrey sought Lord Adare, for he liked to converse with his elder brother's special friend. Adare wrote to William Rowan Hamilton about this "very

clever and metaphysical" youth of seventeen, with "a most beautiful, fine open countenance"[14] (a description which is supported by
an excellent water-color sketch of Aubrey at twenty).

Aubrey de Vere finally met William Rowan Hamilton (later
Sir William), great mathematician and Astronomer Royal, ten
years his senior; and they formed a lifelong friendship. Since
Hamilton had met Coleridge, and since de Vere, like most religious-
minded young men of his time, had accepted Coleridge as a teacher
of wisdom (rather than Bentham with his materialistic utilitarianism), the two new friends had long discussions on metaphysics and
the philosophy of Coleridge and Kant. On Hamilton's visits to
Adare and Curragh Chase, Aubrey and he spent entire nights and
early mornings talking over these subjects of mutual interest. In
an ensuing correspondence (also touching on Hamilton's disappointment over his rejection as a suitor by Aubrey's sister, Ellen
de Vere), Aubrey manifested a maturity and power of analysis
unusual in a youth of seventeen or eighteen.

Now ready, in 1832, to enter Trinity College in Dublin,
de Vere seemed to have no ambition for worldly success; his great
desire was to bring out a translation of Sophocles. At the end of
his first year he wrote "Antigone,"[15] a forerunner of his *Search
after Proserpine,* which was published in 1842 and which was to
merit high praise from Walter Savage Landor. Interest in metaphysics (apparently quite popular at that time) and the philosophy of Coleridge and Kant continued; and de Vere studied
Wordsworth, Keats, Shelley, Tennyson, and Taylor for his dramatic *Philip van Artevelde,* which was then making a popular
appeal. De Vere also gave so much attention to theology that on
graduating from Trinity in 1837 he won the Downes Premium for
Theological Essay Writing.[16]

This abiding interest in theology and religion apparently indicated Aubrey de Vere's inclination toward a clerical life. This
had been the continued hope of his father who had early provided
the boy with books on theology—books which Aubrey had in his
room when he died. Episcopal ministers and close family friends,
Dr. Whewell and Dr. John Jebb, expected him to enter the ministry; Archdeacon Foster offered him a curacy; and eight years

later, when Aubrey was thirty-one, Dr. Pusey "urged" him to take orders. Why did he take no steps towards Angelican orders? Did the Church of England entirely satisfy the aspirations of his early boyhood?[17] Or did the Tractarian Movement, which really had its beginning in 1833, cause him to hesitate?

Be this as it may, he did not move in that direction. The years which followed his graduation from college in 1839 were spent mostly in travel and in an intensive and pleasant social life. For the young Anglo-Irish gentleman enjoyed society and felt at home there, much as did his father. He also enjoyed the congenial home life and what he called "domestic dissipation" at Curragh Chase. There he could indulge his love for study and the outdoor life. It was during these years that his relations with the prominent men of his century grew. His correspondence with them had so impressive a regularity that his brother Horace, fourteen years his junior, had learned to recognize the various handwritings and, on the arrival of the morning mail, would run up to Aubrey's room and call laughingly: "Here you are again: as usual, Newman, Todd and Pusey!"[18]

Was Aubrey making more intensive studies of theology and religion? He met the dignified, ascetical John Henry Newman in 1838 on his first visit to Oxford the year after his graduation. The next year he journeyed to Cambridge to see some of his friends in the "Apostles' Club," which consisted of twelve members, among them Hallam and Tennyson, Thackeray and Stephen Spring Rice. He found Oxford conservative in its religious attitude and Cambridge holding to a self-centered philosophy which, he said, regarded Divine things "as they appear from the little planet of our subjective philosophy."[19] On a later visit to Oxford, in 1841, he was the guest of Dr. William Sewell. In this first-hand view of Tractarianism through its leader, he sensed that "matters ecclesiastical were approaching a crisis."[20]

Love of travel led de Vere to Rome by way of Switzerland. For the sake of economy and liberty, he traveled alone in the Alps; in one hand he carried a change of linen and a guidebook, wrapped in a pocket handkerchief, in the other he held an umbrella. During a midnight storm he lost his way on an abandoned trail and was

almost carried to death by a descending shilly-bed of rocks. Finally
reaching the little hotel at Interlaken, he had "excellent tea and
abundant bread"—the best meal he had ever enjoyed, he said.
Linen and guidebook were drenched, but the faithful umbrella,
which had served as "alpenstock," was uninjured.[21] In Rome, his
destination, de Vere delighted in the social life. For Roman society
was varied and agreeable, "a strange combination of people worth
knowing—such a combination that one could not find elsewhere in
ten years";[22] the wonders of the Eternal City—ruins, statues,
churches and art treasures—seemed less interesting to him.

After spending some months at Curragh Chase, de Vere again
set out for England in the spring of 1841. Crossing the Irish Sea,
he noticed a fellow-traveler, a large, strong man, with a powerful
and crafty eye, a humorous mouth, and a broad, strong forehead,
"well adapted for thinking"—the famous Emancipator, Daniel
O'Connell! De Vere, noting O'Connell's kindness to two little girls,
decided that O'Connell was a demagogue only by necessity, but
not a real democrat—an admirer of the English constitution, but
a hater of the principles of the French Revolution. Stopping at
London, he attended to the publication of his father's *Sonnets* and
Song of Faith, and he met for the first time William Wordsworth,
with whom his father had become acquainted in 1833. Dr. Whewell,
Bishop Thirwall, and Frederick Maurice were also at the breakfast, probably in the home of his uncle, Lord Limerick, in Downing
Street, where Aubrey was a frequent guest when in London. Not
long afterwards de Vere again met Wordsworth in the latter's
own home and thus got an intimate glimpse of the old poet whom
he admired so much. And Wordsworth must have been pleased
with his guest, tall, fair-haired, blue-eyed, spare and athletic.

On his visits to the Lake Country, de Vere formed a lasting
friendship with two remarkable women: Sara Coleridge (Mrs.
Henry Nelson), daughter of the renowned poet, who was twelve
years his senior; and Miss Isabella Fenwick, a close friend of Mr.
and Mrs. Wordsworth, one who had a better understanding of the
laureate than anyone else. Miss Fenwick was thirty years older
than de Vere. Writing to his sister of his new friends, de Vere
described Sara as "most singularly beautiful as well as attractive

—with great blue eyes, into which Coleridge looked down till he
left there his own lustre";[23] and with Miss Fenwick "it was
friendship at first sight."[24] About this time de Vere brought out his
The Waldenses and Other Poems, rather religious in tone, influenced by his talks on Christian evidences with William Rowan
Hamilton, to whom he dedicated the book.

In 1843, he accompanied to Italy Henry Taylor and his wife
—Aubrey's cousin "Dofo"—and a friend's little son, Freddy Elliot,
and proved himself an excellent businessman. Since Henry Taylor,
who held an important position in the Colonial Office, was ailing,
the arrangements for the journey devolved on Aubrey. He attended
to all the details of the nine-month trip and in Naples was even
involved in an encounter with bandits whom he fought off with his
umbrella. His kindness to five-year-old Freddy Elliot was typical
of his fondness for children.[25]

Another journey, this time to Corfu, where his brother Horace
was stationed as a Major Engineer Royal, afforded Aubrey further
opportunity for observation. Traveling alone, as he had done in
Switzerland, he obtained a close view of "these comely Greeks with
their fine heads and flashing eyes," but he felt that beneath majestic
exteriors they were "a false people . . . never ashamed of being
detected in a lie." For them, he felt, there was little hope.[26] Farther
on, de Vere met a Dane who was a lecturer at the military school at
Athens. The Dane predicted (before the middle of the nineteenth
century) "that what he called the fifth great attack on the liberty
and civilization of Europe will one day be made by the Russians;
but he thought that it would be frustrated and would end in the
breaking-up of the great empire."[27] Later de Vere observed in his
book, *Picturesque Sketches of Greece and Turkey:* "How interesting it would be to detect Russia betrayed into something like a
parental affection for Poland, and seeking with her a union not
stimulated merely by ungovernable appetite!"[28]

Aubrey de Vere's Diary (1845-1846) records the principal
interests and events of his thirty-fifth and thirty-sixth years. The
scene shifts to London and neighboring Hampstead, then still a
suburb, to Paris, Scotland, back to London and the Lake Country,
and finally to Curragh Chase. In London he enjoyed the companion-

ship of James Spedding and Edward Fitzgerald, Monckton Milnes
and Alfred Tennyson, who was then at work on *The Princess* and
In Memoriam. He met the Gladstones and the Lockharts, Macaulay
and Carlyle. In Hampstead he hired two rooms at the "Hare and
Hounds," for thirty shillings a week, lunched on strawberries, and
rose early every day to view the distant sky-line of London.

This life was suddenly interrupted by the arrival of Sir
Aubrey, who had fallen ill and had come to London for surgical
treatment. Aubrey visited his father daily, read to him aloud from
Cooper's *Afloat and Ashore* and from Ruskin, bought him illustra-
tions of Giotto's chapel at Padua, and discussed the Rembrandt
and Correggio pictures Sir Aubrey had just purchased. After an
apparent recovery, Sir Aubrey, Lady de Vere and Aubrey went
to Paris for a few weeks and visited the great cathedrals on the
way. Later, Sir Aubrey unknowingly paid his last visit to his
favorite haunts in the Lake Country; to Lady de Vere and Aubrey
he pointed out each scene of his boyhood, even the exact spot where
he had cast his first line. Aubrey was happy to present his friends,
Miss Fenwick and Sara Coleridge, to his parents, who were most
favorably impressed.

Thinking his father entirely recovered, de Vere decided to
take a walking tour through Scotland; and a most interesting trip
it proved. On the way he visited Miss Fenwick; and they had "a
pleasant coze,"[29] in which she told him of her past, and they discussed his future career. He left Miss Fenwick with a copy of
Burns under his arm—the guide she had given him for the trip.
Reaching Glasgow, he admired the buildings and massive stone
streets, visited a queer little penny theater, purchased an oilskin
bag, a portmanteau, and a guide book. Then, after planning his
course, he set out. Whenever possible he walked—along the shore
of Loch Lomond, through the Trossachs, as near as possible to
Loch Katrine—through sunshine and storm, over heather soaked
with rain, trudging along with his pack on his back, sometimes
five, twelve, or even sixteen miles a day. Now and then he received a cup of milk at a highland hut and enjoyed a lunch of
potatoes, butter and milk; nights he spent in an inn or a hotel
along the way. While being rowed through Loch Katrine and view-

ing Ellen's Isle, he read Scott's *Lady of the Lake;* at Inversaid he read Wordsworth's "Highland Girl," and verified the details of the scene; throughout the journey, he found Burns a safe guide. "I saw all things with Burns' eyes: and Scotland became in turn the interpreter of Burns."[30]

Edinburgh delighted him; he called it "the most nobly situated capital north of the Alps."[31] Finding comfortable accommodations at 53 George Street—two rooms on the second floor—he read letters from family and friends; news of the failure of the potato crop in Ireland darkened his day. However, true to his artistic and inquiring nature, he visited art exhibits, and marvelled at the advances in astronomy as he gazed through the immense microscope at the Observatory; he enjoyed the exhilarating air of Calton Hill as he walked rapidly with the short steps of the true pedestrian. During his four weeks at Edinburgh (November 21 until December 19, 1845), de Vere made the acquaintance of Wilson (Christopher North of *Blackwood's*), "a strong, hale, elderly man with a face full of energy and long locks"; Mr. Wilson "spoke with affectionate reverence for Wordsworth, and with the warmest interest and indulgence about Hartley Coleridge."[32] At Lord Jeffrey's social gatherings de Vere sat next to "a young and handsome authoress, a Puseyite"; again at Lord Jeffrey's, de Vere "made the acquaintance of a singularly handsome young lady . . . not very ladylike, being a little forward and not at her ease"; and at Sir John McNeil's he met "a pretty and pleasant young lady . . . extremely high church."[33]

Although de Vere could thus enjoy society to the utmost, his interest in religion did not wane. On his first Sunday in Edinburgh, he visited an Establishment (Presbyterian) church, a "free church," and an Episcopal church. He heard a sermon in a Roman Catholic church, "after which the congregation were exhorted to pray for thousands of English who hung in suspense about their conversion."[34] Diary entries of that time read:

> *Nov. 24*—Read the papers in Waterloo News room and amongst other things a triumphant account in the *Tablet* of the recent conversions.

Nov. 25—Dined at the Tavern and read the *English Church-man.*

Nov. 30 (Sunday)—Went to the Episcopal church . . . After dinner went to the Bishop's church, and finding it closed, to a Presbyterian one—an Establishment one which seemed to be a very sleepy affair as if the fire of the Scotch Divinity had all gone into the free church.

Dec. 2—Went to read the *Tablet,* which gave the names of 5 more clergymen and as many laymen who had recently left our church for Rome—ruminated on the matter and anticipated a constant exfoliation from our church.

Dec. 8—Received a note from Adare and one from Mr. Richards much alarmed at the conversions and prophesying "worse and more of it."[35]

Before leaving Scotland de Vere visited Scott's home (Abbotsford), where he was interested, among other things, in the author's immense shoes. He also paid his respects to the poet's grave.

Reaching home on January 7, 1846, Aubrey de Vere settled down to the usual routine at Curragh Chase. In his diary he mentions his mother's having rheumatism, the reading aloud of Lord Malmsbury's[36] diary, "which exhibits cunning in the character of a restless intriguer"; and of Sir Robert Peel's speech on Free Trade and the Corn Laws, which aroused de Vere's admiration and enthusiasm. On several occasions Aubrey discussed theology with Vere, his eldest brother; other favorite topics were methods of helping the poor—the need of giving employment, of developing the industrial resources of the country, and similar remedies.

For some time Sir Aubrey de Vere had discussed with his sons the necessity of the State's doing something definite for the poor of Ireland: the population was large, and employment was so out of proportion to the population that a man could work but half a week; consequently, wages were necessarily low, industries were non-existent and farms were too small for scientific cultivation. The conscientious country gentlemen who owned the land were unable to effect necessary innovations, but Sir Aubrey recommended emigration aided by the government; that, he held, would not only build up British colonies through industries, but would also provide for such colonies a wholesome population.

Toward the end of June, 1846, Aubrey de Vere recorded: "There was a long discussion on my way of life. I spoke of a political career. H. Taylor replied that I was not fit for it; and Stephen, that it was hardly fit for me, as a poor man. H. Taylor urged some literary task upon me, by way of discipline."[37] Evidently the idea of entering the Episcopal ministry had been laid aside; and meanwhile de Vere had casually and briefly discussed his future career with his friends—Miss Fenwick, who seemed to favor a literary career for him; Mrs. Edward Ernest Villiers, whose choice would probably be that of manufacturer; and Sara Coleridge, who gave him "sisterly counsel." However, tragic events intervened—the last illness and death of Sir Aubrey de Vere, and then the Irish Famine, which extended over a period of four years.

On July 3, 1846, Aubrey was summoned home from London by the unexpected news of his father's critical illness. He hurried to Limerick, and prayed as he was driven the five miles to Adare. On seeing him, Sir Aubrey remarked: "O my dear Aubrey, do I see you again? I am so happy!" Horatio was unable to reach home in time. During the last days of his father's life, Aubrey and the other members of the family, as well as the servants and other dependents, gave evidence of the love, respect and reverence Sir Aubrey had inspired. Shortly after Sir Aubrey's death, Lady de Vere observed that now she would need the special aid of her children. "She seemed to apply this especially to me," Aubrey wrote in his diary.[38]

The horrors and depression of the Famine, the worst of which Sir Aubrey had providentially escaped, caused havoc in the lives of the poor, not only because of the failure of the potato crops but also because of illness, starvation and death that ensued; these conditions also brought worry, trouble, and sadness into the lives of such gentry as the de Veres, who sacrificed days and nights in working for the welfare of their countrymen. Aubrey and his brothers attended relief committees, promoted, as far as possible, the ill-advised public works at first instituted by the government, and later attended to the distribution of Indian meal; but they were well aware of the half-hearted manner in which England helped Ireland, and the blundering methods of those in authority.

During these trying, discouraging times Aubrey de Vere made
some keen practical judgments, which he entered in his diary.
"Nothing can right matters except we can get the labor of the
country back into the hands of the individual employers."[39] And
he analyzed the cause of some of the trouble: extravagance on the
part of proprietors, who, by living beyond their means and becoming burdened with debt, had to beg or bull, thus serving neither
their dependents nor their country. Moreover, the gentry who were
not prodigal were too few and too scattered to effect the good they
desired, especially in promoting peace and preventing violence, to
which starving people are likely to revert.

In a letter to Henry Taylor, written May 31, 1847, de Vere
stated: "I have fulfilled your desire and become a man of public
business. . . . We have set up in the neighborhood all sorts of
industrial employment for the women, which have of course en-
tailed no end of trouble in the management, as well as perplexity
in the disposal of manufactures which nobody wanted."[40] And
another glimpse of his activities is supplied by Henry Taylor:

> Aubrey de Vere has just come to town to give evidence
> before a Parliamentary Committee on Colonisation. He has
> gone through strange adventures, and has become a most
> active man of business and a most efficient mob orator. In
> one instance the troops came to attack a mob of several
> thousands [aroused peasants in Ireland], and finding that
> they were in his hands, who had stopped them and was making
> a speech from the top of a wall, the officer in command very
> wisely took away the troops, and Aubrey brought them to
> reason, and persuaded them to give up their enterprise, and
> disperse . . . His spirits have never failed him . . . One party
> he had to hold with eight muskets and pistols pointed at him
> . . . The people ended by professing great respect for him
> and his family . . .[41]

The right of freedom of speech and of press de Vere fear-
lessly exercised in his publications of 1848, *English Misrule and
Irish Misdeeds*. He indicated the dangers of animosity of many
English toward the Irish. Constructively, he urged systematic
emigration and the development of agriculture in Ireland, as means

Aubrey Moore

of establishing peace and order. Thus he re-echoed his father's sentiments long before the great Famine. Comte de Montalembert, one of many who commended the book, called it "a masterly picture of Ireland's rights, and of her unparalleled wrongs."[42] Since Aubrey was free from all national and religious prejudice, being neither Celtic nor Catholic at that time, the work must have proved very effective because of its objectivity.

After the death of his father, Aubrey de Vere endeavored to distract his mother from her grief by reading Dante with her each morning; this pleased her, for it reminded her of the days she had taught Italian to Sir Aubrey. She liked to talk of the past with Aubrey—of his father and of the daughters, Mary and Catherine, who had died young.

Meanwhile, de Vere "went to choose a site for Farrell's house, as the old man spoke in broken-hearted tone about his rotten potatoes."[43] For this cottage, which was to cost twenty-eight pounds, Aubrey made arrangements; Farrell (one of the dependents) drew some of the stones, and de Vere provided timber and thatch. Willy and Horace, the younger sons, also visited the homes of the poor, while the older sons continued committee work for the amelioration of the victims of the famine. As a result of these meetings Aubrey cleverly outlined the proper procedure at relief meetings: the necessity for good temper and tact, the danger of petty jealousies, the inability of these persons to deliberate in public, the consequent necessity of arriving at an agreement before a meeting, the advantage of placing one responsible person in charge, the impracticability of trying to get tired persons to vote wisely, etc. As public works, instituted by the government, resulted only in uncompleted roads, etc., and since the distribution of Indian meal was by no means a solution of the situation in Ireland, de Vere realized more and more the necessity of reclaiming waste lands, of giving loans to farmers and proprietors, and of working out a good system of emigration.

After de Vere's two years of very active and successful work and the recognition of his ability as a political thinker and writer, the question of public life again presented itself to him. His sister's brother-in-law, William Smith O'Brien, leader of the

Young Ireland party, had suggested Aubrey's "battling for Irish freedom in and out of Parliament."[44] As Stephen, Aubrey's elder brother, was at one time a member of Parliament, the idea was not unusual. However, in a letter to his friend Sir Henry Taylor, de Vere finally weighed the arguments on both sides: being in Parliament would require his living above his "due scale of expense"; his comparative poverty would detract from political respectability; he was able to get on well with others (even the most inimical), but he would assert his independence if he felt it necessary to do so; he disliked political parties, and as member of a party, he might not be able to be independent; if he were in Parliament he would work hard and conscientiously, but would he be able to effect his aims? Moreover, de Vere realized that his studies had not been along the line of those befitting a future parliamentarian.

Marriage does not seem to have ever been seriously contemplated by de Vere. He had many women friends with whom, according to the fashion of the times, he entertained a lively and regular correspondence. Sometimes he visited them during his travels. But these friendships seem to have been platonic. His best friends, Sara Coleridge and Isabella Fenwick, were both many years older than he. Mrs. Edward Ernest Villiers, the widow of Taylor's friend, was apparently one in whom Aubrey was interested. She was a lively, attractive person, interested in social life and devoted to her three children, as her letters show. She, too, was one of his more frequent correspondents. Mrs. Taylor, Aubrey's cousin, and Jane Carlyle also claimed his friendship. And though he often mentioned in letters and diaries other ladies he had met and admired, none of them apparently had made more than a fleeting impression. Once, when Hamilton wanted to draw him out about some romance in his life, the young man replied calmly that the greatest romance in his life was joining the Catholic Church.

But even though he did not take any steps towards an attempt to build a family of his own, in spite of the deep love for family life which he manifested in his life at Curragh Chase, he always showed great interest in children. He was concerned about his sister's little ones, Aubrey and Mary, was interested in the early education of Ernest Villiers, for whom he used to purchase Latin exercise books, and enchanted with Freddy Elliot's quaint remarks, which he found wise and amusing. Writing about Henry Taylor to Miss Fenwick he contrasted the happy life of this friend, the father of two children, with Taylor's life four years before, when the "two blessings" had not yet arrived.

The death of his father as well as the harrowing years of the Famine no doubt matured Aubrey de Vere and also turned him more toward theology. However, letters to his various correspondents contain bits of humor, as well as discussion of such subjects as mediaeval art as a revelation of the mind of the Middle Ages. He greatly admired the Middle Ages, perhaps because of the reading of Scott's novels at Curragh Chase. To Mrs. Villiers (September 1848) he wrote of Alfred Tennyson, then visiting de Vere's home, and mentioned the poet's being delighted with the singing of Mary Lucy (Vere de Vere's wife, much loved by the family). Visiting at "The Grange," the home of Lord and Lady Ashburton, de Vere wrote to Mrs. Villiers: "There is a young lady here who is very fond of poetry, but will never be the cause of poetry in others," and "there is another young lady with a neck as white as this paper . . . but the moment she gets up and walks she walks out of any heart that may have given her a temporary resting-place."[45] Some months later (January 1849) he tells Miss Fenwick of the wedding of his former tutor, Edward Johnstone. De Vere continued: "I . . . acted as his bridesman, signing his papers, etc. Indeed in the confusion, I was rather nearly married myself in his place; but it turned out very well in the end. . . ."[46]

The illness and death of Wordsworth, in 1850, saddened de Vere. "England has lost her greatest man. He had done his work, however," he told Miss Fenwick.[47] Another event, the same year—of a happy nature—was the marriage of Tennyson and his honeymoon at the home of the Marshalls (de Vere's cousins) at Coniston. Of the bride de Vere remarked: "She is very good, sensible, and anxious to make her husband write poetry. She is thirty-seven years old, and has much beauty . . ."[48] Other letters

of 1850 and 1851 contain news of his meeting Archdeacon Manning and of his visit to Mrs. Wordsworth, who gave him six pairs of
woolen socks she had knitted. "I do not know how I am to trample
under foot what has been worked by her hands . . .,"[49] he wrote.

On November 15, 1851, de Vere sent a letter from Avignon to
Sara Coleridge; he had that very day been received into the
Roman Catholic Church. The ceremony was performed by the
future Cardinal Manning. Continuing on his journey to Rome,
with Manning as companion, he later informed Miss Fenwick and
his sister of his change of religion. To his mother (who was
probably the first one to know of his reception into the Church)
he related his experiences, writing to her from the Eternal City,
where he remained several months.

This decision had not come over night, but was an outcome of
a "spiritual odyssey." His interest in theology had always been
an outstanding feature of his character, and ecclesiastical matters
always claimed his attention. He once wrote:

> Traditional prepossessions against the Roman Catholic
> Church . . . I did not share, being already at eighteen an
> ardent disciple of Edmund Burke, who asserted that there
> was no religious body of Europe which represented or at
> least resembled the early Christian Church so much as the
> Irish Catholic of his own day. I looked on her (the R.C.C.)
> as deeply wronged in the past . . .[50]

Yet two years after his graduation from Trinity College,
de Vere, then in Rome, seemed to regard recent converts with pity:

> I fear there are many more likely to follow their example.
> When they wake from their illusion about a perfect Church
> they will be as much discomposed as Jacob was when he found
> that, instead of having married his Rachel, "behold it was
> Leah."[51]

However, his interest in conversions to the Church of Rome
evidently continued, for the diary contains several references[52]
to them, written while he was in Edinburgh. Meanwhile, the early
influence of Coleridge's philosophy became less evident as he
exchanged ideas with the theologians, Dr. Edward Pusey, John
Henry Newman, and Henry Manning.

Five years later, de Vere indicated his progress Romeward:

I find myself daily more disposed to regard the Roman
system as the complete type and permanent form of Christianity. . . . I have not arrived at *convictions* . . . but still I
am most deeply impressed with the fact that so many of the
Roman doctrines . . . appear very different from what they
seem when dislocated from their . . . context . . .[53]

And he told his cousin that a year's meditation and reading, as
well as the reflections of fifteen or twenty years, during which
theology had been his chief study, had led him to see "a great
ship lift her shining sides near our crazy little bark."[54]

De Vere's progress toward the Catholic Church, however,
was not unimpeded by friends he held dear. Dr. John Jebb, Canon
of Hereford, a frequent visitor at the de Vere home, and Dudley
Perceval, another Anglican clergyman, tried to dissuade him from
taking the step he evidently contemplated. Both men believed that
the church of England was the truest earthly witness of the faith[55]
and that desertion from that church was both sinful and un-
patriotic.

De Vere paid a much-desired visit to Dr. Jebb who had once
regarded him as a Champion of the Church of England and now
he tried to steer de Vere from his new course, as de Vere implied to
Sara Coleridge:

I came here to see a very old friend, a man of "High
Church" principle, but at the same time "sound." I hope you
know what that word means, since, *as I do not,* I cannot ex-
plain it . . . He is as much opposed to Rome even as you are
. . . He has a library of 10,000 splendidly bound and well-
chosen folios and quartos . . . Why do not our *minds* tell us
that the Church must be a living voice, not a library?[56]

Mr. Dudley Perceval, in letters written several months after
the visit, urged de Vere to avoid "a most rash, perilous . . . and
most unnecessary plunge."[57] Later he reminded de Vere that the
Church of England regarded the Roman Catholic Church as a
"Schismatical Communion set up in these realms by the Pope in
defiance of every Catholic principle of Church-Law, of all Right,
Truth and Charity."[58]

To de Vere Catholics seemed "to hold all the great truths
of the three Creeds as in eagle-talons."[59] This, he said, increased
his reverence for Rome daily. Also the Gorham Judgement,[60]
which disturbed such men as Gladstone and Manning, also troubled
Aubrey de Vere; and to Hamilton he expressed himself on the
matter:

> I am one of many who have for very many years held what
> is commonly called "High Church" principles, and who find
> the ground cut from under us by the too celebrated Gorham
> decision, which leaves an article of the Creed, "one Baptism,"
> etc., an open question. This circumstance has remanded me
> to the study of the Roman theology . . .[61]

He told Sara Coleridge that he had had "great philosophic objections or antipathies to Rome"; but the reading of Roman tenets in
Roman books made him realize the vastness of that philosophy "in
the most practical and only historical form of Christianity."[62]

A few months later, on hearing of the conversion of his friend,
Henry Manning, he defined his own position: "I lift up mine eyes
to the hills, and see something based on earth but irradiated from
heaven, which changes not in a world of change, and on whose
impassive brow are written Strength and Peace."[63] Although
de Vere's submission to the Church of Rome was probably promoted by Manning, with whom he had discussed theological
matters, he himself was fully convinced of the wisdom of the step
he intended to take. About three months before becoming a Roman
Catholic he wrote:

> My convictions with respect to the claims of the Roman
> Catholic Church seemed to me to reach such a degree of
> certainty and moral urgency as left me no choice, as a con-
> scientious man, desirous of being sincere with himself and
> with others, and of obeying the will of God . . .[64]

Nearly forty years later de Vere told his niece, Mrs. Monsell,
that theology was more to him even than poetry; and when asked
why he had never become a priest he decisively replied that "he
had never had any vocation whatever for the priesthood."[65]

Back at Curragh Chase from his journey to Rome, Aubrey

de Vere resumed his quiet life. Each year, however, in June or July, he went to England; in London, he stayed at the Atheneum Club, where he met his friends—Hutton and Ward, Lord Emly, and others. Every September or October he visited his sister-in-law (Horace's widow) at her old Burke family home, in County Galway. His three nieces and their mother eagerly watched for his visits and were delighted when he arrived. Everyone received a book, and each niece was taken in turn for a walk, during which de Vere spoke of poetry and people, politics and Ireland. In the evenings, surrounded by the family, he would read Wordsworth, Coleridge, or his own poems; and he would have his sister-in-law sing the old songs he loved so well and poems (from *Inisfail*) which Mrs. Horace de Vere had set to music. De Vere's youngest niece, later Lady Shaw, knew her uncle very well, as she had seen him every year during her early childhood and youth; and she believed that, although he was interested in the world and its doings, he was certainly very spiritual. He was also a "gentleman to his fingertips, courteous, kindly, and honorable, strong in opinions and argumentative, enjoying argument but never perverse or provocative."[66] When his sister-in-law married again, de Vere's friendship for the family continued undisturbed.

His daily schedule at Curragh Chase was a simple one—the old-fashioned mutton chop for breakfast, sometimes only a bread pudding for lunch, dinner at seven and generally tea at nine. Conservative in his dress, he wore wide "gill" collars, a black tie, a loose-fitting frockcoat of black-blue velvet, dark uncreased trousers and boots made for comfort. His grand-nephew, J. R. Monsell, whose widowed mother and family lived at Curragh Chase from 1887 until 1897, knew de Vere as an elderly man. He describes him vividly. De Vere had a fine head and a humorous mouth, silky waving hair and a light feathery gleam of whisker. His complexion, no doubt from his outdoor life, was like that of a girl, with a delicate pink on the cheekbones, and he flushed readily with emotion.[67]

Aubrey de Vere was by no means a sportsman; hunting, fishing, and other outdoor sports did not appeal to him. But he was an untiring pedestrian. In County Galway he would start

out at four o'clock in the afternoon for a long walk through fields
and country roads; often he went outdoors on stormy evenings,
sometimes repeating Tennyson's poem on the death of Oliver
Cromwell, whose stormy spirit departed in a wild thunderstorm.
At Curragh Chase he generally spent the morning at his large,
red-baize-covered table in the library containing his fine manuscript copy of his father's *Mary Tudor,* Wordsworth's poems, and
Faber's *Launcelot;* there he did most of his research and writing.
Indoors he wore a skullcap and a velvet coat. For his daily ramble
out-of-doors, however, he put on a "Tavernese" cloak, of fine
black cloth, with a velvet collar and silver clasps; before his
brother Horace had gone to the Crimean war, he had given
de Vere the cloak which he used for many decades and had
renovated by Mrs. de Vere on his yearly visits to Galway. A
slouch hat — similar to those worn by Tennyson — a pair of
black woolen gloves and a large loosely furled umbrella completed
his walking outfit. Early and late de Vere walked in the Curragh
Chase woods; his favorite place was the "Sunset Walk," loved by
his mother. There he liked to sit and watch the sinking sun.
Another haunt reminiscent of his romantic childhood was "Cave
Walk," made for him by his father; he loved it for its castle-like
walls. When the weather was too inclement, he would spend an
hour or more walking up and down the large hall. After dinner
de Vere liked to play backgammon with the daughter of his sister,
Mrs. Monsell. When he joined the family in the drawing-room,
he used an old-fashioned armchair, covered in red velvet. Sometimes he would read or recite poems to the children, or ask them
about their doings. The O'Brien children, who spent much time
with Mrs. Monsell at Curragh Chase, found Aubrey de Vere
most attentive to their stories. If the children had been out
hunting, de Vere would question them about all that had happened
—where the hounds found the fox, what fences they had jumped,
who fell, who rode well.[68]

Mrs. Monsell gives a good picture of de Vere at seventy-four:
his complexion fresh and his step elastic, he showed no signs of
old age. He was so active that at times in the course of a walk
he would climb steep hills. He was fastidious in some matters;

when his nephew, Robert Vere O'Brien, was to be married to Miss Arnold Forster, the choice of the correct tie for such an occasion troubled him. He took two to the church, and after ascertaining the one to use, he put it on as he stood behind a pillar.[69] Of good manners he was most particular.

At the age of eighty-three Aubrey de Vere was a tall slender figure, unbent by age, with an atmosphere of geniality and gladness about him. An American visitor in London in 1897 gives us this charming picture:

> In the presence of Aubrey de Vere there is the vigorous freshness of morning; or else his is one of those rare evenings of life, when the sky is lighted to the very zenith with glow of the sunset. His eyes are clear and bright, kindling as he speaks with rare enthusiasm; he has a keen sense of humor, the gift of all Irishmen, and at the same time a calm, dignified presence . . . We talked of Wordsworth, and Mr. de Vere told us many anecdotes of the great poet . . . He told us of the tomb of his ancestors, the fighting Veres, in Westminster Abbey . . . The next day he came with some sprays of blooming lavender, which he presented with a quaint gallantry to my sister and to me, keeping one piece for his own buttonhole.
>
> That night he dined with us, a stately figure in his velvet coat, and with that gentle courtesy of manner, which seems also to have passed away with much else that belonged to a former time.[70]

Although much of de Vere's life was lived in an atmosphere of solitude and a sort of romanticism, he was keenly alive to the reality of dangers which threatened the country, and he had the foresight to judge their effects. He feared that England and even Europe were giving up Christianity, that they were regarding it merely as a legend and a dream. He worried about the scientific agnosticism of Huxley and Tyndall, seeping its way into the universities; he condemned the godless view of life presented by John Stuart Mill in his autobiography; he attacked the Comtists' reasoning—"Of God you know nothing, not even His existence."[71] Although de Vere admired most of Shelley's poems, he regretted the lyricist's lack of reverence and subsequent conclusion that religion is moral tyranny and that faith implies weakness. Carlyle's unhappiness de Vere attributed to his discarding all revealed religion; and Matthew Arnold's reductions of God to "the tendency of all things to righteousness"[72] filled him with horror.

After his conversion to Catholicism de Vere intensified his correspondence with most of his old friends, Manning and Newman, as well as many Americans. It was his means of keeping abreast of political developments, literary events and other interests. Always averse to a "narrow, money-making profession, pursued with the cant of duty, but in the spirit of trade," he continued writing in the hope to effect good.

By his writings de Vere did all in his power to offset the flood of religious unbelief that he saw advancing with frightful swiftness over England. Speaking of the apparent conflict between science and religion, he remarked: "To disparage Science would be to dishonor one of God's greatest gifts to man. It is to her progress, and that of Liberty, that Humanity looks forward with most trust for her future; but for their progress, nay for their permanence, it is necessary that authentic Religion should maintain in the heart of each man, not only a place, but a power proportionate to the power wielded by its noblest rivals, and should advance with their advance."[73]

Rather apart in politics and even religion, Aubrey de Vere often went his way alone, but in everything he acted with sincerity and from the highest principles. Like his father, he had the comprehensive quality of reverence—"reverence for kings, priests, women (toward whom he always looked with a mixture of tenderness and respect), for children, for all who were aggrieved or oppressed, for all things that were pure, lovely, and of good report . . ."[74] Aubrey de Vere once said that he had always had an exaggerated love of everything that looked like personal liberty; and this independence, guided by high and worthy principles decided his conduct.

Despite so much of his life spent at Curragh Chase, Aubrey de Vere was really a citizen of the world—courtly, polished,

refined, chivalrous and manly. In him there was no backwardness
or shyness, as Edmund Gosse implied in a poem to Aubrey
de Vere (a poem which Lady Shaw disliked very much). Un-
affected by the spirit of the world, he knew its ways, and was
free from morbid self-consciousness. Human and humorous, he
never hurt anyone, but often turned the laugh on himself. He was
natural and simple, self-effacing yet dignified. And he was true
to his numerous friendships because he was interested in others
more than himself. Moreover, with some degree of leisure and
without binding family ties and the strain of business, he was
able to correspond with, meet and help others—with one aim
always in mind—to know better and to make known the life of
the spirit. Spirituality was the well of his character and har-
moniously flowed along with his interest in the world and its
people.

2

DISCIPLE

OF

WILLIAM WORDSWORTH

As a boy of eighteen de Vere voiced for the first time his praise of William Wordsworth when he dedicated an ode to the bard of Rydal.[1] From the laureate's death in 1850 until his own final illness in the first years of this century, de Vere paid an annual visit to Wordsworth's grave.[2] This was the expression of respect and admiration of one who had devoted his long life to championing Wordsworth's cause. According to William Knight, de Vere contributed more interesting and trustworthy reports of Wordsworth than anyone else with the sole exception of Miss Fenwick. Intimate friendship with the poet for more than eight years and the close contact with Wordsworth's most enthusiastic friends—his own father, Sir Aubrey; Henry Taylor; William Rowan Hamilton; Sara Coleridge; William Allingham; Richard Monckton Milnes; Miss Fenwick; and even Wordsworth's old servant, "faithful James"[3]— enabled de Vere to reach an accurate estimate and true interpretations of the poet and his work.

Aubrey de Vere rescued Wordsworth from the charge of egotism, clarified the old poet's moral purpose, introduced Tennyson and Wordsworth to their mutual advantage, and prevented the laureate from altering his verse in later years. De Vere's observations, combined with sympathetic criticism, have produced an authentic and many-dimensioned portrait of Wordsworth.

De Vere left a vivid picture of his own youthful acceptance of Wordsworth before that poet had attained his great popularity. Until then de Vere, like Tennyson and other young men of the day, had assiduously followed the vogue of Byron. However, after some discussion with his father, and the consequent reading of "Laodamía," he discarded the popular "Byronic sulk." As he told Sara Coleridge years later, he "threw off Byron early, as a vicious young horse throws off a bad rider."[4]

The youthful de Vere seemed to find spiritual guidance in the work of Wordsworth. He seemed to reach a new and larger planet, after being "converted" to Wordsworth. The enthusiastic "disciple" cast his own early poems into the sonnet form because of the thought and wide sympathies he found in his "master's" sonnets.

The first meeting with Wordsworth, in London, in 1841, was a notable event in the life of young de Vere. Shortly thereafter he passed a week in the Lake Region in Miss Fenwick's house, and as Wordsworth's guest for a few days, he saw the "old Druid" in his native environment. In a letter to Henry Taylor he gives free vent to the enthusiasm which the days with Wordsworth engendered in him:

> I can hardly tell you the interest with which I listened to Miss Fenwick's conversation . . . He [Wordsworth] speaks still with as fresh enthusiasm on all subjects which present themselves to his moral and poetic sympathies . . . The Old Man of the Mountains is as strong as ever in body and soul. I have seen a great deal of him, and listened to more wisdom than could be extracted from all the conversation going on in London for a week together. We have toiled up the mountainside . . . for hours together . . . It is one of the wonders of the world to hear him talk over his own poetry and give you its secret history . . . There is something very interesting in Miss Fenwick's friendship for Wordsworth . . . What a man he is, and yet hers is a higher moral nature.[5]

It is clear that de Vere liked the laureate, and the latter probably felt himself drawn to this ardent admirer so capable of appreciating his poetry. That Wordsworth esteemed his young friend's judgment, even in the early days of their friendship, is apparent from a letter which he wrote to his publisher, Moxon, shortly after the first meeting with de Vere:

> Mr. Aubrey de Vere is very much interested in the publication of my poems but materially different in the choice from Mr. Hines'. What do you say to that? Dare you venture upon it? He has furnished me a list according to his own choice.[6]

Much later, when Aubrey was asked by his niece, Lady Shaw, to designate his favorites among Wordsworth's poems, he marked the following the *Poems of Wordsworth, selected from the Best Editions* (2 vols., W. Kent and Company, 1880):

In *Volume One:*

Ode on Intimations of Immortality
My Heart Leaps Up When I Behold
To H.C., six years old
The Old Cumberland Beggar
Elegiac Stanzas
To the Daisy
The Brothers
A Farewell
She Dwelt among the Untrodden Ways
'Tis Said That Some Have Died for Love
How Rich that Forehead's Calm Expanse
Of St. Cecilia
Michael
Character of the Happy Warrior
A Poet's Epitaph

Lines Written in Early Spring
The Two April Mornings
The Fountain: A Conversation
Vernal Ode
Ode to Lycoris
Upon the Same Occasion, September 1819
Dion
Memory
Ode to Duty
Yew-Trees
O Nightingale! Thou Surely Art
Three Years She Grew in Sun and Shower
I Wandered Lonely as a Cloud
Ruth
Laodamía

Resolution and Independence
A Song at the Feast of
  Brogham Castle
The Echo

The Pass of Kirkstone
Evening Ode
Lines written a few miles
  above Tintern Abbey

In *Volume Two:*

To a Highland Girl
Stepping Westward
The Solitary Reaper
Departure of Sir Walter
  Scott
The Trossachs
Roman Antiquities
Yarrow Unvisited
Yarrow Visited
Yarrow Revisited
Eclipse of the Sun 1820
Three Cottage Girls
Nun Fret Not
The Spinning Wheel
From Michael Angelo
To the Supreme Being
Sorrow

Death
Imagination
An Evening Thought
The World Is Too Much
  With Us
To B. R. Haydon
On a Portrait of I. F.,
  Painted by Margaret
  Gillis
Parsonage in Oxfordshire
The Builder Virtues
Mutability
Reason and Faith
King's College Chapel
The Primrose of the Rock
Snowdrops
To May

A year later, an anonymous review entitled "Poems of Alfred Tennyson" appeared in the *Quarterly Review*.[7] Wordsworth, who had been informed that de Vere had written the review, was displeased with some remarks in it which he considered disparaging to himself. He wrote to Sir Aubrey de Vere, the poet's father:

> I am confident that unless the critique has been misrepresented to me [he himself had not seen it] the time is not distant when my young friend Aubrey de Vere, if he *be* the author, will sincerely repent of having been so far misled as to write in such a strain, or rather that his judgment had not been thoroughly weighed . . .[8]

Learning that Aubrey de Vere had not written the review, Wordsworth wrote to his young friend two months later:

> Let me express my pleasure in learning that I had been misinformed concerning the article in the "Quarterly." The

thing I have not read nor probably ever will read; but it grieved me to think, from what I heard of it, that it should be written by any friend of mine for whom I have so much regard, and whom I esteem so highly as yourself . . .[9]

De Vere's companionship with Wordworth among his own mountains where he could be best understood,[10] in those regions of which he was "prophet and priest," proved rare opportunities. As they climbed the mountains together, and visited the poet's favorite haunts, Wordsworth gradually revealed his mind and philosophy. "I wish I could send you a list of even the subjects we talked over, but this is impossible," wrote de Vere to his sister. Wordsworth told him that many of his poems were founded on fact, that he was slow in hoping himself a poet, that "Tintern Abbey" was written in his twenty-eighth year, and that from the beginning he had felt called to expound the symbolic "bible" of nature. Wordsworth seemed to converse with nature and to await its messages. As he walked on the mountains, by day or night, he appeared to exchange thoughts with them. Wordsworth felt that inaccurate or untrue descriptions of nature were profanations, heavenly messages falsely delivered. Consequently, he expressed indignation with those ancient writers who incorrectly represented the nightingale as sad, the fox as cowardly, the wolf as ferocious.

Wordsworth, de Vere reported, found fault with Scott[11] for misquoting his "Yarrow"; the substitution of "swans" for "swan" and "sweet" for "still" destroyed the effect of loneliness which he had portrayed in the scene. Such inaccuracy, Wordsworth asserted, implied lack of spiritual discernment. The laureate also criticized Scott's method of working at poetry: he went about the countryside listing in a book the details of nature that caught his attention. Returning home, Scott wove these elements into a poetical description. "Nature does not permit an inventory of her charms!" Wordsworth would indignantly exclaim. The writer of poetry, he explained, should observe and enjoy nature; then after a lapse of several days he should make an artistic poetical picture of the scene as it remains in his mind. Thus the poet will select only significant details and will catch the soul of the scene, for example, "golden daffodils . . . tossing their heads in sprightly dance . . ."

Painting of Aubrey de Vere in Dining Room of Curragh Chase

Park, Lake and Family Memorial Cross

Aubrey de Vere's Birthplace and Home

Entrance Hall with Sculpture Collection

A Corner of the Library

Room Occupied by Aubrey de Vere for more than Seventy Years

Ruins of Franciscan Monastery on River Maigue near Curragh Chase

This "inspired selectness," de Vere maintained, constituted the secret of Wordsworth's power in painting natural scenes.

Wordsworth, too, used a notebook, but in a different manner. De Vere once wrote to Hamilton:

> Did Wordsworth ever tell you, as he did me, that the accident of his being given a manuscript book was the first *occasion* (I do not say cause) of his writing? He thought it a pity, after filling a few pages, to leave the remainder 'white and written still,' and so got into the habit of reducing to shape the thoughts which before had been vaguely haunting his brain, like the body-wanting souls, which wander by the Lethean pools.[12]

Like Ruskin, de Vere compared Wordsworth's attitude toward nature with that of Turner. Poet and artist, he suggested, keenly observed and ardently loved nature. Both interpreted it in its relation with man and in its symbolic significance. Both revealed the soul of nature; and, like Shakespeare, they were faithful in their portrayal of it. Depicting the individual and actual, they also portrayed the universal and archetypal.

Wordsworth's theme, the mutual reaction of human nature and material nature, necessarily emphasized the role of external nature in such a manner that the poet was sometimes accused of pantheism. However, de Vere argued that Wordsworth was too Christian to believe in pantheism, or to content himself with material deities. His fidelity to the true and personal God forced him to relegate external nature to secondary place. As he observed nature with open eyes, however, Wordsworth saw in it heavenly meanings and authentic memorials of the Divine Maker. De Vere noted that as Wordsworth advanced in years his religious beliefs became more orthodox, probably through the influence of Mrs. Wordsworth.

De Vere found a distinct assertion of faith, hope and charity as a means of communion with God in *The Excursion*.[13] Ideas of truth, justice, beauty and good appear in his "Ode on the Intimations of Immortality."[14] Regarding Wordsworth's implications of pre-existence in this poem de Vere stated that the author had assured him that he had held that theory in a poetic, and not in a

religious sense. Nevertheless, Wordsworth's apparent acceptance
of the theory of innate ideas seemed to imply otherwise.

De Vere noticed decided evidences of Wordsworth's religious
faith in his more mature poetry. In his daily life—in conversation,
at family prayers, and in church—he impressed de Vere as a
Christian believer. On one occasion he attempted to alter one of
his odes, in order to remove the old charge of paganism, which
annoyed him greatly. This conviction of the spiritual influence of
Wordsworth's poetry was strengthened during a visit that de Vere
paid to "Grace Dieu" and Charnwood Forest, the scene of the
laureate's Coleorton Poems. Going through the new Cistercian
monastery, de Vere noticed a portrait of Wordworth among those
of saints. When he manifested surprise, the abbot told him that he
had placed it there in gratitude for the spiritual help Wordworth's
poems had given him when he was a young man.[15] The abbot also
stated that his first inclination to the monastic life came with the
reading of these lines of *The Excursion:*

> The life where Hope and Memory are one,
> Earth quiet and unchanged; the human soul
> Consisted in self-rule; and heaven revealed
> To meditate in that quietness.

The unshaken belief that Wordsworth had the power to
inspire and uplift encouraged de Vere through life. That the
laureate aimed to exert a wholesome influence is clear from the
following, quoted by de Vere: "It is indeed a deep satisfaction
to hope and believe that my poetry will be, while it lasts, a help
to the cause of virtue and truth, especially among the young."[16]
And Wordsworth had reason for this hope, for he told de Vere of
many letters of appreciation received from readers who had felt
his inspiration.[17]

De Vere, therefore, was a lifelong champion of Wordsworth's
cause: "his most receptive and sympathetic propagandist since the
world lost him," as Alice Meynell said.[18] In conversation, reviews,
and correspondence he promoted Wordsworth's influence; his
American letters to professors and litterateurs prove his untiring
desire to make the bard of Rydal known across the Atlantic.

De Vere explained the discrepancy between the laureate's

early apparent pantheism and his mature orthodoxy, which rendered some of Wordsworth's poems "confessions of Christian faith." He wrote in his "Recollections of Wordsworth":

> He once remarked to me . . . that when in youth his imagination was shaping for itself the channel in which it was to flow, his religious convictions were less definite and less strong than they had become on more mature thought; and that when his poetic mind and manner had once been formed he feared lest he might, in attempting to modify them, become strained. He added that on religious matters he ever wrote with great diffidence, remembering that if there were subjects too low for song, there were some too high.[19]

Other critics also have offered various explanations for this change in Wordsworth and his work: the end of Coleridge's influence on Wordsworth, the death of Wordsworth's brother, and the realization that nature is insufficient for spiritual needs.[20] De Vere, moreover, answered the charge of egotism leveled against Wordsworth. He regarded the apparent egotism as inoffensive. Wordsworth, he said, studied himself as a typical human being whose thoughts and feelings might be applied to all—to man in general.[21]

While Wordsworth in the role of poet, and moral and political thinker, insisted that the soul of poetry is truth, he also admitted that love is an important theme. He confided to his disciple his reason for not writing more love poetry, which he was capable of producing: he feared that he might write with more ardor than would have been profitable for the young.[22] Wordsworth also told de Vere that concentration on one form of love defrauded many other forms, not less sacred, of their due. Although de Vere knew the poet only as an old man, he felt convinced that he was a man capable of strong passions, as the "Lucy poems" imply. A diary entry in 1845 reads: "Miss Fenwick, who knew Wordsworth most intimately, told me that Wordsworth could not trust himself to write any but severe poetry."[23]

Despite the comparative meagerness of Wordworth's love poetry and the claim of some critics that the laureate's work is cold and unimpassioned, de Vere maintained that passion is one of the most eminent characteristics of his poems. Because all high poetry is impassioned, de Vere insisted, the charge against Wordsworth was injurious. It was also unjust, since it proceeded from a misconception of true poetic passion.[24] Wordsworth himself in his definition of poetry used the words "impassioned expression"; and his "high passion" found expression in keen and sympathetic portrayal of human nature influenced by external nature.

Wordsworth's passion, de Vere explained, was free from sensational phrases and sensuous instincts. It served as a minister of virtue as well as a purveyor of pleasure.[25] He considered it intellectualized emotion, appealing only to those capable of understanding it. So impassioned that it is really at white heat, it appears cold and unimpassioned to the uninitiated. De Vere furthermore distinguished between Wordsworth's "high passion" and that "intellectualized appetite" of the so-called sensual school of poetry, represented by such poets as Swinburne, whose influence he considered pernicious.[26]

While de Vere found this high passion characteristic of Wordsworth's best work, he admitted that some of his poems were over-didactic and uninspired, and consequently lacking in passion. However, he explained that Wordsworth as an avowed teacher[27] sometimes sacrificed poetry to the ethical or philosophical truth he wished to express.[28] It must be acknowledged that Wordsworthian passion is, as de Vere implied, of a peculiar, restrained type.

Considering the mutual esteem with which de Vere and Wordsworth regarded each other, one naturally inquires just how much Wordsworth was influenced by de Vere. As the latter saw a great deal of the laureate, especially from 1841 until 1846, he probably left his impress on the older poet. Aubrey de Vere's diary for 1845 furnishes definite proof that de Vere at least prevented the laureate's spoiling some of his odes. Three consecutive entries read:

> *March 7*—Wordsworth propounded a new reading of a passage in one of his odes . . . which alteration I resisted successfully.

March 8—He proposed another alteration of his ode, with
a view to rescue himself from a charge of paganism. I
resisted the innovation; and we agreed that poetry ought
to put forth great truths, full-faced and singly, without
trying to adjust the balance between opposite truths.

March 9—He made another attempt at altering an ode, but
again promised to give it up.

This inclination of Wordsworth to tamper with poetry written
in his youth is further confirmed in a recorded conversation among
de Vere, Tennyson and Allingham.[29] De Vere had remarked that
Wordsworth should have done great and perfect things, since he
had devoted his entire life to poetry. Allingham replied that the
laureate's mind had become monotonous by reading only his own
poems for years.[30] De Vere agreed with Allingham, and stated
that the older poet was continually retouching, altering and sometimes injuring what he had written.

In regard to the "Laureate Ode," generally attributed to
Wordsworth and often placed at the end of his volume of poems,
de Vere was able to offer authentic and convincing information. He
claimed that the poem, also called "Ode on the Installation of His
Royal Highness Prince Albert as Chancellor of the University of
Cambridge," and written three years before the laureate's death, is
without inspiration. If printed at all, de Vere said, it should be
placed in an appendix with explanatory notes.[31] He based his
conclusions on reliable evidence:

Indeed Miss Fenwick assured me that it was *not* composed
by Wordsworth, but at his entreaty by E. Quillinan, Wordsworth having been strongly urged by the Court to write on
the subject, having failed in an attempt which but for his extreme kindness he would never have made. She said he had
made suggestions and put in perhaps touches here and there
. . . but that it was *not his*.[32]

Three years after making this statement de Vere again insisted
that the poem was not Wordsworth's. Writing to William Knight,
the Wordsworth scholar, he stated:

This is certainly the truth: I should think that he probably
told all that truth to the officials when transmitting the Ode;

but that they concealed the circumstances; and that Wordsworth, then profoundly depressed in spirits on account of
Dora's illness and death, gave no more thought to the subject
and soon forgot all about it. [33]

De Vere further asserted that even had Wordsworth written
the ode, he would not have included it in his works, as he hated
laureate odes. In fact he accepted the laureateship "only on condition that he was to write none."[34] De Vere said that he had
absolutely no reason for believing that Christopher Wordsworth,
the poet's nephew, had anything to do with the ode, as Andrew
George alleged. However, he argued, no matter who wrote the
"Laureate Ode," it should never be placed "on the high altar of
Wordsworth's Cathedral."[35] Finally, de Vere urged Knight to
write to Miss Arnold, an intimate friend of Wordsworth, regarding the matter; she would state "that Wordsworth had *no part in
the Ode*."[36]

De Vere's championing of Wordsworth and his desire to
spread his influence kept pace with their friendship. Perhaps the
most interesting incident during the close friendship of the two
men was the occasion of de Vere's bringing together Wordsworth
and Tennyson, to the great advantage of the future laureate.

3

CHAMPION

OF

ALFRED LORD TENNYSON

The bond of friendship which existed between de Vere and Wordsworth was the result of deep respect: the young poet always regarded the bard of Rydal as a master, to be revered and admired. Consequently, he was to dedicate a great deal of his time and his writings to spreading the fame of the man with whom he had had personal contact only through the last eight years of Wordsworth's life, but whose memory he kept fresh during all of his own lifetime.

Among all the poets who became friends of de Vere, it was Alfred Tennyson with whom he was the most intimate. The close friendship between these two men lasted over half a century: from their meeting in 1842 until the death of the poet laureate in 1893.

Aubrey de Vere's interest in Tennyson began in 1832, when he read Arthur Hallam's essay on the first volume of Tennyson's poetry. He pored over the article in the *Englishman,* which Richard Monckton Milnes had brought with him on his visit to de Vere's home. He became absorbed in this "new" poetry, so different from that of his favorite Wordsworth. Years later he expressed his first impression of it: "There were for me a wild, inexplicable magic and a deep pathos . . . and the character of the language was nearly the opposite . . . of the language of common life among the educated."[1]

So interested were de Vere and his sister Ellen in this new poetry that they read it as they rode up and down the green drives through their Curragh Chase woods while their pony, sensing their abstraction, would almost upset the carriage, or would sometimes remain standing with his head hanging over a gate. Interest in Tennyson was further fostered by de Vere's elder brother and his cousin, Stephen Spring Rice, who were Cambridge friends of Tennyson, as well as by Monckton Milnes, Spedding, Brookfield, and Dr. Whewell. De Vere gradually became intimate with these "Apostles," but not until 1842 on a London visit to his uncle, Lord Limerick, did he meet Tennyson. De Vere was then twenty-eight, and Tennyson five years his senior. The pen-portrait de Vere drew is graphic:

> It was in 1842 that I first met the poet on whom, and on whose work, my imagination had rested so often during the preceding ten years, and I lost nothing when the living man stood before me. The large dark eyes, generally dreamy, but with an occasional gleam of imaginative alertness; the dusky, almost Spanish complexion; the high-built head, and the massive abundance of curling hair, like the finest and blackest silk, are still before me; and no less the stalwart form, strong with the certain step of man.[2]

Feeling attracted to Tennyson, de Vere often visited him while he was "living in a mysterious sort of way on the Hampstead Road—bathing, and learning Persian." According to his diary, de Vere's visits were frequent during 1845 and 1846, the years in which he saw much of Wordsworth also. Often out of spirits, Tennyson railed against the whole system of society, against poverty, and his own miserable state; and de Vere patiently listened to his expressions of self-pity and discontent. On April 18 de Vere recorded: "Sat with Alfred Tennyson, who read Ms. poetry . . . He said he would willingly bargain for the reputation of Suckling or Lovelace . . . Said he was dreadfully cut up by all he had gone through."[3]

De Vere tolerantly heard Tennyson's complaints against

unfavorable reviewers: "I called on Alfred Tennyson, and found him at first much out of spirits. He cheered up soon, and read some beautiful Elegies, complaining of some writer in *Fraser's Magazine* who has spoken of the 'foolish facility' of Tennysonian poetry." Meanwhile de Vere watched with interest the development of *The University* (later *The Princess*) and *Elegies* (*In Memoriam*); and he suggested improvements while Tennyson "crooned till one in the morning." As the poet "intoned" all his poetry, the sound of his deep voice would linger in de Vere's ears as he walked home after spending the entire night with the English poet.

Despite Tennyson's declaration that he cared nothing for fame, de Vere was most eager to see him appreciated. Therefore, while visiting at Rydal Mount, he decided to interest Wordsworth in the work of the depressed and little-known Tennyson, who was most eager to meet the laureate. Accordingly, he tactfully mentioned that a young poet had lately risen up. "Wordsworth answered that he feared from the little he had heard that if Crabbe was the driest of poets, the young aspirant must have the opposite fault. I replied that he should judge for himself, and, *without leave given,* recited to him two poems by Tennyson: 'You ask me, why, though ill at ease' and 'Of old sat Freedom on the heights'. Wordsworth listened with a gradually deepening attention. After a pause he answered, 'I must acknowledge that these two poems are very solid and noble in thought. Their diction also seems singularly stately'."[4]

Two months later, on May fourth, de Vere "brought Tennyson, murmuring sore . . . to see Mr. Wordsworth." Tennyson was pleased and amused when his host, taking his arm, pleasantly said, "Come, brother bard, to dinner." And the laureate was both gratified and flattered by Tennyson's praise of his poetry. De Vere wrote to Miss Isabel Fenwick of this significant meeting:

> I brought Alfred Tennyson up the high hill to pay his respects to the venerable bard. They met at dinner twice, and I was much pleased at finding how much the young poet had liked the old one. There was something at once touching and amusing in the account Tennyson gave me of the evening they

passed together. He had begun by having a certain degree of prejudice against him, but he told me that as he saw the old man with his white hair sitting opposite him, and remembered at the moment that he was the author of "Laodamía" and "Tintern Abbey" and other poems which he had delighted in since boyhood, he could not help a strange feeling of affection for him, which strengthened by degrees.[5]

On July first, after other meetings, the laureate wrote to an American friend: "I saw Tennyson when I was in London several times. He is decidedly the first of our living poets, and I hope will live to give the world better things."[6]

Thus, within four months after hearing Tennyson's poems, which de Vere had read "without leave given" and without consulting Tennyson in advance, the apparently prejudiced Wordsworth declared the younger man the first of England's living poets. The laureate's approval of his younger colleague must have meant much in Tennyson's poetic career; and this approval, as well as Wordsworth's discernment of Tennyson's potentialities, was thus in a great measure due to Aubrey de Vere.

More than thirty years later, de Vere casually told Tennyson of the early championing of his cause. "I read to Wordsworth 'Of old sat Freedom on the heights' and 'You ask me, why, though ill at ease'; and he said, 'Fine poetry and very stately diction'." Tennyson replied, "Hmm," contentedly.[7]

Except for Henry Taylor, Tennyson was to de Vere the most interesting man he had ever met, "so original and yet so rich in sympathy for all that was natural."[8] When the future laureate dolorously remarked that he "cared nothing for fame, and that his life was all thrown away for want of a competence and retirement,"[9] de Vere strongly prescribed for him an "occupation, a wife, and orthodox principles";[10] and Tennyson admitted the wisdom of this advice. "He is as simple as a child and not less interesting for his infirmities,"[11] de Vere wrote in 1848, while Tennyson was his guest for five weeks at Curragh Chase. That spring, Aubrey de Vere had found Tennyson in London, surfeited with dinner-parties and other social events—sixteen engagements between May 3 and 23. Eager to "be alone with God" and to find rest near the sea, Tennyson had decided to go to Devon and Cornwall; but de Vere persuaded him to choose Ireland, where he would see waves of great height. Tennyson went first to de Vere's home, and apparently enjoyed his Curragh Chase vacation, spending the day as he wished, listening to Beethoven and Mozart in the evening, reading his favorite Crabbe to the de Vere family, and expressing disappointment when they did not weep over a sad tale. On one occasion, feeling moody, he refused to go to a dance in the house; whereupon a relative of de Vere's sharply ordered him to put on an evening coat and ask her daughter, Sophia, to dance with him. She inquired of him what the world would be like if others went about growling about amusements in a voice as deep as a lion's. Tennyson took the Irish lady's advice, and danced with delight for several hours.

Tennyson later climbed to the top of Knock Patrick with de Vere, and heard the story of Saint Patrick's famous sermon and his blessing of the land. At Valencia, as the guest of the Knight of Kerry, he enjoyed watching the mighty waves roll in from the Atlantic; and at Killarney he composed the "Bugle Song" for the third edition of *The Princess*. In Ireland Tennyson's swarthy complexion and solitary habits aroused the suspicion of a Fenian; some feared he was a Frenchman and one to be watched, for at that time, a period of great unrest in Europe, there was a rumor of a French invasion of England and Ireland.

Two years later Tennyson finally married; he chose a woman of good sense and orthodox principles. De Vere's impression of her was enthusiastic:

> The poet's wife is a very interesting woman—kindly, affectionate . . . above all deeply and simply religious. Her great and constant desire is to make her husband more religious, or at least to conduce, as far as she may, to his growth in the spiritual life. In this she will doubtless succeed, for piety like hers is infectious, especially where there is an atmosphere of affection to serve as a conducting medium. Indeed, I already observe a great improvement in Alfred. His nature is a religious one . . .; such a nature gravitates toward Christianity especially when it is in harmony with itself.[12]

Undoubtedly, de Vere diagnosed Tennyson's spiritual confusion
correctly. Naturally religious, he had been surrounded from his
youth by young men who "believed no more in Christianity than in
the Feudal System." As Mrs. Tennyson was as interested in her
husband's spiritual outlook as in his poetry, she probably encouraged his friendship with de Vere as one who "might confirm
him in all things wise and healthful." It is an interesting side-
light that de Vere, on learning that Mrs. Tennyson had "a great
horror of Rome," refrained from discussing religion with her,
except, as he expressed it, "just enough to let her see that his
views were different."[13]

Allingham's *Diary* contains an entry, of September 3, 1868,
that illustrates the Tennysons', as well as his own, reaction to
Catholicism as formulated by de Vere. The entry runs as follows:

> "I . . . dined at Farringford. Dinner: A.T., Mrs. T.,
> Lionel, . . . de Vere, and W.A. De Vere's talk of Catholicism
> . . ., sliding into Newmanism and Jesuitry. The T's mildly
> dissentient, I getting angry. T., de V., and I went out under
> the stars. I flared up and asked de Vere, 'Do you yourself
> entirely believe the account given by the Roman Catholic
> Church of God and man?' "
>
> De Vere replied that he did; when Allingham said, "I
> don't believe one atom of it," Tennyson remarked: "You have
> no point of contact then."[14]

Tennyson had certain poetic principles and devices of style
which contributed to the success of his writing. He believed, for
example, that a poem should reflect time and place, the era and
the nationality of its composition. Such notions as these he discussed with de Vere, who made them known to other writers
through his letters and to readers in his essay on Tennyson's
early poems.

De Vere further explained the poet's practice of eliminating
even good stanzas from a short poem, in order that it might not
be "long-backed." Tennyson, said de Vere, held that "every short
poem should have a definite shape, like a curve, sometimes a single,
sometimes a double one, assumed by a severed tress, or the rind of
an apple when flung on the floor."[15] De Vere contrasted Tennyson

with Browning and Swinburne in this regard, and said that the
last-named poets were "constantly spoiling their poems by not
understanding this law of proportion, and thus making them too
long."[16] De Vere told Coventry Patmore that Tennyson in his
solicitude for poetic form applied this rule to *In Memoriam,* lest
anything superfluous distort the poem and spoil its shape.[17]

De Vere did not accept all Tennyson's poetic views, however;
in his critique of *The Princess,* published in the *Edinburgh
Review,* he wrote in part:

> The reader . . . will perceive that although the discordant
> materials of the tale are put together with much skill, it
> does not propose to itself the highest objects of narrative
> poetry . . . The faults of "The Princess" are, in the main,
> faults of detail . . .; the heroine is a little too metaphysical in
> her discourse . . . There are too many classical allusions
> in the hero's mouth. The diction seems too familiar.[18]

Evidently de Vere had proposed some changes in *The
Princess,* for Tennyson wrote to him:

> I had Moxon send you the new edition of "The Princess."
> You will find that in some measure I have adopted your sug-
> gestions, not entirely. Many thanks for your critique in the
> *Edinburgh* . . . I have every reason to be grateful to you,
> both for the ability of the article and for the favourable view
> you take of me in general; too favourable surely. I dare not
> believe such good things of myself.[19]

Later, Tennyson informed de Vere that he experienced a very
lively gratification in finding that his recent alterations had met
de Vere's approval as well as that of de Vere's mother and sister.[20]
Thus de Vere was indirectly responsible for the second edition of
The Princess.

On other points the two poets disagreed. Although one of
the links which held them together was a common esteem for
Wordsworth, de Vere revered the old bard more than did Tennyson. The latter felt that Wordsworth's poetry lacked artistic skill
and that his "small things" were the best. On one occasion Tennyson remarked that even "Tintern Abbey" would be better if com-

pressed. Trying to justify his "master," de Vere replied that
Homer and Milton could be as dull as Wordsworth at times; but
Tennyson "grunted 'No, no!'" He added: "The man I count
greater than them all—Wordsworth, Coleridge, Byron, Shelley,
every one of them—is Keats. . . . Thousands of faults! . . . but
he's wonderful."[21]

De Vere, who had discovered Robert Burns for himself
during his tour through Scotland, found that Tennyson and
Wordsworth disagreed in their judgment of the work of the
Scottish poet. Wordsworth had little regard for Burns' "foolish
little amatory songs," generally considered his best work; Tennyson chose to forget the bard's "stupid things, his serious pieces."[22]
Writing to de Vere from Scotland, in 1849, Tennyson told him
he had visited Kirk Allaway, in order to see the monument of
Burns as well as the "banks and braes of Bonny Doon." "I know
you do not care for him," he wrote, "but I do, and hold there
never was immortal poet if he be not one."[23]

One of the richest fruits of de Vere's contact with Tennyson
consists in his criticism and interpretation of the poet's work,
especially in the article entitled "The Reception of the Early
Poems—1832-1845." The diction of Tennyson's first volume, according to de Vere, was elaborate and somewhat artificial, in
keeping with the prevailing style; but the later poems proved
that Tennyson discarded his early elaborateness for a style
"especially marked by its purity." Beauty and pathos and an
interpretation of nature, new to de Vere, continued to survive in
the later poems.

De Vere called attention to the haunting melancholy of
"Marianna in the Moated Grange" and "The Dying Swan," both
excellent examples of the poet's skill in the use of long vowels.
"The Dream of Fair Women" suggested Dante to his mind. And
he found in "The Recollections of the Arabian Nights" a world
of bright vision set floating in sound." (A look at this poem,
"Kubla Khan-like" in images and meter, proves the aptness of
de Vere's statement.)

Tennyson's second volume of poems, published in 1854, impressed de Vere as less spontaneous than the first collection, but

richer in taste, artistry and versatility, especially embodied in English idyl, classic poem, and fantasy. "The Miller's Daughter," "The Lotus Eaters," and "The Dream of Fair Women" exemplify respectively these three types.

De Vere analyzed "The Palace of Art" keenly and discerningly: a subjective topic objectively handled, full of vividness and concentration, with images for a moral end. He related an interesting anecdote connected with the origin of this poem. While visiting Tennyson, Richard Trench, a poet (and later Archbishop of Canterbury), decried the "art for Art's sake" theory, later so popular with the aesthetes. On his departure, Tennyson wrote "The Palace of Art" as an answer to the "heresy" of substituting art for faith, and beauty for sanctity.

In the two poems he had quoted to Wordsworth, de Vere discerned Tennyson's attitude toward liberty: it must be a moral power founded on wisdom, mutual respect and self-control. He felt that the poems attained force through brevity, simplicity of diction and perfection of form. The fact that de Vere himself held that the value of liberty lies in its moral and spiritual, rather than its political aspect, probably attracted him to these poems.

Tennyson's 1842 collection, de Vere believed, excelled the earlier work both in form and content. This volume manifested the author's "largeness of sympathies," delight in knowledge, unity of purpose and singular common sense (which last de Vere regarded as a form of inspiration). The idyls of country life, the critic continued, were unlike anything written by any preceding poet. Such poems as "The Gardener's Daughter" caught the atmosphere of the countryside as well as the life of the people. In "The Talking Oak" the poet reached the heights of harmonious, expressive, and richly colored language; and "The Brook" de Vere considered a good companion poem for it. He correctly noted definite evidences of dramatic skill in the English idyls, so delightfully different from the work of former poets, whose "stock-in-trade" consisted of fauns, piping shepherds, and stereotyped descriptions of outdoor life.

Of *In Memoriam,* which he considered Tennyson's finest poem, de Vere remarked: "It showed how great a thing man's love is, by revealing the greatness of that love; that grief and deliverance from grief, of which it is capable." Of "The Idylls of the King": "It showed how high is that aim which every commonwealth of men is bound to propose to itself; and it showed that that aim, political at once and spiritual, when frustrated, owes its doom not to mischance or external violence chiefly, but to moral evil that saps the State's foundation."

Aubrey de Vere took considerable pains to point out the purity and nobility of Tennyson's teaching, even though he came to object to the overly-didactic tone of the poet's later work. He stressed, too, Tennyson's originality, his new interpretation of nature and his artistic workmanship, the result of careful and patient effort. He argued that Tennyson, although a born poet, had reached success not only through his intellectual and moral gifts, but also by his absorption in the all-important duty of writing praiseworthy poetry and of giving his entire attention to it. Thus Tennyson became not only a student of character and an exquisite artist, but also the most representative poet of his time.

Writing of Tennyson's volume of 1842, really representative of his best work, de Vere made a statement which may be regarded as a general estimate of his friend.

> It was the heart of England even more than her imagination that he made his own. It was the Humanities and the truths underlying them that he sang, and he so sang them that any deep-hearted reader was made to feel through his far-reaching thought that those humanities are spiritual things, and that to touch them is to touch the garment of the Divine. . . . The Heroic is not greatly appreciated in these days, but on this occasion the change met with a response.[24]

Despite differences of character and temperament, de Vere and Tennyson were alike in their quest for love and beauty, by which, however, de Vere implied divine love and beauty. Of Tennyson, his appreciative friend wrote: "It was easy to see that to discern the Beautiful in all around us, and to reveal that beauty to others, was his poetic vocation."[25]

Speaking of Tennyson and de Vere, both of whom he knew,
Wilfrid Ward made some significant remarks:

To my mind, the friend of Tennyson whose saintliness
most completely had his sympathy was Aubrey de Vere, of
whom Sara Coleridge said that he had more entirely a poet's
nature even than her own father, or any other of the great
poets she had known. Aubrey de Vere's simplicity and deep
piety were as remarkable as his keen perception and close
knowledge on the subject which most interested Tennyson
himself. I wish I had seen more of the intercourse of two men
whose friendship was almost lifelong, and showed Tennyson
at his very best in conversation.[26]

It was in the house of this friend, Wilfrid Ward, that de Vere
made Tennyson acquainted with Herbert Vaughan, later Cardinal.
The incident is amusing:

. . . In 1874 Bishop Vaughan was the guest of Mr. and
Mrs. Ward at Weston Manor. De Vere, who was visiting the
Tennysons at Farringford, decided to go to Weston to see
his former companion at Rome; and Lord and Lady Tennyson
accompanied him. Mrs. Cameron, the famous photographer,
who had long been seeking a subject for Tennyson's "Launcelot," suddenly entered the room where Bishop Vaughan,
"the most knightly of priests" was standing before the fire.
Transfixed by his appearance (as de Vere had been twenty
years before) she enthusiastically called to Tennyson, "I have
found Sir Launcelot." But the Laureate, whose sight was
poor, failed to see Vaughan; and he replied in a loud voice:
"I want a face that is well worn with human passion." The
Bishop smiled and blushed. Laughter ensued, and the Laureate and the future Cardinal became acquainted . . ."[27]

It cannot be denied that Tennyson's later poems inspire because of the spirituality which permeates them. The question arises
of how much the Irish poet and friend through half a century contributed to Tennyson's point of view. Their very long friendship,
their agreement on so many vital questions, and Tennyson's admiration for de Vere's nobility of character may have affected the
personality and work of Tennyson. Letters and diary, moreover,

prove that the self-effacing de Vere was neither an inactive nor a negligible factor in the life of Tennyson.[28]

Moreover, de Vere promoted interest in Tennyson by propagating his works, both in the British Isles and America, as his enthusiastic correspondence with Alice Meynell and Charles Eliot Norton of Harvard indicates. He became in large measure the literary critic and interpreter of the laureate and thus bequeathed to future generations Tennyson's valuable ideas and literary "discoveries." What he himself thought of his friend, he expressed best in a sonnet entitled "Poet," which he wrote in honor of the laureate:

> None sang of love more nobly; few as well;
> Of Friendship none with pathos so profound;
> Of Duty sternliest—proved when myrtle-crowned;
> Of English grove and rivulet, mead and dell;
> Great Arthur's Legend he alone dared tell;
> Milton and Dryden failed to tread that ground;
> For him alone o'er Camelot's faery bound
> The "horns of Elfland" blew their magic spell.
> Since Shakespeare and since Wordsworth none hath sung
> So well his England's greatness; none hath given
> Reproof more fearless or advice more sage;
> None inlier taught how near is earth to heaven;
> With what vast concords Nature's harp is strung;
> How base false pride; faction's fanatic rage.[29]

4

FRIEND

OF

THE COLERIDGES

The greatest of all great men . . . Samuel Taylor Coleridge . . . I never had the good fortune to meet, but his daughter was one of my chief friends . . . and her brothers I knew well . . . She was certainly the most wonderful woman I have ever known,"[1] wrote Aubrey de Vere in 1900 at the age of eighty-six, almost a half century after Sara Coleridge's death.

As a youth de Vere had chosen Coleridge as a philosophical guide because of the underlying spirituality in the poet-philosopher's teaching; this choice was made against the materialistic tenets of Bentham, then popular.[2] Naturally de Vere gradually became interested in Coleridge's poetry, in which he found music, spirituality and a subtle sweetness. He believed, as did Wordsworth, that no other poet had so exquisite an ear as did Coleridge; and he also felt that Coleridge would have been the greatest poet of his time had he written poetry ten years longer.

Although de Vere early turned from Byron's poetry, and later even that of Shelley, he retained forever his reverence for "the aged man with the dreary eyes—lips once brightened by Parnassian springs, and still breathing Elysian airs."[3] Each year throughout his long life de Vere visited the grave and haunts of

Coleridge. In later years he spoke of the poet-philosopher as one
of the inspired writers who had assisted his early spiritual development. Even de Vere's change of religion did not alter his allegiance to the memory of Coleridge. Although the old poet had
said hard things against Rome,[4] he considered the "Catholic
Church the normal means of preserving faith in an invisible world
among the mass of men";[5] and this "admission" pleased de Vere.

Aubrey de Vere first met Sara Coleridge in 1841; he found
her almost as interesting as Wordsworth, with whom he became
acquainted about the same time. Mutual interests—literature,
theology and religion, philosophy, and S.T.C.—drew them together and led to a prolific correspondence. Although they disagreed on many matters, theirs was an ideal friendship, based on
mutual respect and understanding, kindred interests, and proper
evaluation of each other's gifts.

Sara Coleridge certainly was a most unusual woman of many
accomplishments. At twenty, she translated, from the Latin of
Martin Dobrizhoffer, *An Account of the Abipones* (Equestrian
People of Paraguay), in three volumes. She also wrote *The Life
of Bayard*, in two volumes. Moreover, with her cousin-husband
she edited her father's *Biographia Literaria* (two volumes), *Notes
and Lectures upon Shakespeare* (two volumes), *Essays on His
Own Times* (three volumes), and *Poems of S.T.C.* As her husband
died in 1843, and these books were published respectively in 1847,
1849, 1850 and 1852, Sara must have done a vast amount of work
on them. Probably she had not time for her own writing; her only
original works are *Pretty Lessons in Verse for Good Children*
and *Phantasmion, a Fairy Tale*. This lyrical fairy tale of mingled
verse and prose makes the reader regret that Sara Coleridge did
not give the world more original writings. Her work proves her
learning and acuteness as well as her industry and patience, despite ill health. In a letter to Henry Reed, in 1851, she gives this
picture of de Vere:

> I have lived among poets a great deal, and have known
> greater and better poets than Aubrey de Vere—but a more
> *entire poet*—one more a poet in his whole mind and tempera-
> ment, I never knew or met with. He is most amiable, uniting

a feminine gentleness and compassionateness with the most perfect manliness, both negative and positive. He is all simplicity—yet so grateful and gracious! A polished *Irish* gentleman is the most polished of all gentlemen—and Aubrey de Vere is such—sportive and jestful—yet with a depth of seriousness in his nature ever present. His height is 6 feet 2 —slender and graceful, with a fair, clear skin emblematic of the perfect purity of mind.[6]

The long and extensive correspondence between these two gifted persons furnishes a great deal of information about them and provides insight into their characters. There was hardly a topic which was not touched on with poetry, criticism, and theology taking the lead. Letters and diary entries testify to the intensity of this correspondence and to its influence on their lives. For example, de Vere notes that he could not bring Sara to praise his father's *Mary Tudor*. De Vere once offered her a volume of Keats in exchange for her father's poems. She read *The Imitation of Christ* of Thomas à Kempis, which de Vere had given her. She was frankly grateful for de Vere's condolences on the death of her mother in October 1846.[7]

Discussing *Endymion,* Sara told de Vere with characteristic frankness, "I am afraid you like nothing that is *horrid,* that you are too fond of the 'roses and the thistle-down'; and find such things too flinty for your nice touch."[8] And in another letter to de Vere, who had acquired a liking for Burns as he traveled through the Highlands, she replied: "I am glad you are not too genteel to like Burns."[9]

While de Vere and Sara Coleridge were both strong Wordsworthians, they did not see eye to eye regarding his poems. Sara insisted that in Wordsworth's earlier poetry alone, the genuine Wordsworthian inspiration uttered itself. She believed that de Vere rated Wordsworth's later poems too high; the "Triad," in which Sara, Dora Wordsworth and Edith Southey are eulogized, she considered definitely second-rate, in contradiction to de Vere's admiration for it. No doubt, de Vere's friendship with Sara Coleridge increased his knowledge of Wordsworth, for she gave de Vere her own notes on Wordsworth.[10] She wrote to de Vere:

"I knew dear Mr. Wordsworth perhaps as well as I have ever known anyone in the world—more intimately than my own father, as intimately as I know my Uncle Southey."[11]

She disagreed, then, with Aubrey de Vere in her evaluation of Wordsworth's work; however, with him, she disapproved of Wordsworth's altering his early poems. She found Thomas Babington Macaulay, as did de Vere, a clever, agreeable man, though rather fond of showing off in conversation. While she considered Elizabeth Barrett Browning the most literary woman of the age, she greatly disliked her rugged, harsh versification and imperfect rhymes; so did de Vere. On the relative merits of Milton and Dante, Sara preferred Milton; de Vere called him the sublimest of the sublime, but chose Dante, whose work he read assiduously. Sara admired Thomas Gray, but did not feel drawn to Walter Savage Landor, whereas de Vere took the opposite stand regarding each.

De Vere's articles on Tennyson, Shelley and Keats, published in the *Edinburgh Review,* evoked praise from Sara Coleridge. She wrote to him:

> Nothing can be more admirable than your characterization of Keats. . . . What you say of Shelley is excellent too; but this on Keats is more *entirely* new, and the whole article is worthy of you.[12]

In one *Review* article he proved his appreciation of the great lyricist and clearly indicated the reasons for his youthful mistakes:

> He [Shelley] taught when he had but begun to think, and before he had begun to learn; and the perverse error which blinded his eyes made void one-half of the work of his hands . . . With the weapon of an idle and ignorant scorn he struck, not only at abuses and corruptions, . . . but at the truths older than either science or song, and higher than his highest hopes for man . . . Great indeed is the bequest which Shelley left us: and it is not without somewhat of remorseful sorrow that we remember what life gave him in return. . . . He had his intellectual raptures, and he had his friends—one of them fatal to him, because the supplanter of his youthful faith—Godwin.[13]

Keats's poetry, de Vere continued, shows a genius more Grecian than Shelley's. "His sense of beauty is profounder still; and is accompanied by that in which Shelley's poetry is deficient —Repose." Keats's work, de Vere held, implies a constant enjoyment of the beautiful, as well as an insatiable thirst for it. "Beauty was the adornment of Shelley's poetry; it was the very essence of Keats'." In his narrative poems, wrote de Vere, Keats proved his rare gift for invention and his power of diction. His most remarkable characteristic, however, was his perfect combination of the sensuous and the ideal; his ideality, explained de Vere, prevented the sensuous from degenerating into sensuality.

Interest in theology and religion appears again and again in the course of Sara Coleridge's and Aubrey de Vere's correspondence. Although their beliefs were at variance, they talked and wrote constantly on theological questions. With the utmost candor de Vere wrote on his religious progress "toward Rome." While visiting his old Anglican friend, Dr. John Jebb, de Vere wrote to Sara, inquiring:

> "Pray, is it true that Manning has 'joined Rome'? If so, how many has he taken with him?"[14]

De Vere again wrote to Sara while he himself was on his way to Rome and in the company of Henry Manning. Evidently de Vere wished to offer some consolation to Sara, then "very much out of spirits." Perhaps drawing from his own experience, he sent this message:

> God is most with us when His hand lies heaviest on us; and it is then chiefly that He endeavours to draw us to Himself. Could we but yield to that gentle violence and be with Him indeed, how soon should we find ourselves in the very centre of spiritual peace . . .[15]

And the very day of his reception into the Catholic Church, he told her in his letter from Avignon: "I was this morning received into what I believe to be the one Catholic and Apostolic Church . . ."[16] Three months later he assured her that Catholicism had cast no fetters on his mind.

De Vere's candor regarding his spiritual odyssey no doubt afforded Sara Coleridge a clearer and more sympathetic understanding of the Anglo-Catholic movement. His change of faith evidently made little or no change in their friendship, as it did in the case of other friends of de Vere. She greatly admired his "Nine Letters on Irish Affairs," published in *The Morning Chronicle*. She commended his style and ability to "preach about agriculture." This information she used in her introduction to her father's *Essays on His Own Times,* which she edited.

De Vere's high esteem for Sara Coleridge was reciprocated. Five years after they became acquainted, Sara wrote:

> I have found de Vere's conversation delightful. He lives in a region of poetic thought, an "unsubstantial faery place," outside the workaday world. To my weary, heavy spirit communion with him has ever been most soothing and refreshing; and the more so as his poetry . . . does not prevent him from considering realities of the life to come.[17]

His habitual optimism—his desire to "give *this earth* a fair trial, to have it show what it can be at its best, in the highest perfection of which it is capable"[18] cheered the last decade of her life, that otherwise would have been melancholy and ineffectual. That de Vere, "the warmest friend of her widowhood,"[19] re-awakened her creative ability finds verification in an entry in her notebook:

> My conversation with Mr. de Vere in the Years 1843, 4, 5; and our discussions of W— especially, re-excited my little weak poetic faculty. The poems which were produced under this influence I shall mark thus—for *A de V.*—as they were sent to him in letters during our early correspondence.[20]

Visiting Sara, de Vere had the opportunity of becoming acquainted with the rarely mentioned mother of Sara, Mrs. Samuel Taylor Coleridge, whom he found most attractive. He enjoyed sitting with the old lady, as she rambled along, recalling stories of the past, as well as giving interesting bits of information, not always in logical order. De Vere said he admired Mrs. Coleridge's garrulity more than Thomas Macaulay's bombastic pronouncements. Speaking of Sara, the old lady said that when her daughter was but thirteen, a gentleman proposed to her; that all Sara's admirers, including her husband-cousin, Henry Nelson Coleridge, had died when young; that, therefore, Sara would have been a widow no matter whom she married; that although Sara and her future husband became interested in each other when she was nineteen, they waited six years before marrying; that Sara had elevated and refined her husband, and their marriage had been happy. For three years, moreover, Sara had suffered from spine and nerves, yet she wrote her only original work, *Phantasmion*, while in bed. Sara's mother also told de Vere that her daughter's translation, made when she was young, brought her £130; this is probably the Latin work, *Abipones* of Dobrizhoffer.

Mrs. Coleridge said she married S.T.C. when he was less than twenty-three. Hazlitt, she continued, worried them with his visits; and de Quincey used to say to Coleridge, "I should be so much obliged if you would speak a little more on the level of my comprehension!" She herself often remarked to her husband, "Man, do you really understand yourself?"[21]

De Vere's friendship with Hartley Coleridge, Sara's brother, and his sympathetic critique of Hartley's work, published in the *Edinburgh Review,* in 1849, also won him Sara's gratitude and admiration. She appreciatively wrote to him:

> It is by far the best in every way that I have seen; it presents the poems in their deepest and most dignified aspect, and the dear man's character along with them. Yet there is nothing . . . exalting them too highly . . .; nothing that seems violently partial and exaggerated.[22]

Aubrey de Vere probably first heard the name of Hartley Coleridge when he was only nine years old. Sir Aubrey at that time had written the drama *Julian the Apostate,* and Hartley had contributed to the *British Critic* a favorable criticism. Impressed by the ability of the critic, Sir Aubrey asked Hartley to undertake the education of his two sons for a considerable remuneration. But Hartley preferred to remain at Ambleside rather than be under the patronage of a wealthy Irish country gentleman.

However, it was not until 1845 that de Vere met Hartley. He recounted his first impression of Coleridge's son:

> One day Miss Fenwick drove me to the Nab Cottage . . ., the residence of Hartley Coleridge. She sent for him, and at once he came. It was a white-haired apparition—wearing in all other respects the semblance of youth . . . He could hardly be said to have walked, for he seemed with difficulty to keep his feet on the ground, as he wavered about near us with arms extended like wings. Everything that he said was strange and quaint; . . . and, though always amusing, yet always represented a mind whose thoughts dwelt in regions as remote as the antipodes. After fifty years of ill-fortune the man before us was still the child described by Wordsworth in his poem to H.C. at three years of age.[23]

De Vere found Hartley touchingly reverent when referring to religious subjects, and apparently possessed of a certain tenderness. In his diary de Vere made the following note:

> Hartley Coleridge . . . read us two beautiful poems (one on his sister's bereavement),[24] tried to write a sonnet to the picture, and was very delightful just before going away. My father and mother very much and sadly, though kindly, impressed by him.[25]

Discussing Hartley's *Essays and Marginalia,* de Vere remarked that the essayist united exact thought and brilliant wit in his descriptions of Chaucer, Shakespeare, Daniel Defoe, Dryden and Donne. Hartley's poems he considered meditative, like Wordsworth's, but without the passion of that poet, or of Samuel Coleridge, although they resemble the latter's in being fitful and sanguine, buoyant and sweet. De Vere attributed Hartley's compartively small output to his weakness of will and an inability "to systematize." For self-control, de Vere asserted, is the " 'leathern girdle,' which, seeming to restrain, braces the adventurous artist for his ascent up the mountainside . . . He [Hartley] needs something of ascetic discipline and renunciation."[26]

De Vere's estimate of Hartley Coleridge and his work is confirmed by later writers. For example, Hugh Walker, eighty years later, implies that Hartley's failures had their source in his desultory education, based on his own father's ideas. S. T. Coleridge had decided: "Thou, my babe, shalt wander like a breeze . . . ";

and this "wandering," says Walker, "left Hartley's will undisci-
plined, and his fancy unrestrained."[27] In his *Coleridge Fille,* published in 1940, Earl Leslie Griggs states: "To the end of his days
Hartley continued, as his father had once written, to 'wander like
a breeze'; but he remained innocent and humble . . ."[28] De Vere,
in his *Recollections,* noted: "There must have been a vein of bitterness in Hartley's nature, or he could not have addressed that
sonnet to his father which contains the line: 'Thy prayer was
heard—I wandered like a breeze'."[29]

Consideration of the relations of Aubrey de Vere and the
Coleridges recalls the often forgotten fact that in the last years
of his life Samuel Taylor Coleridge was regarded as the foremost
religious thinker of his day.[30] Many men of the time were happy
to consider themselves his disciples, even though, like de Vere,
each perhaps said later: "I am beginning to transfer my allegiance
from Plato and Coleridge, and to value facts almost as much as
ideas."[31] From a review of the friendship of Sara and de Vere
and their correspondence evolves a new appraisal of the only
daughter of the celebrated poet-philosopher, the niece of the poet
Robert Southey (in whose home she grew up), and the close
friend of the bard of Rydal and his family.

Both Sara Coleridge and Aubrey de Vere loved poetry and
religion, yet in each they differed. Sara liked de Vere's poems for
personal reasons, but she thought they lacked power of expression.
In her interest in America, Sara was one with de Vere, for she
wrote: "America—a land in which I shall never cease to take an
interest."[32] Sara asked for no beauty in her religion and refused to
believe such doctrines as original sin and the resurrection of the
body; meanwhile, as has been noted, de Vere continued his journey
"Romeward." Despite differences of opinion and conviction, these
strong characters remained true friends. De Vere's high regard
for Sara Coleridge arouses interest in her varied literary work,
which, because of its scope and scholarship, places her high among
literary women of the last century. In his *Recollections,* in a
passage written half a century after their first meeting, de Vere's
estimate of her had remained unchanged:

"She was certainly the most wonderful woman I have

ever known, but it was not to her intellectual faculties chiefly that the term 'wonderful' would ever have been applied, so much more wonderful would her moral and spiritual being have appeared by comparison."[33]

The final estimate of Sara Coleridge, a beautiful and fitting tribute to the gifted poet-translator-editor, de Vere wrote for Edith Coleridge's *Memoir and Letters of Sara Coleridge* and also placed it in his *Recollections:*

> With all her high literary powers she was utterly unlike the mass of those who are called literary persons. Few have possessed such learning . . . But in the daughter, as in the father, the real marvel . . . was the spiritual mind. . . . Her great characteristic was the radiant spirituality of her intellectual and imaginative being . . .
>
> There is a certain gentleness and modesty which belong to real genius . . . It was these qualities that gave to her manners their charm of feminine grace, self-possession and sweetness. . . . It is only a fortunate few who will appreciate her yet higher gifts, those that belong to the moral being . . . wide sympathies and high aspirations, courageous love of knowledge, devout submission to revealed truth; domestic affections so tender, so dutiful and so self-sacrificing; the friendships faithful and so unexacting.[34]

5

INTIMATE

OF

SIR HENRY TAYLOR

Aubrey de Vere's chief friend,[1] most constant and helpful, was Henry Taylor—later Sir Henry Taylor of the Order of St. Michael and St. George, an honor conferred on him for his many years of outstanding service in the Colonial Office.[2] Taylor, de Vere's senior by fourteen years, was a prominent civic and literary figure of the nineteenth century. Community of interests, especially in literature, mutual friends, and love of family life linked these two men. Their friendship was further strengthened by Taylor's marriage to de Vere's first cousin, Theodosia Alice Spring Rice.[3]

As an influential civil servant—he was in the Colonial Office from 1823 to 1872—Taylor necessarily kept abreast of the times. Various contemporary problems came to his attention: for example, Benthamism, the Catholic Emancipation and the Irish Question, the Reform Bill of 1832 and Chartism, the freeing of negro slaves in Jamaica, Gladstone's policies and the American Civil War. Even the pros and cons of vivisection in the eighties interested him.[4] Taylor knew personally all the statesmen with the exception of Disraeli, Canning and Brougham. Among his acquaintances were the historians Hallam and Macaulay, Carlyle,

Lecky and Froude. With de Vere as a trusted friend, Taylor discussed passing events, foreign affairs, and trends of the times. For
here again the gentle and unassuming Irish aristocrat played his
favorite role of adviser and observer.

Taylor started his literary career in 1822 (at the age of
twenty-two) with a critique of Thomas Moore's *Irish Melodies*.
The critique was published in the *Edinburgh Review*,[5] which, like
the *Quarterly*, exercised great power over literary and political
judgments and couched its criticism in language often harsh and
invective.[6] Following the vogue, Taylor wrote his review in a
sarcastic vein. Two years later, he reviewed Landor's poems in
the same disparaging tone and thereby received a rebuke from
the affable Robert Southey. Through the years Taylor revealed his
own mind and art in lyric poetry, six dramatic romances (closet
dramas), an autobiography of two volumes, and his *Correspondence* (edited by Edward Dowden), which marks him as a connois-
seur in the art of letter-writing. Henry Taylor himself counted
among his friends many poets and writers of distinction: Wordsworth wrote to him as early as 1823;[7] Southey's personality and
work merited his admiration; Scott as an elderly man enjoyed
meeting Taylor; and Coleridge, despite his illness, read *Philip
van Artevelde* shortly before his death, in 1834. Moore and Camp-
bell, Spedding and Rogers, Tennyson and Browning, Sara Coleridge and Isabella Fenwick, Jane and Thomas Carlyle were also
among his friends. In fact, when Taylor married de Vere's cousin,
friends of husband and wife united in a wider circle, which continued to grow with the years. Thus de Vere's friendships increased in number; for instance, Isabella Fenwick, a relative of
Taylor, took a keen interest in de Vere, although to her Taylor
was the dearest person in her life.[8]

Although Taylor and de Vere shared an ardent love for
literature, they did not see eye to eye on all questions. For example, Taylor was in early life affiliated with the materialistic
Benthamites, whereas de Vere, as has been stated, followed the
more spiritual ideas of Burke and Coleridge. Taylor disliked
America, especially during the Civil War period; de Vere, on
the other hand, in his letters to Charles Eliot Norton of Harvard

and other American friends, evinced a sympathetic interest in America and a love for those literary persons whom he knew on the other side of the Atlantic. Taylor's prejudice against the Irish people is manifest in his correspondence;[9] de Vere, who knew and understood conditions in Ireland, loved the peasants. No doubt Taylor, a man of integrity, lacked the knowledge necessary for forming just judgments in these cases; but throughout his life de Vere seemed free from prejudice.

Taylor, like de Vere, early turned from the poetry of Byron, and later from that of Shelley, which he regarded as lacking in intellectual appeal. Therefore, in writing his own plays he ran counter to popular taste; he deliberately departed from the sensational, unintellectual, "weakened Byronism," in vogue at the time. His aim as poet and as dramatist was to portray life as it is, and to imply in that portrayal an underlying philosophy of life.[10] Although his closet dramas, or dramatic romances (as de Vere terms Taylor's plays), have their defects, the characters appear three-dimensional.

In 1834 Taylor's *Philip van Artevelde* appeared, and because of its new appeal it became a tremendous success. Coleridge, we know, read it; Lockhart's approving article on it was published in the *Quarterly,* and the first edition of five hundred copies was soon sold out. Taylor became famous overnight; as the lion of society,[11] he was immediately welcomed at Lansdowne House and Holland House,[12] each a rendezvous for distinguished persons. Meanwhile Aubrey de Vere, filled with admiration for both book and author, immediately started to interest his friends, especially William Rowan Hamilton, in the new drama.[13]

Four years later de Vere finally met Taylor at the Colonial Office. He found the author remarkably handsome, the most stately person he had ever seen; his manner was serene and almost cold, his speech slow and measured.[14] They discussed Wordsworth, and the play on which Taylor was then working, *Edwin the Fair.* About this time de Vere became friendly with James Spedding, an intellectual and kind-hearted man, who worked at the Colonial Office for some time, and later published *The Life and Letters of Lord Bacon.* On more than one occasion Taylor brought de Vere to the famous literary breakfasts of elderly Samuel Rogers (that patron of artists and litterateurs), who had the distinction of entertaining, at some time or other, every hero or man of genius of his era.

The friendship between de Vere and Taylor, both prolific letter-writers, led to a correspondence which is not only revealing but also delightful to read. Taylor's chief occupation, in the Colonial Office, consumed many hours of the day and often of the night; and writing was more or less a hobby which formed the chief delight of his life. He regretted that he had not more time to give to this "higher calling." De Vere, on the contrary, regarded writing as a vocation which demanded (as Wordsworth had often remarked) "the whole man"; to him writing was the chief occupation in life, and the aim of his writing was to effect good. In this attitude he again resembled Wordsworth, whose motive also, especially in his later years, was to promote good. While Taylor's writing brought him satisfaction in his power of creation, de Vere's meant more or less a satisfaction of conscience. De Vere, who considered the "life poetic" paramount, would not sacrifice literary ability to public life. As he stated in a letter to Taylor: "Modesty as well as avarice or vanity often seduces people into sacrificing literature to public life, the remote good to the immediate; because every man of ability *sees* the result of his own practical efficiency, whereas the results of his genius belong to the regions of Faith."[15] Taylor, though renouncing promotion in favor of his literary ambition, was first and foremost a Civil Servant.

Ideas on literary technique, as well as valuable criticisms of such writers as Wordsworth, Shelley and Hartley Coleridge, also appear in de Vere's letters to his friend. His remark on the purpose of rhyming is original:

> When lines salute each other with that sort of "kiss of peace," which we call rhyme, I suppose it must give them great pleasure . . . What the rhyme does is to recall the *memory* of the line foregone, and thus link different parts of a stanza into a whole.[16]

De Vere disliked the heroic couplet and argued, "The lines rather exchange resonant slaps on each other's faces than any gentler form of salutation." Dryden's and Pope's imperfect rhymes[17] (such as "drawn" and "scorn") made him quite indignant, yet he did not object to imperfect rhymes "when the *mind* perceives at once that the words are corresponding words, such as 'enter' and 'winter'."[18]

Writing to Taylor of Southey, whose letters he had read,[19] de Vere stated that the former laureate must have been gifted with "infused knowledge"; Southey could not have acquired all he knew by mere reading. He believed that had Southey lived, he could have accomplished great things in the mythological tales he had planned. The drudgery of history, according to de Vere, drained away the poetic fire, and left his imagination somewhat chilled.[20]

Discussing his own "Autumnal Ode" (similar to his "Ode to a Daffodil"), which he had written to please Taylor, de Vere stated the purpose of the poem. In it he wished to express a great truth, the opposite of that contained in Wordsworth's "Vernal Ode." In the latter, the poet stated that the seasons (the "cyclical revolutions of nature") make time an image of eternity. De Vere, on the other hand, tried to show that the soul, having an eternal destiny, never finds complete satisfaction in the beauties of earth.[21]

De Vere's essay "Sir Henry Taylor's Poetry"[22] is as valuable for its sound, original opinions on literature in general, as it is interesting for its estimate of Taylor's work. De Vere, incidentally, contrasts the beginning of Greek tragedy with the development of the English ballad. In treating Taylor's *A Sicilian Summer,* de Vere develops the thought that Shakespeare's comedies (for example, *The Merchant of Venice, The Tempest, As You Like It*) are as serious in their purpose as are his tragedies.[23] In dealing with *Saint Clement's Eve,* the critic deplores the fact that the drama contains no noble characters to balance the ignoble. In the third part of his essay "Minor Poems," de Vere considers truth in poetry and the advantages of short poems over long. He holds that Taylor's short poems, like his dramas, are characterized by strength and truth, grace and beauty.

Taylor, in turn, criticized de Vere's work, and tried to as-

certain why it did not make a wide appeal to the reading public.
Writing to de Vere he indicated that absence of passion was the
reason:

> I have read and considered your volume, . . . curious to
> know if you be not a great poet, wherein you fail. Not in
> intellect, not in art or the rhythmic sense . . . not in fancy . . .
> Is it then in human and imaginative passion? That, I think,
> is the only question . . . If passion be the only element which
> is defective in your poetry . . . that will account for its want
> of popularity . . .[24]

Almost two decades before, William Rowan Hamilton had told
de Vere that his poems appealed too little to passion.

Again in reply to de Vere's deep and metaphysical explanation of his *May Carols* and their purpose, Taylor remarked:

> One other reason for your unpopularity as a poet is your
> non-exercise of that preliminary act of the imagination by
> which a man conceives his audience.[25]

Two decades later, Taylor presented another idea in explanation of de Vere's lack of success: the subject matter did not appeal
to popular taste. He found *The Foray of Queen Meave* admirably
executed, but the subject, being Irish, would not interest English
readers. Nor would the book appeal to de Vere's countrymen who
unfortunately then lacked educational advantages and even the
means to purchase it.[26]

Taylor, however, said of de Vere: "He is not the *most* poetical
poet of this century; but of the poetical poets he is by far the most
intellectual next after, if after, Coleridge and Wordsworth . . ."[27]
In de Vere, therefore, we find, as did Henry Taylor, that classic
restraint and natural serenity developed in his discipleship of
Wordsworth were in some part the causes of lack of passion. And
this, with de Vere's choice of subjects, hindered his popularity.

Aubrey de Vere himself offered an explanation for his lack of
popularity; he was looked on with suspicion by some Irish because
he stood out against violence of any kind, although he had a
keen love for and interest in the Irish peasants; and he was
without favor with the English because of his change of religion.

Moreover, as Wilfred Meynell has pointed out, the forties offered little encouragement to new poets.

Again, Taylor wrote rather humorously of de Vere's personality:

> As to Aubrey de Vere's faults, he has fewer than anybody else that I know, and it would be well for you and me if we could throw our faults and virtues into hotchpot with Aubrey's and share and share alike accordingly. I should ride off like a beggar on horseback, and you would be lifted . . . to a situation in which you would look down upon the kingdoms of the earth and the glory thereof.[28]

De Vere's letters to Taylor reveal, among other characteristics, his optimistic wistfulness in recalling old friends and experiences. For example:

> Weeding among old letters does, indeed, make us feel that the past is full of ghosts; but ghosts differ in their classes as much as the other spirits, black, white and gray; and the ghost which you sent me in the form of a recollection of 1844 is, indeed, a "spirit of noonday." Everything that belongs to old days wears for me a magical brightness, and a coloring like that of mountains a little before sunrise. You see I do not say a "little before sunset.". . . One knows, looking back on them, that somehow they were not all that they seem to have been.[29]

And twenty-five years later he expressed himself in a similar mood:

> Your letter has given me a strange day—one with an indescribable mixture of sadness and sweetness . . . The sad thought is, "Can such tracts of happiness, indeed, lie behind me?" with the question, "Did one, indeed, while passing through golden regions, fail so much to value their full worth?" The sweet thought is . . . that nothing of good vouchsafed to us has been given in vain.[30]

Here we may discern the keen pleasures that de Vere found in his lifelong friendship with Taylor. We know de Vere better through his sincere and intimate letters to his friend. Their correspondence reveals also de Vere's genius for literary criticism. Moreover, it affords us a keen appraisal of de Vere's work.

Through contact with Taylor, de Vere became more intimate with many literary figures and Taylor benefited in like manner.

During their long friendship of fifty years, de Vere and Taylor shared pleasures as well as ideas and convictions. As a relative, de Vere was always a welcomed guest, especially during the summers that the Taylors spent at Bournemouth. Their eldest boy was de Vere's namesake and godchild; and the other children always eagerly awaited de Vere's visits. In the early days of the Taylors' married life de Vere, as has been noted, accompanied them on a journey to Italy, where Henry Taylor went in search of health. Recalling that trip, Taylor wrote: "I do not know that a generous affection has ever wrought a more wonderful work than it did on our travels, in converting Aubrey de Vere into a practical man. The most experienced courier could not have made arrangements for us day by day and hour by hour, or bargained with hotel-keepers and vetturini more successfully or with more care or assiduity."[31] Both de Vere and Taylor enjoyed visits to "the Grange," the home of Lord and Lady Ashburton, renowned for their gatherings of all types of celebrities. As Mrs. Taylor would go nowhere without her children, the hospitable Ashburtons (according to Taylor) welcomed the Taylors "with all their encumbrances" for weeks at a time, to meet "a cloud of 'savants'— physiologists, chemists, mechanists, historians, poets, artists, Dr. This, and Professor That."[32] And among this heterogeneous group Carlyle "flashed," and the Brookfields "glistened and gleamed," while de Vere remained affable with all.

Taylor, on account of his occupation and his poor health, was unable to keep up with the world of society, which he enjoyed. However, he found that it interfered with happy home life, appreciation of spiritual values, time for literature, and the enjoyment of nature. De Vere, on the other hand, thoroughly enjoyed meeting his friends in London and elsewhere since he had many months of the year to spend amidst the quiet joys of Curragh Chase.

Through the years, and even after the death of his beloved friend in 1886, de Vere continued to promote interest in Taylor's work. He retained his high regard for *Philip van Artevelde*.[33]

Although it failed on the stage, even with Macready as the leading actor and director, de Vere always admired it as a dramatic
romance; and in 1900 he urged Professor George Edward Woodberry of Columbia to make it known in America.[34] (Incidentally,
he also mentioned his own father's *Mary Tudor*, admired by Gladstone and Manning, and still rated high by literary critics.) In
1898, de Vere asked Charles Eliot Norton of Harvard to introduce to the students Taylor's *Autobiography*, of which thirteen
hundred copies were sold in England.[35] To William Knight, American Wordsworthian scholar, de Vere, in 1882, recommended Taylor's valuable articles on Wordsworth (published in the *Quarterly*),
the fruit of a fifty years' friendship with the bard of Rydal.[36]

6

CRITIC

OF

COVENTRY PATMORE

$\mathbf{A}$t the home of Richard Monckton Milnes (Lord Houghton), which was a gathering place of the men of letters of the period, Aubrey de Vere, in 1844, met a despondent young man who made it clear that he had selected poetry as his profession.[1] Coventry Patmore, then twenty-one years old, had just had his first disappointment: his first volume, *Poems*, had received such an unfavorable reception by the critics that he had destroyed all unsold copies.[2] De Vere, however, who took an immediate liking for the young man, came to feel that young Patmore showed signs of genius and that it would be only a question of time before he was recognized.[3] A strong link of friendship was established between the two men and was destined to last fifty-two years, in the course of which de Vere proved an interested critic and sometimes a confidant of Patmore.[4]

On their frequent meetings in London the two men discovered many mutual interests: both had a high regard for Coleridge, great admiration for Tennyson, and profound reverence for Wordsworth.[5] They differed greatly, however, in temperament. Patmore was pessimistic by nature, inclined to be turbulent and eccentric; de Vere was an optimist, even-tempered, serene, and conservative.

This difference in disposition is seen in Patmore's diary entry made in the early days of their friendship. The two friends had been invited to visit the Greenwich observatory together, and Patmore jotted down:

> Mr. de Vere as we walked back . . . in the morning, was in a very elated frame of mind about the bigness of the starry heavens: but I maintained my view that they were only created "to make dirt cheap" as was Coleridge's theory also; but de Vere would not see it.[6]

A glimpse of Patmore's family life is caught by de Vere, who visited the Patmores on a particularly "starry" night, and thus recorded in his diary:

> A wonderful night had come to them, a night rare in misty climate; one of those which breed a confusion among the constellations, but which may have suggested to the poet of "The Seasons" written in *The Germ* the line—"Poured all the Arabian heaven upon this night". . ."Our child must see it," the poet exclaimed. "It is worth while breaking her sleep for it. She will never forget it. She will see in it even more than we do! We must wait patiently for her earliest word!" The father snatched her [Emily] from her small bed; the mother wrapped the blanket carefully about her. They carried her into the garden. Slowly they drew the veil from her eyes. They stood in silence waiting for the oracular word. At last it came.—It was this: "Oh, papa, how untidy the sky is!"[7]

In 1848, through the influence of Lord Houghton, Coventry Patmore, who sorely needed the means of earning a livelihood, was appointed assistant librarian of the British Museum. Soon he and his wife Emily were entertaining the circle of the Pre-Raphaelites, and two years later a poem by Patmore appeared in Rossetti's *The Germ*.[8] But another volume of poems, *Tamerton Church Tower*, published in 1855, shared the fate of Patmore's first poems: it met with little success.

One day in the year 1850, Patmore, in a state of great excitement, called on de Vere, and with much enthusiasm told his friend of his original idea; he had discovered a new theme for poetry: "love in the deeper and softer sense of the word."[9] He wished to represent marriage as the road to spiritual truth and love as the mystical way to God. The fruit of this idea appeared four years later under the title *The Betrothal,* the first of six proposed parts constituting *The Angel in the House.* An advance copy of the book was sent to Tennyson, who then happened to have as his guest Aubrey de Vere; and the two friends read the poem as they sat on a cliff close to the sea, on the Isle of Wight. Both poets admired the poem, and Tennyson remarked that the completed poem would be numbered with the great poetry of the ages.[10] De Vere wrote to encourage Patmore; and Mrs. Patmore was evidently delighted over the good news, for she wrote to a friend, quoting from de Vere's letter:

> . . . Aubrey de Vere, himself a poet, writes, "Alfred told me" (he was with Tennyson when he received the book) "that your poems when finished will add . . . to the small number of great poems which the world has had." Do not laugh at my boasting; but somehow I feel as if you would sympathize with me in the pleasure these words of praise have caused me[11]

In 1858 a critique of *The Angel in the House,* written by de Vere, appeared in the powerful *Edinburgh Review* and helped a great deal to publicize the novel in verse. The book sold in thousands of copies. At the time of Patmore's death in 1896, the sales had reached a quarter million copies. For some time *The Angel in the House* was the only rival of Tennyson's *Idylls of the King.*[12] This success was probably due in part to the simple meter and fluency of the verses; many readers, however, failed to discern the underlying theme of analogy between human and divine love.

In his critique of *The Angel in the House,* de Vere considered only the first two parts (*The Betrothal* and *The Espousals*), published respectively in 1854 and 1856; the other two parts were not written until 1860 and 1863. De Vere wrote in part:

> Of the longer poems which attempt exclusively to describe the finer emotions of modern society, the most original and the most artistic is Mr. Coventry Patmore's *Angel in the*

House. . . . The task Mr. Patmore has undertaken is to trace
. . . the ebb and flow of those feelings which are in every rank
of life, the well-head of poetry . . . The merit of it consists
principally in its refined and delicate execution. . . . The
author's desire is to illustrate ordinary, not exceptional,
modern life. . . . The poet has derived the interest of his work
from the philosophic analysis of the affections, and a descriptive power equally harmonious and vivid. The poem
divides itself into two classes of compositions . . .; reflections
on life and character, and descriptive pictures.[13]

De Vere claimed that *The Angel in the House* was an effectual
protest against the less wholesome poetry of the age; in its serenity it contrasts with that "Spasmodic School" (represented by
Sydney Dobell and Alexander Smith and defined "as a blend of
Keats with Byron"),[14] "which delights in jerks and jolts, and
tolerates no music that has not a dash of discord in it."[15]

When the third and fourth parts of the poem came out in
1860 and 1863, readers discovered that *Faithful Forever* and *Victories of Love* were inferior to the other half of the work; and the
prestige of Patmore and his work suffered. In view of this, he
abandoned the thought of writing a fifth and a sixth part to *The
Angel in the House;* Swinburne's parody of the work naturally
may have made Patmore realize that his theme did not lend itself to
lengthy treatment. Throughout all his work, even in *The Angel in
the House,* Patmore's philosophy was wholesome. In an essay,
"Love and Poetry" in his *Religio Poetae,* he stated: "The world is
finding out, as it has often done before, that it cannot do without
religion. Love is the first thing to wither under its loss. What love
does in transfiguring life, that religion does in transfiguring love.
. . . Love is sure to be something less than human if it is not something more."[16]

Writing to Patmore, January 16, 1863, de Vere suggested
omitting two passages in *Victories of Love;* although poetic merit
and philosophic interest characterized the passages, de Vere maintained they were liable to be misunderstood and attacked. After
de Vere and Dr. Richard Garnett assisted in revising the poem,
de Vere felt that the "rejection of some philosophical passages"

had improved the work, for, he held, "poetry refuses to take up more of philosophy than it can hold in solution. . . ."[17]

Continuing his role of critic, de Vere warned Patmore against prolixity and repetition. Superfluous words, he insisted, prevent any poem of considerable length from being effective.

This principle of selecting only the best and necessary applies also to collections of poems. No poet, said de Vere, should publish his poorly written poems in the volume with his best; if he does so, the collection will be spoiled. Wordsworth, Coleridge, and Shelley erred by not eliminating their uninspired work from their collections of poetry. To illustrate this point, de Vere remarked:

> The statue is spoilt by the heap of rubbish at its base, and the building half hidden by the remains of what should have been regarded as mere scaffolding. . . . A poet's less good things betray him: they show us how he worked. The Muse, if wise, no more admits us to her dressing-room than any other lady.[18]

Evidently Patmore heeded de Vere's admonition concerning compactness (which Tennyson attained with much industry), for the *Odes* of Patmore are noted for their economy and coherence.[19] Again de Vere elucidated this principle with a comparison: "The Greeks used to say, 'Art is long, but life is short'; and omitted many details in their poetry . . . just as they omitted the bridles of their sculptured horses." De Vere also cited causes for obscurity: a doubtful "antecedent," an allusion unexplained, the lack of title to a poem, and the writer's becoming preoccupied with his own thoughts, as in philosophical themes, and thus forgetting the "hooks and eyes" of style then most necessary.[20]

Patmore evidently consulted de Vere on personal and religious matters, as well as on literary problems. Emily Patmore was ill (from 1857 until her death in 1862,), and Patmore was naturally worried, for they were devoted to each other. Moreover, there were six children to be cared for. But Patmore seemed also to be in a state of spiritual unrest; true to his literary conscience and mystically minded, he felt the poet's responsibility to the public as well as to himself. Herbert Read, the English critic, suggests that Patmore's "very concentration on the nature of poetry led him toward the wider mysticism of the Catholic faith."[21] However, Emily felt that her husband was too keenly interested in Catholicism, for which she had an inherent dislike. She also feared the influence of her husband's Catholic friends, de Vere and Manning; on one occasion she remarked to Patmore, "When I am gone, they [the Catholics] will get you, and then I shall see you no more."[22]

A letter from de Vere to Patmore, written February 14, 1857, contains the following:

> I earnestly trust that nothing will induce you to remit or postpone the great duty of religious inquiry. . . . The more He [God] has in store for any soul, the more he makes it acquainted with the great Realities both of sorrow and of joy. . . . In His eyes each of us exists as the whole universe exists, or as He would do if the universe contained no creature but Himself. . . . All will go well if we can but learn to trust God *enough,* and serve Him with absolute disinterestedness.[23]

Also the diary note written by Patmore suggests his confused state of mind:

> The conversations of Mr. Aubrey de Vere and Dr. Manning on the Roman Catholic religion, in which she [Emily] answered all their most subtle arguments, which were wholly beyond my power to see through, so as to set my mind at rest on this point . . . Emily read de Vere's essays on the Roman Catholic Religion and, though shaken at first, answered everything in them to her own satisfaction, which certainly would have been to mine.[24]

In a letter to his wife Patmore indicates his regard for her judgment, as well as his opposition to Victorian style and method:

> Aubrey de Vere spent another evening here. He challenged me to a public defence of my thesis (which I learned from *you*): that there was little real feeling, much less passion, in Tennyson's poetry. We took the *In Memoriam* for our proofs; and after examining one after another all his favorite pieces, he was forced to conclude that they each and all contained indications of consciousness, artifice, and other qualities in-

consistent with the existence of any very lively flow of feeling at the time of writing.[25]

Emily died in 1862, and to the bereaved Patmore de Vere wrote from Coniston:

> Your note has a very sad sound; but I ought to be all the more obliged to you for having, notwithstanding, remembered your promise; for it is when we are most out of spirits that we find it most troublesome to write in general. I am not at all surprised at your return to your home having a very depressing effect upon you. It is most sadly natural that this should be the case; and, also, the more so when a house already empty is made more empty by your children's being away from it, though not, fortunately, far away. I believe that, when we begin to lift up our heads again after any great bereavement, the progress we make, even under the most favourable circumstances, is far from being an even or equal progress. . . . What I have tried to write will at least show you how strong are my hopes that in proportion to present suffering will be your future consolation.[26]

About a year and a half after his wife's death, "Patmore felt he needed a holiday. His health, never very robust, showed the strain and worry of the last two years. Aubrey de Vere, who seems to have taken a solicitous interest in him during these difficult years, urged him to go to Rome. . . ."[27] In a letter to his daughter Emily (dated January 18, 1864) Patmore wrote: "Mr. Aubrey de Vere is gone to Rome and I am not sure that I shall not go, too, in a little while. . . ."[28]

He also told her:

> I expect to be very dull and miserable for the first two or three weeks until I get to Rome; but when I am there I shall be all right, for nobody can be dull or miserable where Mr. de Vere is. Don't you remember how *he looked like sunshine* whenever he came to see us at Hampstead or Highgate Rise?[29]

Later he records his experience:

> . . . I went to Rome and through the kindness of a friend, for whose many kindnesses to me I can never be grateful

enough, Aubrey de Vere, I was admitted into the best Catholic society of the great center of Catholic life. Here the concrete argument which had hitherto been more or less wanting to complete my abstract consent, was rapidly built up; and I gave most of my hours—of which for the first time for many years I had abundance at my disposal—to the most serious consideration of any remaining doubts; doubts which had a hundred times been disproved to the understanding, but which somehow rose again and again in my conscience . . .[30]

In letters to a friend, Patmore expressed his appreciation of Aubrey de Vere: both de Vere and Mr. Monsell had brought him among a society which interested him more than anything else in Rome. And again, he stated: "Aubrey de Vere, who knows Rome like his native land, says that a man might walk on his head, and no Roman would think or say other than that happened to be his taste, and that he had a right to do it."[31] And he made this comment:

> . . . Priests are very much the pleasantest, best informed and most conversable people in Rome . . . I have seen equal —never superior—refinement in other men . . . Certainly Roman Catholicism has some claims (I do not know how much the claims may be worth) to be called, as it is written, "the religion of gentlemen."[32]

As Aubrey de Vere and his friend, Mr. Monsell (later Lord Emly), both Roman Catholics, belonged to the aristocratic colony of English Catholics, Patmore soon found himself launched in social life. And he felt happy among these friends: "their ways," he said, "convinced me that I should not be leaping into any strange gulf of uncongenial life if I became a Catholic, but no one helped me nearly so much to remove this fear as a lady whom I now met in this society."[33]

Patmore entered the Catholic Church in 1864, and the following year the lady mentioned, Marianne Caroline Byles, became his second wife—the inspiration of his truly poetic odes. Patmore left his position at the British Museum, bought a country estate, and devoted the next thirty years of his life exclusively to writing. In the new surroundings, in a new attitude towards life, he produced a new type of poetry, far superior to his former somewhat commonplace work.

In discussing *The Unknown Eros and Other Odes,* in his article "Coventry Patmore's Poetry," de Vere termed it a remarkable volume of poems altogether unlike most of the poetry that had appeared recently. The odes, both in the strictest as well as a wider sense of the word, contain lofty and occasionally mystical thoughts in subtle, expressive and musical language. "The Unknown Eros," with its long and short lines, reminded de Vere of the cadences of an Aeolian harp following a law of its own. And he found the affections celebrated in the poem spiritual and eminently human also.[34] The irregularity of the iambic lines—from two to ten or twelve syllables—conveys the idea of freedom and impetuous force that de Vere suggests. These odes, dealing with high ethical truth, add to Patmore's stature. They are characterized also by elevated sentiment, vigor, expressive diction, and metrical felicity.[35]

In January, 1890, de Vere commended Patmore for his essay, *Principle in Art,* which showed "vigor and conciseness"; he also praised its temperance, dignity and grace of style. A few days later, however, de Vere advised Patmore, about to publish his *Lyrics,* to omit three of his "Psyche Odes," because of their excessive development of the analogy between human and divine love. In his *The Angel in the House,* as has been indicated, Patmore attempted to show that affection between husband and wife should aid in the perfection of each individual, but in the *Odes* he compared God's love for the individual soul with the married love of man and woman.

De Vere, who had approved of the *Odes* of 1877, feared that the three odes then in question would, if published, injure Patmore's reputation. These were his words:

> Those three poems would *greatly* impair circulation of *your* poetry and thus diminish its power of benefiting well disposed readers, although doubtless poetry of many writers owes much of its fame to what we should regard as the least commendable part of it. Those poems are the least liked by those who most appreciate the rest of your poetry. The

more you rise in general estimation, the more will those three poems be turned against you—by more than one class of hostile readers . . .[36]

De Vere's circumspection and restraint did not harmonize with the passionate and daring expression of Patmore's theme in these *Odes*. Patmore felt that he had entered on the darkest period of his poetic career:

> Just at the moment when he felt at the height of his powers, the friends who had so rapturously admired *The Angel in the House* turned a deaf ear to his new poems. Ardent admirers of his talent, such as Aubrey de Vere, strangely disapproved of them.[37]

In his letters to other correspondents, Aubrey de Vere was constantly interested in Coventry Patmore and his work. Writing to Charles Eliot Norton, he said: "You must let me know what you think of Patmore's Odes."[38] To Reverend Matthew Russell, S. J., Editor of the *Irish Monthly*, he remarked of the *Unknown Eros and Other Poems*: "It seems to me a volume far and away superior to the ordinary run of recent poetry. . . ."[39] A much later letter, also to Father Russell, dated February 1, 1890, mentioned "Patmore's beautiful book" (probably his *Principle in Art*, published in 1889). To another friend he wrote, some years later: "I am sure you were very sorry for Patmore, who died October 26, 1896—a man of real genius and appreciated by a few, among them the Meynells.[40] To the same correspondent, Aubrey de Vere, less than three years before his own death remarked: "I wish you would write a review of Coventry Patmore's Poetry! I am sure you would make it a highly interesting thing . . ."[41]

Undoubtedly de Vere and Patmore regarded each other with admiration. They were in agreement in their philosophy of literature: "bad morality is bad art." Both held noble and lofty aims, and felt that the writer is primarily a teacher. However, Patmore said of de Vere: "He has all the gifts that make a poet, excepting the last degree of individuality which is most essential of all."[42]

De Vere's final estimate of Patmore, written after his death, and on his own eighty-fifth birthday, recalls his impressions of more than a half century before. On their first meeting in 1844, de Vere had noticed Patmore's simplicity and quiet enthusiasm, as well as his evident genius. And in later meetings in London he had discovered Patmore's originality and his sensitive and impassioned intellect. Throughout the decades de Vere remained true to his first impressions:

> I need not tell you how much I regret Coventry Patmore. I look upon him as a poet of very high merit and also of a very peculiar character of genius. His *Odes* I should place far higher than his "Angel in the House"; and of that I wrote in the *Edinburgh Review* in a way which, as he told me, had given a considerable impulse to its circulation. But many of his odes are of a higher strain and some of one strain very much higher, and a very peculiar one. He was eminently a sincere poet. The verse expressed the man in a most remarkable degree—both his opinions and his feelings; and his nature was a high one . . .[43]

7

ADVERSARY

OF

THOMAS CARLYLE

Aubrey de Vere's relationship with Thomas Carlyle differed totally from any other of his friendships. Here were two men of contrasting personalities and opposing views of life. The rugged Scot was born near wild moorlands and reared in stern Calvinism; the Anglo-Irish gentleman claimed landscaped Curragh Chase as his birthplace and grew up in a loving and cultured family of the Church of England. Carlyle's religion dwindled to "Calvinism without the Christianity";[1] de Vere's led him to the Church of his Norman ancestors. De Vere was at ease and displayed a happy temperament under all circumstances, whereas Carlyle—an enigma, especially in politics—seemed always "audience-conscious" and unhappy, as his pathetic face suggests.

Yet de Vere was attracted, even fascinated, by Carlyle. He disliked the Scot's unorthodox prejudice and irreverence but admired his sincerity and probity. For fifty-five years—from their first meeting in 1845 until Carlyle's death in 1881, and as late as 1900—de Vere's interest in Carlyle never flagged. He also felt constantly challenged by the views Carlyle expressed, but took up the challenge in letters and conversations with his opponent.

The two men became acquainted at the home of Lady Ashburton, for years "the most brilliant phenomenon of London society" and "one of Carlyle's most valued and cherished friends."[2] De Vere made an entry of that event in his Diary of May 28: "Dined with the Ashburtons and met Mr. and Mrs. Lockhart, Mr. Carlyle, and Lady Harriet Baring—a dull, easy dinner. . . . Carlyle inveighed bitterly against Lord Brougham[3] and 'oratory,' pronouncing them both the merest shams."[4]

Later the same year, de Vere again visited "The Grange" and while there wrote to a friend:

> The Carlyles are here, and Diogenes-Samuel [Carlyle] denounces all things as sharply as ever. To one who never heard him before, his talk must be striking . . . He certainly loves Truth and Justice, but our moral nature requires something more definite than an affection for abstract qualities . . . He will decry the most sacred and fundamental truths on hazard, and without taking the trouble to inquire whether they are true or not, merely to round out one of those sentences to which, as a victim of phrases,[5] he is subject.[6]

However, like all who ever listened to the broad Scotch accent of this great conversationalist, de Vere enjoyed him more than he did most persons he met in society. "His expressions are pointed always and often significant—his doctrine pungent; and I suppose that where every dish is insipid, the one you like best is that which has the sharpest sauce," de Vere remarked.[7]

Carlyle's wife, the clever Jane, also interested de Vere. To him she appeared sincere and severe, "with a still and quiet will which is always tragic because one remembers against how many things in this world it will blunt itself, and how many of its victories will cost it dear, owing to the infirmities of the judgment associated with it."[8]

Jane's impressions of de Vere are expressed in a way typical of her:

> I have made two new acquaintances which I mean to keep up in London—a male and a female— one has already reached its culmination—and no more can come of it than has come.

... With the male it is better ... that may develop itself into a real friendship—the name is romantic enough—very handsome—young—religious—to the extent even of eating fish on Fridays and fasting in Lent. A Poet—highly accomplished every way, despising "wits" (wonderfulest of all) and in sort a rare mortal as men go . . .[9]

Some months later, she wrote to her husband, then in Ireland, of a visit from de Vere. The tone is characteristic of Thomas Carlyle's "necessary evil":[10]

The day before yesterday I . . . was going to have "my simple repast" (wing of a chicken) at four o'clock when Aubrey de Vere came and staid till after five. He asked your address to send you his paper on Ireland; and I gave it to him as I then had it: Post Office, Dublin. So you must call at the Post Office in case. I said to him as one says all sorts of polite things, "Farewell, then; I suppose I shall hear no more of you till I find you again in London."

To which he answered, with the down still on the cheek of that beautiful enthusiasm, "Nay, Mrs. C. That depends on *you;* if you will only be kind enough to send me your address in Scotland, I shall be only too happy to write!" — Another letter of twenty-four pages I can well believe! At last he went, and I sat down to my chicken . . .[11]

It was in 1849 that Carlyle traveled in Ireland with Charles Gavan Duffy, and before going he asked de Vere to "put down on paper his notions of a set of Irish *notabiles* and *notabilia*"[12] for him. But Carlyle had little sympathy for Ireland in the aftermath of the Famine and did not show interest in de Vere's *English Misrule and Irish Misdeeds*. In fact, he found in it "much to dissent from," although the book, published in 1848, had won the commendation of John Stuart Mill, Sir James Stephen[13] and the Comte de Montalembert. Carlyle wrote to de Vere:

It seems to me of no use when one has fallen into misfortune to blame one's enemies, one's friends, or one's government; or indeed any creature or entity whatever, till once one has thoroughly blamed one's own poor self . . .[14]

And after visiting Ireland the following year, he expressed himself with apparent prejudice:

> The reasonable men I talk with, not to speak of poor
> wretched serfs and savages, miscalled free citizens, seem to
> consider the potato their one dream of happiness. If the potato
> will revive, we live; if it die, what can we also do but die?
> More grievous stupor and stolidity I never witnessed on as
> wide a scale before . . .[15]

About this time Henry Taylor, visiting at "The Grange,"
where Carlyle and de Vere also were guests, wrote to his wife:

> Carlyle talks more bright and forcible nonsense than men
> ever did before; Aubrey de Vere distributes himself equally,
> is easy, and appears to advantage, showing the desire to please
> without the care to conciliate, and showing most of it, I think,
> when he is addressing himself to Mrs. Carlyle. With Carlyle,
> I hear that he had a passage of arms yesterday on theological
> grounds, and they say that Carlyle was furiously and extrava-
> gantly irreverent. Aubrey no doubt would be calm and strong;
> and Carlyle, I suppose, had repented afterwards, for at dinner
> he took an opportunity of observing that he was "bound to
> say Mr. de Vere had talked a great deal of excellent sense that
> day . . ."[16]

Different opinions, however, did not interfere with the friend-
ship of these unlike men, for the following year (1849), while de
Vere was staying with the Taylors at Mortlake, Carlyle, as well as
Tennyson, visited him. It was probably after closer observation of
Diogenes-Samuel that de Vere, some time later, expressed this
opinion:

> Poor Carlyle fancies that he looks down on all forms of
> Christianity from some supposed height—probably in the
> moon—deciding that this doctrine was suited to one time, and
> another tolerable at another.[17]

Naturally, Carlyle attacked things that de Vere held sacred.
On one such occasion, when Carlyle was rude, de Vere calmly said
to him: "Mr. Carlyle, many persons regard you as a prophet; and I
do not dispute the title, on condition that it is borne in mind that in
the old Hebrew days Prophets were classed in two categories—the

True Prophets and the False Prophets."[18] And Carlyle replied with a loud, good-humored laugh.

De Vere, moreover, withstood Carlyle's attempts to dissuade him from becoming a Catholic. Shortly before de Vere's conversion, in 1851, Carlyle visited him and broached the subject.

"I hear you are thinking of becoming a Roman Catholic. Now I give you a warning. You were born free: do not put yourself into that prison."

De Vere replied, "But you know I am already a Christian and I have often heard you say that Catholicism, little as you like it, is the only form of Christianity that has any coherence, solidity, or power about it."

"That is quite true," answered Carlyle, "but Protestantism is a much better thing, for all that, for Protestantism has its face turned in the right direction." (He probably meant that it was turned toward reason.)

De Vere then said, "I have long since cast my lot with Christianity, and I grow daily to see more plainly that Catholicism is the permanent form of Christianity; and likewise that the objections brought against both, however plausible, are equally fallacious, and for the most part are substantially the same."[19]

William Knight's judgment concerning Carlyle harmonizes with the foregoing views:

He [Carlyle] was full of prejudice—*steeped* in it, I should say,—so far as the genius and the work of the Church Catholic was concerned. He had a very genuine appreciation of moral goodness . . . but with his width of vision he could not appreciate the work that was being done and done admirably by labourers in grooves that really ran parallel to his own; and when that work was referred to, he often grumbled and became taciturn . . .[20]

De Vere's sincere appreciation of Carlyle's fundamental goodness and potentialities is implied in a letter written after his own conversion. Expressing the hope that others might know "what Catholicism really is . . in *life* as well as in *mind*," he wrote:

If, for instance, Carlyle were a Catholic, to what a height would not spiritual elevation rise, built upon a basis so strong

. . . and rendered adamantine by faith divine . . . How soon
would all who know him shake off at least the prejudice, that
Roman Catholicism is in some way connected with weakness
or want of integrity.[21]

The publication of Henry Taylor's *Autobiography,* in which
Carlyle is a dominant figure, occasioned further remarks from de
Vere. Writing to Taylor, he stated:

> Your sketch of Carlyle is admirable; but I do not think his
> love of truth, either in matters concrete or contemplative, bears
> any large proportion to his scorn of "shams."
> The revolutionary people really forgive his phrases in
> praise of despotic rule, just as the Whigs forgave Moore for
> his Irish patriotism when they found he was contented to hang
> his harp on the orange-trees in the conservatories at Holland
> Park. Carlyle's admirers feel that *his works* are at the revo-
> lutionary side . . .[22]

Although Carlyle's habitual declamations sometimes displeased de Vere, he was always kindly toward him. In a letter of
1880 he cited instances of "old Carlyle's" friendly relations with
those who failed to agree with him. Regretting that Carlyle was
not the writer of a newspaper article against atheists and material-
ists, although it was signed with his name, de Vere remarked:

> I think that such a protest with his name, against a philos-
> ophy to which he might well have applied an epithet he was
> fond of . . . "hog's wash," might have been more useful than
> elaborate arguments to some persons. It is a great thing to
> help people to trust their higher *instincts.*[23]

Visiting Coniston in 1878, de Vere detected evidences of
Carlyle's unwholesome influence on John Ruskin. "I cannot but
believe," he wrote to Charles Eliot Norton of Harvard, "that if
Ruskin had not in some matters been carried out of his natural
course by an exaggerated admiration for Carlyle, he would before
now have reached a happier goal."[24] Later, Norton, editor of
Carlyle's *Letters,* gave evidence that he, too, had become imbued
with the philosophy of the Scot. Only two years before his death
de Vere expressed his opinion to Walter George Smith:

I wonder whether you know another American friend of mine, Charles Eliot Norton. In him a singularly vigorous intellect is united with a most remarkable sweetness of nature: but I fear that a closeness of intimacy with Carlyle may have been injurious to him in many respects . . .[25]

With characteristic understanding, however, de Vere analyzed what he thought was the source of Carlyle's trouble:

Great allowance is due to Carlyle's harsh judgments when one remembers that dyspepsia, of which he gives such a touching description; but I think his sadness, increasing as it did with years, proceeded yet more from the inadequacy which any religious views adopted by one who has discarded the Christian Faith must ever have . . . Carlyle was deep-hearted—though by no means, as his votaries fancy, deep-minded . . .[26]

Again and again de Vere insisted that Carlyle was not a philosopher, not a prophet, but a prose-poet:

To me he never seemed a Philosopher: for his thought appeared to me always to be but a fiercely cerebral declamation without the intellectual self-possession or the stillness which belongs to deep thought; but I regarded him as a man of warm affections as well as vivid imagination, and very high in the ranks of Prose-Poets . . .[27]

Six years later, on receiving copies of Carlyle's *Letters,* de Vere held to the same opinion: "A man of genius . . . the greatest of Prose-Poets; . . . not in any degree a philosopher because he had not sufficient intellectual self-possession to be one."[28] More definitely de Vere touched on effects of Carlyle's religious views:

He might have had an impassioned religious sentiment, like his impassioned love for his country, had he lived before John Knox had bedeviled his country's religion, leaving behind the sour John-noxious Doctrine, which Carlyle early discarded, taking, however, very unfortunately, the wrong turn.[29]

De Vere's amicable defiance of unfounded statements and pseudo-philosophy was not unheeded by Carlyle, who admitted that his own lectures were "a mixture of prophecy and play-acting."[30] In a letter to Miss Norton, sister of the editor of Carlyle's *Letters,* de Vere expressed his final pronouncement.

After a forty year association with Carlyle, he gave a keen and true appraisal of the Victorian. He believed that Carlyle's extraordinary enthusiasm for Goethe had proved injurious to him, for Carlyle's earlier letters show a marked difference in tone. He praised his ardent and courageous heart, vivid imagination and perceptive powers but still maintained that Carlyle was not a great thinker. Once more he hinted at the cause of Carlyle's gloom:

> It seems to me that as poor Carlyle grew older he got deeper and deeper down into a forest, lion-haunted and black with trees. Much of his gloom doubtless came from his temperament, but how much of it would have been spared to him had he clung fast to Faith, that Faith which is one with Hope, no less than with Charity—not that earthly Hope of which the type is a sail; but that Heavenly Hope, the symbol of which has ever been the anchor, at rest because it has gone down into the depth of things . . .[31]

8

ADVISER

OF

ALICE MEYNELL

To the young poet Alice Thompson, who was later to be Mrs. Wilfrid Meynell, Aubrey de Vere became a literary adviser. Their first meeting, in the early seventies, is recorded by her daughter Viola:

> A home for the Thompson family was established in South Kensington and there social intercourse broadened for the girls, Elizabeth[1] and Alice. Catholic society—a thing rather apart in those days—had Lady Herbert of Lea for one of its hostesses; and at her house Alice met Aubrey de Vere, whose advice, after further meetings elsewhere, she ventured to ask.[2]

It was after a gathering at the home of Lady Georgiana Fullerton, novelist and philanthropist, that de Vere received a humble request from Miss Thompson:

> I am in great need of friendly guidance in the art I have chosen and loved for years and years. Many things that you said . . . have opened my eyes to my own ignorance and to the errors of taste and judgment which mark my work.[3]

With the grace characteristic of de Vere, he replied that he was a firm believer in "female poetry" and its wide possibilities.

He put the shy young woman at ease by telling her:

> The sympathies to which I should wish any verse of mine
> to come home are not the sympathies of pretentious critics,
> but the smpathies of the young; . . . of those who, like your-
> self, have a keen relish for poetry, and whose lofty ideal of
> it has not been blunted.[4]

Alice Thompson sent her poems in manuscript to de Vere,
and he in turn proved the "helper of the young woman."[5] Manuscripts, letters and other documents, all furnish a record of Aubrey
de Vere's "comments on her verse made during her maidenhood."[6]
These sources of information include a series of eleven letters
written by de Vere to Miss Thompson from 1874 to 1877,[7] a record
of his comments on her poetic translations from the French and
on her early verse,[8] and a little manuscript written by Miss
Thompson after a literary interview with de Vere.[9]

Throughout his letters, de Vere urged clarity, care in the
choice of words, avoidance of elisions and contractions, the necessity of polishing an apparently finished production, and constant
and whole-hearted effort. He advised the reading of Coleridge's
Biographia Literaria (Chapter XVII) for better understanding of
proportion, grace and harmony—so well exemplified in the work
of ancient and medieval poets. In this connection he wrote: "Had
Mrs. Browning and her husband appreciated the truth here af-
firmed, their poetry might have quadrupled its value. Tennyson
and Landor have understood that matter, and few besides in our
day . . ."[10]

For "rich and varied metrical effects" he recommended the
study of Crashaw's poems. "As regards Chaucer," he remarked,
"I suspect it is as we get on in years that his freshness becomes
precious—just as, when we grow autumnal ourselves, we appreciate the spring."[11] In the spiritual welfare of Swinburne, whose
connection with the "sensualist school" he deplored, he showed a
keen interest:

> Is it true that Swinburne has lately professed himself a
> Christian? Was it in a speech or a letter? If this is a real
> conversion, it is deeply interesting. I have heard that he

was deeply religious as a boy. He belongs to an old family, Catholic till early in this century.[12]

When Alice Thompson's *Preludes* was about to appear, de Vere again offered advice:

> I am very much interested at hearing that you have made up your mind on the subject of publication, and intend to bring out a volume of poetry soon. There is much to be said both for and against very early publication. . . . I believe that when we discussed the subject I was rather on the side of waiting a little; but if you have determined the other way, it may turn out all for the best. A young poet is sometimes the slave of what he has written so long as it remains in his desk. When it is once published, he feels more free . . . and more able to strike any new style, or modify his earliest one in any way that may seem best. . . . Most earnestly do I trust that the poetic career on which you are entering may be a long and happy one. There is still a great work in the world for poetry to do, if it is sound at heart and fresh in spirit—which, alas, cannot be said of much of the poetry now most popular . . .[13]

In the last letter of the series, de Vere turned aside from criticism and technical suggestions to refer to Alice Thompson's approaching marriage:

> As I dare say you are seeing Wilfrid Meynell every day, may I ask you to give him my best thanks for the little note written on receiving my congratulations; and tell him . . . that as Elizabeth Barrett, when going to be married, enriched our stores poetic with her "Sonnets from the Portuguese," he has a perfect right to insist on your writing a series either of sonnets, or some other form of poems "from the Spanish" . . . Most ardently do I hope that your marriage may be as rich as the happiest marriage has ever been in good to both —and I hope it will make you all the more disposed to *write* as well as *live* poetry.[14]

Perhaps less interesting but more influential than the letters is the second source of information: a manuscript, in de Vere's handwriting, of his comments on Alice Thompson's early poems. His definite suggestions and his advice were carefully weighed and heeded, as comparison with her published poems proves. Ten poems[15] are briefly discussed in the manuscript, which gives tangible evidence of the development of the poet's art and of de Vere's method. For example, of "Builders of Ruins," de Vere remarked:

> There are many good thoughts and felicitous expressions in this poem; but it seems to me deficient in clearness.—A line as rough as "Her quiet time out, and we aspire" is only allowable if there is some special reason to justify it. Many of our later English poets seem to prefer such lines to regular lines. If "calm" were substituted for "quiet" the lines would flow smoothly. The poem wants bracing and clearing, I think.[16]

The present form of the poem [17] shows that the young woman had listened to the criticism. The "rough" line has become: "Through her still time; and we aspire." "Still," not "calm," was substituted for "quiet."

Clearness, conciseness and smoothness form the theme of de Vere's criticism. Discussing one of her sonnets, de Vere offers interesting ideas on that poetic form:

> Unity of thought and sentiment . . . are the first requisites of the sonnet, which should not be an enclosure of several thoughts, but the development of one. It should be "mult*um* not mul*ta*," much and not many, in a compact form. Shakespeare's are exquisite short poems rather than sonnets, in most instances. Wordsworth's have almost always, like Milton's, the still and lustrous simplicity of the sonnet. Even in his "Scorn not the sonnet, Critic," beneath the marvelous aggregation of images, there is a latent unity of thought.[18]

De Vere's critical comments on Miss Thompson's translations of French verse reveal a subtle knowledge of French style.

The third and most interesting source of information concerning de Vere's literary relations with Miss Thompson is the manuscript "in Alice's handwriting." It contains notes evidently written for her own use after a "private audience" with him. The manuscript is headed: "The most spiritual, truly blessed Aubrey de Vere himself said some things I must remember." Naive, humorous and

sincere, these remarks catch the spirit of the interview; they reveal
the charm of the young poet and the sympathy and judgment of her
literary adviser. Miss Thompson's attitude throughout is one of
confidence in de Vere's opinion. Her questions and answers manifest simplicity and charm.

De Vere recommended the thorough study of classic models—
Homer, Dante, Spenser, Shakespeare. When Miss Thompson remarked that women had been barred from the study of Greek, he
suggested a translation of Homer, which she resolved to get.
He called her attention to Homer's "wide sympathy with *all*
humanity." She noted:

> Also Homer passes over an incident with a light and delicate
> touch and immense tact which leaves the bloom on it, where
> a modern world would work and work, laying colour on colour,
> and losing the whole beauty of the incident—for its beauty
> may entirely consist in a certain indistinctness. As an example
> of this Aubrey de Vere cited Nausicaa and her feeling for
> Ulysses.[19]

De Vere quoted Wordsworth's advice to him: "Study nature
in reverence and simplicity *as she is*—in her truth . . . not only in
the works of God in the world, but . . . in the human heart . . ." and
continued that one's attitude should be humble, studious, penetrating, observant.

For Shelley de Vere expressed sympathy and appreciation. He
told Miss Thompson how, on a visit to Italy, he had haunted
Shelley's places at La Spezia. There he had met an old boatman
who called Shelley "l'Angelo," because of his solitary life and habit
of silence. De Vere felt that the great lyricist might have become
a great Christian. Alice Thompson cited de Vere's two theories
about Shelley:

> One, that he was *good*, blinded by tremendous prejudices
> which were partly owing to his education. The other, that all
> the evil, the errors of that exquisite genius, were owing to pride
> —his *one* sin.[20]

Her notes on de Vere's ideas concerning Browning should be
read just as she wrote them, without thought of publication.

He said: "Do you admire Browning? I suspect you do."
(He had seen my study, but I did not know it then.)

He considered Browning had two faults; one was his obscurity, which was caused by this—that he had been so long
accustomed to "think in shorthand" (that was Aubrey de
Vere's expression), that he forgot that others had not acquired
the art.

He [de Vere] was with Browning and his wife, and he spoke
to Browning about the obscurity. "I have been told that before," said B., "and I have taken down all my books, and I
have read through every line, and I can't for the life of me
find one obscure passage in the whole!"

"Browning's other fault is—?" de Vere continued.—"Now
can you tell me what his other fault is?" (This was because
it was mine also, and de Vere wished to instruct me in this
kind manner. But I guessed wrong.) I guessed worldliness and
clever shrewdness in analyzing character, which is not for
poetry. He agreed as to this, and said then, "That is a third
fault; but the second is *roughness* in versification."

He had mentioned this also to Browning, and Browning
had vociferated, "I have been told that, too, and I can't for
the life of me find a single rough line in all my poems, my dear
fellow!"

"He had trained his ear then," I said, "to find sweetness
in discord and roughness": and Aubrey took the expression and
spoke of that false training of the ear.

"As to Mrs. Browning," I asked, "what do you think of
her?" He said she was the greatest of poetesses (which displeased me). He also said she had great imagination and
thought, but he spoke with great regret of her constant *effort,*
and spasm. He told me of the old dancing-master that taught
him and some other children. The old man used to turn his
head over his little violin, and say to them with a smile, "With
ease to yourself, Master Johnny. With ease to yourself, Miss
Fanny!"

What excellent advice to a poet! I laughed at this and
enjoyed it.

During the interview, de Vere also talked of Tennyson. Touching on the popular "sensualist school," de Vere said, "How *can*
they bring evil into poetry? Why, if I were the most wicked of men

I could not put my wickedness into verse. . . . Poetry is Earthly
Paradise. . . . The popularity of much of the poetry of the day is
entirely owing to its latent infidelity."[21]

These letters and manuscripts, and also Viola Meynell's
Memoir of her mother, attest to the importance of Aubrey de Vere's
role in Alice Meynell's literary development. His emphasis on form
and conciseness, his condemnation of vagueness and his insistence
on "taking pains" must have contributed notably to the formation
of her style.

Generally, at the end of his suggestions for improving Miss
Thompson's work de Vere would add in his kindly way, "You
will think of something better than my suggestions," or "A fresh
eye occasionally sees what the author's eye does not at once
observe."[22]

But de Vere did more than offer criticism and advice to this
young friend, thirty-six years his junior. He brought her early
poems to the attention of Tennyson, Henry Taylor and Coventry
Patmore, and tried to broaden her circle of literary acquaintances.
Through him the two Thompson sisters, Elizabeth and Alice, visited
Tennyson's "high-hilled house" at Aldworth so that the poet laureate could see for himself "which was poet and which was artist."[23]
De Vere encouraged the young woman to continue seeing Tennyson:
"I am glad you mean to pay the Tennysons another visit and hope
you will be often with them. He will give you many a useful hint as
to poetry considered as art."[24] In 1877, after Alice's marriage to
Wilfrid Meynell, de Vere wrote to his cousin, Lady Taylor: "I
hope you will like my young poet friend, Alice Meynell. To me she
is very interesting, but you will find her shy."[25]

After her marriage Alice Meynell assisted her husband, who
was also a writer of verse, criticism and biography, with the editing
of the London periodicals *The Weekly Register* and *Merrie England*. The latter carried a great share of the work of Francis
Thompson, the lyric poet and essayist for whose discovery the
Meynells were responsible. Alice Meynell's later poetry was more
distinguished than her early work, but her bid for fame came from
her essays and criticism in which she revealed her finesse and distinction of thought and style.

The Meynells formed the center of a large circle of literary friends. For a long time, during the closing years of the nineteenth century and through the first decades of the twentieth, their home in Palace Court was the gathering place for the leading writers of the time,[26] and many a young talent received inspiration and encouragement from the Meynells. Yet with all her literary activities, Alice Meynell found time to bring up a family of eight children.

"A notice of Aubrey de Vere's work, which she [Alice Meynell] wrote in the comparatively early days of our married life," said Wilfrid Meynell, "I printed in my paper, *The Weekly Register,* and it was quoted in a Ceylon paper, in the issue of September 23, 1881."[27] This rather lengthy article was published more than twenty years before de Vere's death.

> No mental life has ever been more uniformly guarded, guided, restrained, admonished, and inspired by his literary conscience than Aubrey de Vere's must have been, if we may judge by the rightness and uprightness of his whole career of poetical work.
>
> And besides this intimate love of letters, he leads and has led a life more literary in its outward circumstances than falls to the lot of many men in these complicated times. For he was the friend of Wordsworth when that great philosopher and poet was an old man, and has been his most receptive and sympathetic propagandist since the world has lost him. De Vere was also the friend of Landor, the most loved member of that literary society of which Crabb Robinson noted the annals, and the correspondent of Coleridge's daughter. He is the friend of Sir Henry Taylor, of Tennyson, of Browning, of all that is foremost and best in that literary life which is the complement of the life of fact and sorrow.[28]

Alice Meynell's poetry and prose prove that she took seriously what de Vere had told her about taking pains and throwing her heart into her work. She followed his advice by publishing only the best of her work, which won the praise of Ruskin, Browning, Rossetti and others. She has been called fastidious for her exact and delicate handling of words. Her essays—"Mrs. Johnson," "Prue," and "Ceres's Runaway"—illustrate her prose style. "The

Shepherdess" and "Renunciation" are typical of her poetry. Like de Vere, she maintained high standards; and, like him, she kept informed of the universal interests of her time, and was aware of life in a modern world. Also she showed intense interest in others. But unlike de Vere, Alice Meynell makes an emotional appeal by means of the passionate (though restrained) emotion that she put into her poetry; "Renunciation" furnishes an excellent example of this really throbbing emotion. De Vere, on the other hand, did not put passion into his poetry, as Henry Taylor has pointed out; he did express feelings, as in "Sorrow," but the emotion was rather intellectual.

9

ASSOCIATE

OF CHURCHMEN

Perhaps no other Victorian lay-man had so many eminent ecclesiastical friends as did Aubrey de Vere, whose life was dominated by his love of theology and his attachment to the Church. Before his reception into the Catholic Church, he was a friend of Anglican leaders: of Dr. Edward Bouverie Pusey, who, in his concern and alarm over the growth of rationalism in the Anglican Church, had joined Keble and Newman in the Oxford Movement; of the Reverend Mr. Sewell, a high-church Oxford divine and "self-forgetting, enthusiastic philoso-pher, whether one liked his philosophy or not";[1] of Dr. William Whewell, Oxford professor of moral philosophy, "a hearty, genial and honest man with an enormous physical force of intellect, which beat down all obstacles like the brow of a bull";[2] of the Reverend Frederick Denison Maurice, who followed the Broad-Church Movement and became the founder of Christian Socialism; of the Reverend William Whately, founder of the Broad-Church policy and later Archbishop of Dublin. Dr. John Jebb, the nephew of Bishop Jebb of Limerick, was considered an old friend of the family by all the de Veres.

Moreover, de Vere became the correspondent of Henry Edward Manning, the loyal friend of John Henry Newman, and the champion of Herbert Vaughan—all three destined to become Car-

dinals of the Catholic Church. For all these churchmen de Vere
retained a high and constant regard. No friendship interfered with
the other, and his feelings remained the same for those who continued Anglicans and those who did not. In the case of Newman,
Manning and Vaughan, the friendship was destined to last until
death. The churchmen who remained Anglican, like Dr. Jebb, disapproved of de Vere's leaving the Church of England, and some of
them, despite de Vere's wishes to the contrary, withdrew their
friendship.

JOHN HENRY NEWMAN

Of all the churchmen with whom de Vere entertained close
contact, it was probably Newman who exercised the greatest influence upon him. Theirs was the friendship of longest duration—
from 1838 when they first met at Oxford, to 1890, the year of the
Cardinal's death. De Vere himself once stated that Newman was
one of the two men he had loved best; the other, of course, was
Wordsworth.[3]

De Vere's interest in Newman was first roused when he received news from Richard Monckton Milnes, who had been visiting
at Oxford:

> I heard . . . Newman preach on the building of churches, in
> a manner that a Bishop urging the people to contribute to the
> "Osian Basilica" in the time of Theodosius might have envied
> and imitated. He is surely a great man. . . .[4]

Oxford made an indelible impression on young de Vere on the
occasion of his first visit, which he made shortly after receiving
Milnes' letter. In his pocket he carried a letter of introduction to
John Henry Newman from Dr. J. H. Todd, eminent fellow of
Trinity College in Dublin.

Concerning his first meeting with Newman, de Vere wrote to
his sister, Ellen: "He is very dignified, very ascetical, and so very
humble and gentle in manner . . .";[5] after having attended the
morning service at Saint Mary's, he added, "Newman's reading is
beautiful, a sort of melodious, plaintive and rather quick chaunt. . . .

He looks like a very young man made old by study.—His forehead
is very high and not very broad."[6] Almost sixty years later, in 1896,
de Vere vividly recalled this first glimpse of his friend:

> The emotion of seeing him for the first time was one of the
> greatest in my life. I shall never forget his appearance. I had
> been waiting some time, and then the door opened, and New-
> man, in cap and gown, entered very swiftly and quietly, with a
> kind of balance of the figure, like a very great lady sweeping
> into the room. That was my first impression; the second was
> of a high-bred young monk of the Middle Ages, whose as-
> ceticism cannot quite conceal his distinguished elegance.[7]

On one occasion de Vere went to Saint Mary's to hear Newman
preach on "Unreal Words." Since he was late, he took a seat remote
from the pulpit and regretted that he would be unable to hear well.
But to his surprise he heard every syllable. Although Newman's
voice was low and musical, it had carrying power.[8] One seemed to be
listening to Newman's thinking rather than his speaking. For Newman's definition of style was "a thinking out into language"[9]—
quite true of his pure, simple and transparent prose.

Three or four years later, de Vere met Newman again, but
this time under entirely different circumstances. In the interval,
Newman had incurred the disapproval of the Oxford authorities
because of his *Tracts for the Times,* and especially for his "Tract
90," which was directed against the Thirty-nine Articles of the
Anglican Church. Asked to discontinue such writings, Newman had
resigned from Oxford, and with some companions he had retired to
a kind of hermitage at Littlemore, three miles from Oxford. De
Vere went there on foot to visit Newman. He found the churchman
reserved, grave and even depressed; he was apparently suffering
from the pain of broken ties, for separation from his beloved Oxford
must have hurt him deeply. Newman accompanied de Vere part of
the way back to Oxford and gave every evidence of a great internal
struggle. Shortly afterwards, in 1845, Newman joined the Catholic
Church and went to Rome to prepare for the priesthood.

In the intervening time, de Vere read Newman's *Essay on the
Development of Christian Doctrine,* which was not entirely to his

liking, although in it he found light on the distinction between
principles and doctrines—something which he had missed in the
works of Maurice.[10] In 1850 de Vere attended Newman's lectures
on "Anglican Difficulties," which he considered impressive, sug-
gestive, spiritually helpful, and delivered with impassioned eloquence.[11] About this time he expressed his candid opinion of Newman in a letter to Sara Coleridge:

> As a fact, I know that Newman is wholly free from tempta-
> tions toward infidelity [in religion]; that he anticipates an un-
> precedented outburst of infidelity all over the world;—that
> to withstand it he deems his especial vocation. . . . There is
> occasionally an iron hardness in J. Newman; but in him, as in
> Dante, . . . an exquisite and surpassing sweetness. . . . The only
> part of his mind which I do not like comes out in his vein of
> irony. I must say I thought his lectures full of matter. . . .[12]

The following year, in November 1851, six years after Newman, de Vere became a Roman Catholic. What really occasioned
this step, over which he had reasoned and prayed, was the Gorham
Judgment, a decision that earlier in the year had also impelled
Henry Manning to leave the Church of England, which he pas-
sionately loved.

Five years later, John Henry Newman was placed in charge
of the new Catholic University in Dublin. The task of establishing
and organizing this undertaking proved most difficult. The student
body consisted mainly of Irish young men and of some foreign
students, coming from distinguished families and attracted to
Dublin chiefly by Newman's prestige. In 1856 Aubrey de Vere
was asked to deliver a course in English Literature at the University
of Dublin; and in a private report to Cardinal Cullen, Newman, who
was responsible for the invitation, stated that de Vere's name as a
poet was "high in England."[13] Two of de Vere's twelve lectures
were later published in his *Essays Literary and Ethical;* one of
them, "Literature in Its Social Aspects," is considered remarkable.

Newman, who presided over the larger of the two University
houses, invited de Vere to live at his house. Thus the Irishman had
the opportunity to observe Newman most intimately and to realize
the appalling difficulties that confronted him. The buildings were

poor in comparison with those of Dublin's Trinity College and the
imposing structures of Oxford and Cambridge. Government and
Parliament refused the University of Dublin public endowments,
proper buildings, and even the charter: the claim was that the
Queen's Colleges were sufficient for the demand, but, with the sole
exception of Belfast, they were not agreeable either to Protestants
or to Catholics because of their lack of religious instruction. The
Irish poor, though they really had no interest in the university,
helped financially, but the middle and upper classes were not generous. Lack of funds prevented Newman from hiring necessary help,
and proper equipment was never forthcoming; yet patiently and
humbly, as de Vere states it, he "carved for thirty hungry youths."[14]
In some cases jealousy—which de Vere does not dicuss—misunderstanding and even suspicion of insincerity increased Newman's
feeling of frustration.

During de Vere's residence at Newman's house at the University he was taken ill with scarlatina. In order to avoid contagion,
he desired to leave the house, but Newman insisted that he remain
and he himself visited the sick man regularly, sitting and talking
with him every day. When de Vere later went to Bray to convalesce
in the sea air, Newman drove out to see him. On this occasion, de
Vere offered to take his friend through the beautiful countryside of
County Wicklow, but Newman replied that "life is full of work
more important than the enjoyment of mountains and lakes."[15]

After seven years of worry and difficulties at the University
Newman resigned the rectorship; he realized that an Irish Oxford
was then far from possible. Weary and depressed, he left Dublin
for Birmingham. There, each year, de Vere visited him on his way
to the Cumberland Mountains and the grave of Wordsworth. He
often wished that Newman had met Wordsworth, for he considered them both profoundly English. De Vere's estimate of the
older Newman is expressed in a letter of 1868 to his cousin:

> The specialty of Newman is that he has always invited the
> heroic daring . . . with the keenest intellect of the time, and
> with the most tender character, and sensitive temperament.
> I believe that his not writing more proceeds chiefly from his
> deep spirit of self-sacrifice, and a belief that in hearing the

confessions of poor factory girls at Birmingham he is making
a better oblation to God than he could make by writing more.[16]

But probably there were other reasons for Newman's not writing
more. When de Vere congratulated him in 1864 on his *Apologia*
and asked him to write more in the same vein, Newman replied:

> I have had a great trial and am very wearied but I trust
> that on the whole I have done my work—though, of course, it
> might have been done better. . . . I have no wish at my age to
> be involved in controversy, and spend my strength in self-
> defence. . . .[17]

Yet, six years later, encouraged by the success of his *Apologia*
and his subsequently restored prestige, Newman gave de Vere an
interesting account of his new book, *The Grammar of Assent,* and
a few words about himself:

> As to my *Essay on Assent,* it is on a subject which has teased
> me for these twenty or thirty years. I felt I had something
> to say upon it; yet, whenever I attempted, the sight I saw
> vanished, plunged into a thicket, curled itself up like a hedge-
> hog, or changed colors like a chameleon . . . At last, four
> years ago, when I was up at Glion over the Lake of Geneva,
> a thought came into my head as the clue, the "open sesame"
> of the whole subject, and I at once wrote it all down, and
> I pursued it about the Lake of Lucerne . . . You must not
> think . . . I am sure myself that I have done any great thing . . .
> I think that sometimes a man's failures do more good to the
> world or to his cause than his best successes. . .[18]

De Vere probably knew Newman as very few did. He had seen
him at various crises in his life and at all his significant stages: as
the popular Rector of St. Mary's church at Oxford; at Littlemore
when Newman was about to sever his strongest ties; at Dublin
where disappointment and failure were his fate. De Vere had
known about Newman's frustrated hopes to edit the *Rambler,* which
he felt could become a power for good. He had noticed his disappointment when Oxford refused to admit Catholic students and
had been a witness to Newman's disillusion when he was unable to
continue his revision of the English Catholic Bible, a Papal com-
mission: the opportunity was suddenly withdrawn in a confusion

over publication rights. But de Vere rejoiced with his friend when the cloud of misunderstanding was finally lifted, and mourned when, after a period of storm and darkness, Newman closed his life in quiet splendor.

In de Vere's opinion the most remarkable thing about Newman was his intense personality—his strong belief in his own powers, the conviction that he had a special vocation from God to fulfill his mission. Yet he was humble. It was really he who was the leader of the Oxford Movement, but he insisted that Pusey and Keble should be considered first. Kindness and humility, thoughtfulness and courage, veneration and zeal were the characteristics of this man who was also keenly interested in earthly affairs. This interest, de Vere points out, is manifest in the character studies in Newman's historical essays. Cardinal Newman had a high regard for the humanities and disagreed with any system of study which ignored Latin and Greek. The great master of English prose in his *Idea of a University* proves his concern, however, for fitting students for life in the world. But such a life must be motivated by humanistic and religious ideals. In a letter to de Vere, in which he thanked the Irish poet for having sent him a copy of his own *Alexander the Great,* Newman expressed his admiration for true heroism. Of Alexander he wrote:

> Who was there but him whose object it was to carry on civilization and the arts of peace while he was a conqueror? Compare him with Attila and Tamerlane. Julius Caesar, compared with Alexander, was but a party man to a great general.[19]

De Vere and Newman shared a great admiration for the Middle Ages and both loved Scott's novels and chivalrous poetry. Newman and Taylor admired each other, though they never met. Through de Vere it is known that Newman had written, but forgotten, his *Dream of Gerontius,* until a publisher solicited a contribution. Newman sent him the manuscript—which was promptly published. *Callista,* so Newman told de Vere, had been written in pencil in railroad coaches. Newman evidently liked de Vere's poetry, for his "Docens" and "In Epiphania" were sung daily during May at the Oratory, and Newman placed de Vere's "Reality" on the title page of his *Callista*.

"Nothing was more characteristic of Newman," de Vere wrote, "than his unconscious refinement. It would have been impossible for him to tolerate coarse society, or coarse books, or manners seriously deficient in self-respect and respect for others. There was also in him a tenderness marked by a smile of magical sweetness, but a sweetness that had in it nothing of softness."[20]

At the same time de Vere stated that the severity apparent in Newman's face was a severity "which enables a man alike to exact from others, and himself to render, whatever painful service or sacrifice justice claims."[21] In Newman more than in any other person he knew, de Vere found realized that "out of the strong came forth sweetness."[22] The coldness which some attributed to Newman was probably a cloak for his sensitiveness or the result of his early training, or perhaps an acquisition from Oxford; his *Apologia* has been called "eminently and emphatically literature, . . . the revelation of a great and fiery soul"[23] aroused by injustice.

In a letter to Miss Norton, the sister of his friend Charles Eliot Norton, de Vere wrote in the year following Newman's death:

> The outburst of enthusiastic admiration for Newman on the part of writers from every school of English thought was very cheering to those who remembered how entirely he had been misunderstood and misrepresented for many years after his submission to that church which had converted the English race to the Christian faith. . . . I published a sonnet[24] expressing the hope that those who now praise Newman so eloquently will also read his works, especially those of his maturer days.[25]

De Vere's sonnet "Cardinal Newman" expresses the hope that the influence of the great man will live:

> Thy ninety years on earth have passed away.
> At last thou restest 'mid that heavenly clime
> Where Act is Rest and Age perpetual prime;
> Thy noblest, holiest work begins this day—
> Begins, not ends! Best work is prayer; and they
> Who plead, absolved from bonds of space and time,
> With lordliest labor work that work sublime,

Order our planet with benignest sway.
So, work, great Spirit! Thy toils foregone, each year,
Bear fruit on earth! Thousands but praise thee now;
Those laureates soon will bend a brightening brow
O'er tomes of thine; on each may drop a tear
For friends that o'er blind oceans pushed their prow,
Self-created of a guiding light so clear.[26]

De Vere's *Recollections,* written in his eighty-fourth year and
published in 1897, seven years after Newman's death, contain this
picture of a man who already is being proposed for canonization:
the message implied is as applicable today as it was six decades ago.

> He had ever retained a faith, firm and fixed, that the
> Christian religion came from God, that it was God's chief
> gift to man and the one hope of the world. . . . He believed that
> before his England, and before the world there remained
> greater perils, and also greater possible glories, than at any
> preceding time; that only through a pure and a complete
> Christianity, in its integrity and in its unity, those perils could
> be surmounted, and that glorious inheritance attained.[27]

HENRY EDWARD MANNING

A greater contrast of personalities than that which existed between Newman and de Vere's friend Henry Edward Manning can
hardly be imagined. Yet, profound friendship united de Vere and
Manning just as it did de Vere and Newman.

The two men met for the first time at a dinner party at the
home of the Earl of Dunraven in Adare, where the Irish poet had
occasion to observe the man of whom he had heard so much. In his
"Reminiscences of Cardinal Manning,"[1] de Vere draws a sympathetic picture of "the popular and picturesque figure that appealed to the imagination of the multitude."[2] These reminiscences,
perhaps more personal in nature than those of Cardinal Newman,
present a defense of the sometimes misunderstood and perhaps
maligned churchman.[3]

At the time of their meeting, both men had a profound attachment to the Church of England. "I well remember saying to myself
on meeting Manning for the first time, 'I see a word written on the
forehead of that man, and that word is Sacerdos',"[4] de Vere wrote

forty years later. In a letter to his mother, written the year before Manning left the Anglican church, de Vere remarked:

I returned after passing three or four delightful days with Archdeacon Manning. How I wish you knew him! He is the most spiritual, and at the same time most ecclesiastical-looking man I ever met. . . . His manners are not less interesting, including a marvelous union of grace, decisiveness and sanctity. His hopes for the church are not apparently very high.[5]

During these visits to Manning's rectory at Lavington, de Vere learned that his host considered Dante and Thomas Aquinas the greatest of human minds. He termed Dante's poetry "Saint Thomas Aquinas put into verse."[6] One evening they read to each other passages from Dante's "Paradiso," and de Vere and Manning agreed that Dante knew theology better than did many bishops of their own time.[7] De Vere commemorated this visit to Manning and his love for Aquinas and Dante in a sonnet, "Cardinal Manning":

I learned his greatness first at Lavington.
The moon had early sought her bed of brine,
But we discoursed till now each starry sign
Had sunk. Our theme was one, and one alone,
"Two minds supreme," he said, "our earth has known;
One sang in science, one served God in song.—
Aquinas, Dante." Slowly in me grew strong
A thought: "These two great minds in him are one.
Lord, what shall this man do?" Later, at Rome,
Beside the dust of Peter and of Paul
Eight hundred sires of Christendom
In council sat. I marked him 'mid them all.
I thought of that long night in years gone by,
And cried, "At last my question meets reply!"[8]

Manning's love for Dante indicated his preference for verse of a severe intellectual and spiritual order. In this he resembled Newman, as he did in his attitude toward Wordsworth. Neither of the two regarded the former laureate so highly as did de Vere. Like Newman, Manning loved music but wished to hear only liturgical music in churches. In the later school of painting Manning had no interest, as de Vere discovered when they both visited art galleries

on the Continent; Fra Angelico was his favorite artist.[9] Like Newman, Manning admired the works of Henry Taylor; and both
praised Sir Aubrey de Vere's *Mary Tudor,* about which Manning
was particularly enthusiastic:

> It is the work of a mind high, large and good . . . Perhaps
> my feeling may be tinged by sympathy and the "Idola Ec-
> clesiastica." But Gladstone is not; and we agree in considering
> *Mary Tudor* the finest drama since Shakespeare's time. It is
> to me one more evidence of the injustice or the incapacity of
> readers and critics that it should be unknown.[10]

Regarding literature in general, de Vere thought Manning
narrow in one sense. Manning did not believe that every book should
be didactic, but he held that a certain reserve should be observed
in writing. "He could not forgive those who, in Christian ages and
Christian lands, wrote as nobler writers of pagan days would have
regarded as a sin, not only against decorum, but also against
letters."[11]

De Vere admired Manning's extreme self-possession and self-
control; he contrasted the churchman with Carlyle, who seemed
unable to do his thinking until he had worked himself into an intellectual passion.[12] Manning's singular deliberateness, serenity and
control gave the impression of coldness; but de Vere maintained
that "some of Manning's affections were intense and indelible,
especially in the case of his father."[13]

It was on April 6, 1851, that Manning was received into the
Catholic Church; several months later he and de Vere set out for
Rome. However, they stopped at Avignon, where on November 15
Aubrey de Vere became a Roman Catholic.

An incident which occurred when the two were at Avignon
throws light on Manning's character. He lost a small black bag
containing his "most precious memorials"—his deceased wife's
letters, his journals, and one hundred pounds. In reply to de Vere's
sympathetic words, Manning said: "Say nothing! I can just endure
it when I keep perfectly silent."[14] Later he told de Vere: "The
loss was probably necessary—necessary to sever all bonds of
earth."[15] De Vere found in Manning a remoteness regarding not
only temporal things, but also all human ties except the closest.[16]

He saw Manning's spirituality grow with the years—a progress borne out by his Journal and Diary.[17]

De Vere successfully defended Manning against the charge of insincerity by referring to several columns of the former Anglican's early sermons in which the sincerity of his ecclesiastical opinions seems manifest.[18] The popular accusation of ambition raised against Manning is refuted by de Vere:

> A man conscious of great powers will generally wish to have a sphere in which he can exercise them for the benefit of mankind. . . . Without ambition of an unworthy kind, strong faculties may, by natural instinct, crave a field for their exercise, as bodily energies do without reproach. Manning would never have desired a position which he knew might be occupied by another, with more benefit to mankind; neither would he have been slow to suspect that he might himself be unequal to its duties.[19]

In 1881, thirty years later, Manning spoke in his own defense:

> If it be ambition to desire to see work done that ought to be done, and to be done as it ought to be done, and when ill done to be done better; and to be done without being the doer of it, if only it be done at all . . .; and if it be ambition to say, "Let me try," I acknowledge ambition and I hope to die in it. When ambition gains its summit, He will judge whether I have entered into my rest. . . . Three times at least in my life I broke the line where ambition would have led me.[20]

And, again, eight years later, Manning weighed the accusation:

> I have been accused by both friends and enemies of ambition. Every man who rises is supposed to have desired and sought it. Have I done? Three times I acted in direct contradiction of ambition. Some have said that when I saw it was impossible for me to be an Anglican bishop, I aimed at a Catholic bishopric. If so, it was a vaulting ambition, and deserved success. . . . Why not believe in a divine government of the lives of men?[21]

Manning's letters indicate that he regarded de Vere as a confidant. When made Bishop of Westminster in 1885, Manning wrote to de Vere: "You were one of the first I thought of when this thing came on me, and I wish I could see you. . . ."[22] And ten years later, when Manning was created Cardinal, he sent this message from Rome to his old friend:

> I wish you were here with me. . . . If I can better serve the Church, so be it! For myself, it is a restraint upon the liberty I have hitherto enjoyed. Moreover, anyone who in the world's eyes rises high is thought to seek it, and love it; and that hinders his work for souls. God knows whether this has been so with me. And I will wait for the last day. . . .[23]

The whole matter of Manning's ambition was well summed up by de Vere when he stated that the churchman possessed "that union of qualities that almost inevitably leads to eminence unless a man is resolved not to accept it."[24] He had shown great energy, circumspection, the practical qualities of a man of business, and the contemplative faculties of a theologian.

Manning's chief asset, in de Vere's eyes, however, was his unbounded energy, which enabled him to work all day and preach at night—for he considered preaching as restful; to him it was simply a thinking aloud. He was happiest when he was working for his fellow-men. He possessed great administrative sense, the ability to systemize his various duties and the discernment to discover the special aptitudes of those around him and to make the best of those aptitudes.[25] In politics and public affairs he was entirely unlike Newman, who had told de Vere that since 1832 he "had had no political views at all."[26] Newman was a student and scholar; Manning, essentially a man of affairs. He played an important part in the Oecumenical Council of 1870 and threw himself into such social questions as the great London dock strike of 1889.[27] In a letter to de Vere Manning referred to his work at this time:

> Your affectionate and interesting letter . . . came to me in the midst of strikes. Since then I have been again and again trying to avert new contentions. And now as to the strike: I can only say I never thought of it until I found myself in it; and I believe that our Lord used me as He did Balaam's ass. I have been so long working with working men that it is not difficult to me; and somehow I am known to the English work-

ing men as well as to any. They listened to me readily from the
first . . .[28]

Like Newman, Manning met disappointments and frustrations
with courage, and apparently without resentment. False and mali-
cious rumors about him and his views, circulated after his submission to Rome, probably caused him pain; but as the years
passed, "rumor, which had come in as a lion, went out as a lamb."[29]
Long before Manning's death (as in the case of Newman) all pre-
judices and bitterness against him had gradually disappeared. His
own lack of prejudice was manifested in 1890 when he wrote of
the Salvation Army: "If General Booth can gather under human
influence and guidance those whom all other agencies for good have
not yet reached, who shall forbid him?"[30] And he remarked that "it
was the Quakers who had originated the Anti-slavery Society."[31]

HERBERT VAUGHAN

Herbert Vaughan, later Bishop of Salford and Cardinal, was
but twenty-two when Aubrey de Vere met him in Rome. De Vere
was seeking rooms in the Eternal City on his arrival from Avignon.
He was told that a young ecclesiastic who had an excellent sitting-
room near the Piazza della Minerva would probably share it with a
compatriot.[1] De Vere wrote, announcing his intended visit, and
soon knocked on the door of the young man's room. Hearing
"Avanti!" he entered and stood amazed at the beauty of the young
Englishman. "Good heavens!" de Vere said to himself, "if you are
like that, what must your sister be?" The two, although very unlike
in character, became fellow-lodgers and fast friends.[2]

The following passage is from one of de Vere's letters to his
mother, written in Rome at this time:

> I like my companion in my lodgings better every day. I
> must have mentioned him to you; he is a Mr. Vaughan, the
> eldest son of one of the great old Catholic families of England.
> He renounces prospects as brilliant as almost any man in Eng-
> land can command, to be a priest in some out-of-the-way
> village in Wales, and seems as happy as the day is long at his
> studies and devotions. He is very handsome and refined and

as innocent as a child. He sits up half the night reading Thomas Aquinas, and tells me in the morning that he had been dreaming that people had been burning him alive; and that it had given him no pain . . .[3]

And six months later, when he had returned to England, de Vere went to Herefordshire, to become acquainted with the Vaughan family—"noble, generous, devout and humble people." Nearby was the home of Dr. John Jebb, but de Vere dared not go there. To Miss Fenwick he expressed his feelings:

> Almost within sight was the house of my old friend Jebb, who, while dissuading me from Rome last year, had yet confessed that, if he had lived at the time of the Reformation, nothing would have induced him to join the Innovators. . . .
> You can imagine how strange it must have seemed to me to reflect that while I was so warmly received by perfect strangers, I should have created nothing but embarrassment at the house of an old friend, who wrote to my brother, on his change[4] to say that friendship must now be at an end. Yet he is a particularly kind-hearted person, steady and strong in his nature as well as constant, and attached to justice. . . . Friends find it hard not to resent changes of this sort as a personal wrong, while nothing is farther from the fact than that, in such changes, they were forgotten *even for a moment*.[5]

It is clear that kindred interests in theology formed a strong link and a lasting friendship between Vaughan and de Vere. The Irishman, devoted from early youth to theological studies, could not but admire his young friend who had early "resolved to be not only a good priest, but also the best possible sort of priest."[6] De Vere enjoyed the companionship of an Englishman whose family had never given up the old faith; and no doubt Vaughan felt drawn to the enthusiastic poet—Irish by birth, English by heritage—who had just returned to the religion of his Norman ancestors.[7]

SOME OTHER

VICTORIANS

The wide circle of Aubrey de Vere's friends and acquaintances included many other eminent Victorians, some of whom are little known today. In his extensive correspondence de Vere revealed himself always as an assiduous observer of the Victorian literary scene. He noted the role of Maecenas in which Richard Monckton Milnes (Lord Houghton) placed himself, and was interested in Walter Savage Landor's love of classicism. He called attention to Ruskin's appreciation of the Middle Ages and stressed the value of Robert and Elizabeth Browning's poetry.

He praised Thomas Macaulay's conversational powers and encouraged Edward Dowden in his study of Shakespeare and other poets. The correspondence with Wilfrid Ward reveals de Vere's own keenness as a critic and evaluator of passing events and of their significance for the future. His relations with Richard Holt Hutton clearly confirm the judgment of this prominent Victorian critic that Aubrey de Vere excels in literary criticism far more than in poetry.

RICHARD MONCKTON MILNES

Richard Monckton Milnes, who had been one of the Cambridge "apostles," played a significant part in the social, political and literary life of his time. This man, who helped many a struggling

writer to become famous, never achieved fame for himself, though
he often seemed to be on the brink of lasting fame. Having breakfast with Milnes one day, de Vere noted that his friend was divided
between literature and politics and "incommoded by a partial discovery of the necessity of earnestness for success."[1] Apparently
Milnes sometimes skimmed over the surface of each undertaking
and failed to concentrate his energies, conviction and hard work on
a definite goal. But through Milnes de Vere became interested in
writers before unknown to him, and he acknowledged his debt:

> Through him, we became acquainted with the refined and
> classical poetry of Landor. . . . Through Milnes also we
> acquired a thorough knowledge of Shelley and Keats (before
> unknown to us). . . . And I became familiar with those noble
> works of Kenelm Digby, *The Broad Stone of Honor* and
> *Mores Catholici,* in which what was best in the Middle Ages
> is so vividly mirrored and to which I have felt myself much
> indebted for the light which they cast on religious history and
> philosophy.[2]

Besides introducing de Vere to the poetry of Tennyson, Milnes
continued to suggest other books, such as Browning's *Strafford,*
which he compared rather amazingly with a drawing of Michelangelo, Harriet Martineau's *America,* and Carlyle's *French Revolution.*[3] He shared his interest in religion and churchmen with de
Vere: "Have you seen Newman's new book on the prophetical
character? . . . I hear he said he was conscious of dealing a severe
blow to actual Protestantism. His volume of verses is very interesting and pleasing, with nearly as much poetry as one wants in that
kind of thing."[4] And again: "By-the-bye, by no means omit to get
The Kingdom of Christ, volume first, published by Darton, High
Holborn. It is by Maurice, the 'caposetta' of our [Cambridge]
apostles, and will interest you exceedingly."[5] Milnes also discussed
the soul after death, and showed a keen interest in the Newmanites;
of the Roman Church he said, "She never forgot that her foot was
on earth, though her head was in heaven."[6] Later Milnes wrote to
de Vere concerning a visit to Oxford:

> I heard Pusey lecture on the mystical interpretation of
> Scripture . . . unintelligibly to the greater part of his audience.

He [Newman] is surely a great man, and I sorrow that my plain judgment of things as they are will not permit me to hope for him any fair scope for realizing and formalizing his high notions . . .[7]

Milnes met de Vere occasionally in London; and fourteen years after his first visit to Curragh Chase, he returned and remained at de Vere's home "a good many days, though when he left they seemed too few."[8]

De Vere, who had won the esteem of Milnes,[9] urged his friend to publish his best poems;[10] Milnes did so and left four volumes of reflective lyric verse, published in 1844, and his important biography of Keats, which came out four years later. To T. Wemyss Reid's *Life, Letters and Friendships of Richard Monckton Milnes* de Vere contributed "a vivid picture of the brilliant youth" of Milnes.[11] In this article de Vere related an incident that concerned Milnes and Wordsworth, who had both been invited to a masked ball at Buckingham Palace. When the laureate heard that Milnes was going to the ball in the role of "old Chaucer," he explained: "If Richard Milnes goes to the Queen's ball as Chaucer, it only remains for me to go to it as Richard Milnes."[12]

The Library of Literary Criticism contains de Vere's appraisal of the poetry of Richard Monckton Milnes:

> Some time or other the world will discover, with much pleasure and surprise, what a true poet there lived in a man whom it regarded chiefly as a pleasant companion with odd ways and manifold accomplishments. . . . His poetry did not assert itself; it had a modesty about it which the poet himself did not claim. It shunned the sensational, and the refinement which so marks it presented probably the greatest obstacle to its popularity. Though rich in fancy, it is grave-hearted, and in an unusual degree thoughful; it is full of pathos, and that pathos often rests gently, like Wordsworth's "lenient cloud," on scenes and incidents not only of modern but of conventional life.[13]

WALTER SAVAGE LANDOR

On a memorable visit to de Vere's home, in 1831, Milnes interested Aubrey, as well as other members of the family, in the

work of Walter Savage Landor.[1] His poetry and "those imaginary
conversations which take perhaps the highest rank in prose poetry"[2]
won de Vere's lasting approval. The following year de Vere wrote
of Landor as a classical writer, "in mind most Grecian, most
thoroughly accomplished and refined . . ."[3] Once, in discussing
Plato, de Vere remarked:

> Plato seems to me to write as Coleridge and Landor would
> have done if they constituted a single mind. He unites the
> vast comprehension and subtle insight into spiritual Beauty
> of the former with that sustained elevation, that bland and
> equable nobleness, and that exquisite appreciation of Definite
> Beauty, which distinguish the latter. . . . In Coleridge's Muse
> you see nothing but the forehead and eyes, and in Landor's
> little more than the mouth and chin: in Plato you have the
> full countenance of perfect and placid Wisdom—that union of
> "Science and Song." . . .[4]

Although de Vere found in Landor a kindred love for the
Greek, their ideas on other subjects did not always harmonize. For
example, Landor considered Homer and Dante together only equiv-
alent to Milton "shorn of his sonnets and 'Allegro' and 'Penseroso'
. . .";[5] but de Vere, always somewhat severe with Milton, disagreed
with this opinion. This Victorian habit of comparison appears often
in de Vere's correspondence with Sara Coleridge and elsewhere.
De Vere contrasted and compared Landor with others: "Southey
and Landor flung their poetry adrift in oceans of prose. Coleridge
talked his away in monologue."[6] And again:

> Landor was proud, not only of his style, but of the pains
> he took with it. That care, he said, should be only in part con-
> cealed; light touches of the chisel should remain on the marble.
> Newman also wrote with extraordinary care, but his care was
> only to be plain.[7]

It is surprising that de Vere included none of Landor's poems in the
two anthologies he edited;[8] probably he preferred the prose *"Imaginary Conversations.*

"Landor's Poetry"[9] is an essay in which de Vere discussed
Greek thought and its expression in poetry and commended Lan-

dor's devotion to ideal beauty and classical associations. De Vere
noted a classical love for order and symmetry and a Greek spirit
manifested in definite gracefulness, sensuous and imaginative treatment of nature, and aversion to the mysterious and spiritual. De
Vere met the charge of Landor's deficiency in pathos by pointing
out that the poet usually presented life in its most ordinary course,
in the "exhilaration and equable light of day," rather than "tinged
with the lights of a low horizon and clouded with the shadows of
eve."[10] He cited examples of deep and tender, though unostenta-
tious, pathos in "Corythos" and "The Death of Artemedora."
Terrible, yet merely suggested, pathos appears in "The Madness
of Orestes."[11]

Landor's shorter dramatic "fragments" (as in the *Imaginary
Conversations*) de Vere considered richer in delineation of passion;
the author, he held, lacked power to build plots in which incident
resulted from incident, rested on moral support and illustrated
character.[12] He remarked on the excellence of the philosophical
passages in the poem "Regeneration"; the fine description in
"Gebir";[13] the poet's Greek treatment of love as "a plain, honest
passion . . . free from all morbid consciousness"; and his concise and
clever manipulation of episodes.[14] De Vere attributed Landor's
occasional obscurity to condensation, subtlety and elaborateness.
He noted the poet's preference for the idyl and the ode, rather
than the more modern forms of ballad, sonnet and song.

The critic concluded his essay by saying that the poetry of
Landor possesses the unobtrusiveness of genuine poetry, free from
studied effects and exaggeration. Its extreme refinement, however,
hindered its popularity, for "music which is music only, without
the jar of wood and wire, will be heard but in the still gallery or
lonely grove."[15]

Throughout his life de Vere continued to be interested in
Landor's work and to propagate it. In a letter to George Edward
Woodberry regarding his *Makers of Literature,* de Vere, in his
eighty-sixth year, mentioned Landor as an especial favorite from
his youth. He urged Woodberry to make Landor's prose and poetry
better known in America.[16]

Landor, although "very sparing of admiration for poetry,

bestowed it unsparingly upon de Vere";[17] he praised the Irish poet's more classical work and wrote verses[18] which prove the sincerity of his praise. As Henry Taylor expressed it: "When de Vere's poems were but little read, and when Landor was, I think, seventy-four years of age, he gave as cordial a salutation as ever old poet bestowed upon a young one."[19]

Admiring de Vere's "Greek spirit," Landor wrote to a friend:
I would recommend your reading the Poems of Aubrey de Vere. Nothing of our days will bear a moment's comparison with them, nor indeed do I find anything more classical among the best of the ancients. . . .[20]

De Vere's *Search after Proserpine* made an especial appeal to Landor, who wrote enthusiastically to John Forster:

Have you the *Masque of Proserpine?* If not, I will lend you mine. He has raised her not only up to earth again, but to heaven. It is delightful to find one figure who has escaped the hairdresser and the milliner. . . The most envious of them [poets] does not envy me more than I envy Aubrey de Vere; but envy with me lowers her shoulder to let a Love mount upon it. These are revolutionary times . . . but old forms of poetry start up again. I can imagine Milton reading to Proserpine the beautiful Masque, and Proserpine saying in her simplicity, "You have succeeded with me."[21]

This copy of de Vere's *Search after Proserpine* had an interesting history. De Vere inscribed it and sent it to Landor probably shortly after publication, in 1843; but for some reason Landor paid no attention to it. Finally five years later, he found it under a pile of books that had long remained undisturbed. So fascinated was he with the *Masque* that he remained up all night to read it and almost immediately wrote to de Vere:

Although it is almost morning, I am resolved to continue the Masque until I have read it through, for nothing (I am convinced) in the best of Greek dithyrambics was better than p. 15. It is the first time I have felt *hellenized* by a modern hand. . . . Shelley and Keats breathed the air of the Aegean. . . . Had these two wonderful men lived, they would have done what it appears to me is reserved for you to do.[22]

De Vere replied to this high praise:

> Landor's remarks on my volume are, of course, immeasurably above its merits; but they illustrate the exuberance of his imagination and the generosity of his genius. He enjoyed praising, as inferior men enjoy sneering.[23]

Undoubtedly, Landor's most natural, and consequently most sincere, criticism of de Vere's work appears in the remarks written on the margins of a copy of the *Search after Proserpine* found in an old bookstall in Chicago, in 1897. (Apparently it is the volume which de Vere sent to Landor in 1843.[24])

Of de Vere's sonnet "Allegory" Landor remarked: "Like Shakespeare, but better." The octave of this poem runs:

> You say that you have given your love to me.
>   Ah, give it not, but lend it me; and say
> That you will oftimes ask me to repay,
> But never, to restore it; so shall we
> Retaining, still bestow perpetually:
>   So shall I ask thee for every day,
>   Securely as for daily bread we pray:
> So all of favor, not of right, shall be.[25]

De Vere's "Sunrise," now called "The Sun-God," Landor called "the noblest sonnet that was ever written." He rated de Vere's "Power" "magnificent." Other comments in the margins are: "finer than the best in Homer," "very Attic," "Greece never produced anything so exquisite."

Landor's remarks on de Vere's "Coleridge" are amusing and cynical. De Vere's poem runs:

> His eye saw all things in the symmetry
> Of time and just proportion,
> Yet dim that eye with gazing upon heaven . . .

And Landor wrote of Coleridge: "The greatest liar that ever did gaze upon it." To de Vere's lines of the same poem:

> Adown Lethean streams his spirit drifted
> Under Elysian shades . . .

Landor added: "Drunk with gin and opium." After the passage expressing the hope that the poet (de Vere) may be awakened by

Coleridge when he (Coleridge) awakes, Landor scribbled: "And let me nap on!"[26]

Landor also appreciated de Vere's prose work *English Misrule and Irish Misdeeds,* praised by Comte de Montalembert.[27] Landor called it a "work which unites the wisdom of Bacon with the eloquence of Burke."[28] This must have pleased de Vere, for he always retained his youthful admiration for these two writers.

Landor greeted de Vere with the following:
Welcome, who last hast climbed the cloven hill
Forsaken by its Muses and their god!
Show us the way; we miss it, young and old.
Roses that cannot clasp their languid leaves
Encumber all our ways of poetry.
The satin slipper and the mirror boot
Delight in pressing them; but who hath trackt
A Grace's naked foot amid them all?

Or who hath seen (Ah! how few care to see!)
The close-bound tresses and the robe succinct?
Thou hast; and she hath placed her palm in thine;
Walk ye together in our fields and groves.
We have gay birds and graver; we have none
Of varied note, none to whom harmony
Late hours will listen, none who sings alone. . . .

. . . Come reascend with me the steeps of Greece
With firmer foot than mine; none stop the road,
And few will follow; we shall breathe apart
That pure fresh air, and drink the untroubled spring.
Lead thou the way; I knew it once; my sight
May miss old marks; lend me thy hand; press on;
Elastic is thy step, thy guidance sure.[29]

JOHN RUSKIN

Walter Savage Landor admired de Vere for his ability to put his love for Greek into verse; John Ruskin appreciated him for his character and personality. De Vere first became interested in Ruskin in 1843, when his *Modern Painters*[1] was published. "I am told that the author's name is Ruskin, and that he was considered at

college as an odd sort of man who would never do anything,"[2] de
Vere wrote at that time. Two years later de Vere read Ruskin to
his father, who enjoyed it very much,[3] and they decided that the
author "seemed to make out his case in favor of the modern land-
scape painter."[4]

Five years later Ruskin and de Vere met at the home of
Carlyle, whose influence over Ruskin began about that time. Present
were Mrs. Ruskin, Mrs. Carlyle, Mrs. Wedgwood, Erasmus Dar-
win, as well as Ruskin, Carlyle, and de Vere. Carlyle's biographer
mentions the gathering:

> Ruskin and his wife called at Cheyne Row. Ruskin set him-
> self to badger Carlyle about religious opinions in presence of
> Mrs. C., Mrs. R., Mrs. Wedgwood, Erasmus Darwin, and de
> Vere (poet and Puseyite).[5] John persevered until he made
> sure of the joyful discovery that the Devil had not personal
> existence at all! The only Devil he need fear was that within
> each of us;—what may have upset poor de Vere—that no
> power can "clip the wings" of that Devil but one's own.[6]

More than a decade after this meeting Ruskin wrote to a
friend:

> Aubrey de Vere is the noblest person I've yet heard of your
> getting hold of. He will do you good; he is one of the very,
> very, *very* few religious men living. You may tell him (I knew
> him once, and know his work still)—that if ever I get better
> I mean to be religious again, too, but my religion is to be old
> Greek. It will do quite as well as his, and is entirely "certain"
> also, which is an immense comfort.[7]

Perhaps de Vere's peace of mind and serenity pleased Ruskin, who
restlessly "vacillated all his life."[8] Eleven years after this letter
was written, de Vere discussed Ruskin in a letter to an American
friend of Ruskin and disciple of Carlyle, Charles Eliot Norton of
Harvard:

> Ruskin has been a considerable time bringing out a sort of
> monthly letter addressed to the working classes. The speci-
> mens that I have seen contain much that is eloquent; but I
> fear that when he gets within the domain of political economy
> and social science many of his views are unsound and danger-

ous.[9] Poor fellow, he seems to me to be unhappy in the present, and to have but little of a better outlook as regards the future; but how far this represents a permanent condition or one of those moods of judgment at times, it is impossible to guess, and probably he does not know himself.[10]

A few months later de Vere discerned in Ruskin a state of mind which probably indicated his future mental condition.[11] In another letter to Norton de Vere stated:

> He has evidently much genius and high aspirations; and what you say of his heart is high praise still. He has, I am afraid, much incoherency of mind—a lack of "hooks and eyes" in his thoughts. . . . Ruskin sometimes speaks as if he were very near to Catholic belief, and an hour after as if he believed nothing at all.[12]

Three years after this, de Vere pleased Ruskin with a visit, quite different from Ruskin's visit to Matthew Arnold at Ambleside —a visit which much disappointed the art critic.[13] The following year (1878) de Vere again journeyed to Coniston, and reported his reactions to Norton:

> Ruskin seems to me very much as when I saw him last year. . . . He is sooner fatigued with head-work than he used to be; but of this one sees nothing during a visit of a few hours. He speaks on the same subjects as of old, with the same animation, and the same admirable felicity of diction as well as charm of imagination. He was speaking of you with the greatest affection.[14]—Also on art and literature, as well as on various topics philosophical and social. His remarks were always most suggestive and interesting, though in some cases too much influenced, as it appeared to me, by what might be called Carlyle's declamatory way of thinking. . . . I cannot but believe that had Ruskin in some matters not been carried out of his natural course by an exaggerated admiration for Carlyle, he would before now have reached a happier goal.[15]

Again in 1879, ten years later, de Vere went to see Ruskin; his interest and fidelity never waned. Both men appreciated nature and the work of Wordsworth, and they loved the Middle Ages, in which they found a joy in living. Ruskin said: "The Middle Ages had

their wars and agonies, but also intense delights"[16] and for de
Vere they "constituted the devout, joyous though often incoherent
childhood of Europe."[17]

THE BROWNINGS

De Vere's association with Robert and Elizabeth Barrett
Browning was less intimate and of shorter duration than that with
Ruskin. In 1837 the literary Milnes discussed *Strafford* in a letter
to de Vere, and eight years later de Vere noted reading "The
Piper" to his family. Shortly after, in a letter to Sara Coleridge,
he indicated his interest in Elizabeth:

> I wish you would persuade your friend, Miss Barrett, to
> write with as much grace and refinement as ever, and not talk
> about "garrulous God—Innocence," and such extravagant
> over-strained things, which are as objectionable as great
> unfeminine strides, abrupt movements. I wish she had less
> ambition, or rather more and of a nobler sort, that of writing
> like a woman of genius—as she is—not like a man. . . . She is
> injured by taking men models.[1]

To another correspondent de Vere stated that her poetry was "full
of genius, though over-strained and injured by eccentricities and
want of simplicity."[2]

De Vere's condemnation of Elizabeth's poetic form was echoed
almost three decades later, when he said of Robert Browning:

> I admire his abilities and energies, but I can never keep
> company long with a book which does not seem replete with
> beauty as well as truth, and many of his poetic capriccios are
> intended to illustrate the beauty of ugliness.[3]

And to Alice Thompson Meynell[4] de Vere specifically indicated the
defects in both poets:

> Had Mrs. Browning and her husband appreciated the truth
> affirmed in Coleridge's "Biographia Literaria," Chapter XVII,
> regarding the superiority of ancient and mediaeval poets over
> modern ones in proportion, grace, and harmony, their poetry
> might have quadrupled its value.[5]

De Vere's surprise over the growing vogue of Browning's work appears in a letter to Allingham:

> One of the most remarkable turns that literary things have taken of late is the *sudden popularity* of Browning's poems. His publishers told me that in fifteen years he had hardly sold fifteen copies of them: and all at once they leaped up into popularity so great that I hear the young men at the Universities run after him more than Tennyson.[6]

De Vere's literary judgments on the Brownings, uttered sixty years ago, were entirely his own; yet they bear a close resemblance to the opinions of modern critics. Such phrases as "faults of rhyme and rhythm," "passages of powerful thought," "adoption of the masculine tone"[7] recall de Vere's remarks on Elizabeth Barrett. And "needless harshness and obscurity," "profundity of thought," "style and rhythm . . . often intolerably rough and unmusical"[8] remind one of de Vere's attitude toward Robert's poetry, formed without modern literary perspective.

Interest in Browning and his gifted wife prompted de Vere to visit them in Florence on his return journey from Rome a few months after his reception into the Catholic Church. The new convert's enthusiasm in his faith was evidently expressed, for they discussed the problems of religion until the early hours of morning. As a result, Browning wrote a letter which seems to be a reply to one of de Vere's:

> I was much interested by the hours you gave me on that last evening of yours in Florence, and grateful, too, and *not* "tired." The sense of the spiritual, the exercise of the soul's instinct, the attitude of the life toward the Truth and the Love are always interesting to me. *I am never tired of sunrises.*[9] That I believe you to be mistaken in much is obvious; but you think worse of the act of mistaking than I do—which is obvious too—and so it is true (though a paradox) that I differ less from you than you differ from me. In spite of which, you were very patient and at the same time loyal with me, for which I thank you entirely.[10]

Obviously, Browning respected de Vere's philosophy of life although he disagreed with it. At Browning's death in 1889, almost

four decades after their meeting in Florence, de Vere spoke of
him as "a truehearted man and poet, and a great thinker in verse."[11]
His sonnet of the following year expressed de Vere's final decision
on Browning's work:

Gone from us! That strong singer of late days—
Sweet singer should be strong—who, tarrying here,
Chose still rough music for his themes austere,
Hard-headed, aye but tender-hearted lays,
Carefully careless, garden half, half maze.
His thoughts he sang, deep thoughts to thinkers dear,
Now flashing under gleam of smile or tear,
Now veiled in language like a breezy haze
Chance-pierced by sunbeams from the lake it covers.
He sang man's ways—not heights of sage or saint,
Not highways broad, not haunts endeared to lovers;
He sang life's byways, sang its angles quaint,
Its Runic lore inscribed on stave or stone;
Song's short-hand strain—its key oft his alone.[12]

THOMAS MACAULAY

Thomas Macaulay did not excite the admiration of de Vere,
as did his contemporary Browning. He seems to have been but a
casual acquaintance. Yet de Vere's appraisal of the historian
matches those of his contemporaries[1] and of more modern critics.

After meeting Macaulay at the home of Lady de Vere's
brother, Lord Monteagle, de Vere wrote his impressions:

We had a great dinner party...Whewell, Hallam, Macaulay
and Milman, the first three such inordinate talkers by reputation that I was on the watch to see which would put the others
down . . . Whewell I like very much . . . Macaulay is far from
ill-conditioned; but he is rather bluff and good-humoured than
genial. His mind is evidently a *robust* one—it has also ardor
enough to fuse together into strange combinations the mass of
strange and disorderly knowledge with which his great memory
litters him. It has also a self-confidence[2] which belongs to
narrowness, and an utter unappreciation of all matters which
it cannot wield and twist about . . .; but I could observe in it
no trace of originality, depth,[3] breadth, elevation, subtlety,

comprehensiveness, spirituality[4]—in one word, none of the attributes of greatness.[5]

Yet, de Vere justly admitted that Macaulay was a strong man who would do his day's work honestly, before his day was done. In his opinion Macaulay liked "if not Truth, at least the exhilaration of a hunt after Truth or the animation of the battle for the cause of Truth." Contrasting him with Lecky many years later, de Vere remarked that although the latter was thoroughly prejudiced against Catholicism, his work "showed up the extraordinary inaccuracies"[6] of Macaulay's statements as to the conduct of the Irish Parliament in 1680.[7]

EDWARD DOWDEN

Edward Dowden's connection with de Vere came through Sir Henry Taylor, for Dowden edited Taylor's letters.[1] The correspondence which passed between Professor Dowden and de Vere is a source of valuable information. It proves de Vere's influence on Dowden's work and something quite different—de Vere's critical ability in the later decades of his life.

The correspondence (from 1874 and 1892) was occasioned by Dowden's literary work, especially that on Shakespeare and on Wordsworth. Dowden appealed to de Vere for ideas concerning the proper approach to a study of the great dramatist.[2] Modestly, de Vere asserted that his knowledge of Shakespeare was limited,[3] although his later criticism on Dowden's book would seem to prove the contrary.

Shakspere: His Mind and Art, which was published in 1875, met with de Vere's approval. After two readings he pronounced it better than August Wilhelm Schlegel's work in the same area; he praised the author's keen insight and power of expression.[4] However, de Vere did not hesitate to tell Dowden that he was too severe in his attitude toward Ophelia and much too lenient with Juliet, Helena and Cordelia. He also took exception to Dowden's interpretation of the character of Henry VI, in which Dowden reveals an apparent misconception of a saint in the Catholic sense.[5] In answer to Dowden's portrayal of Henry VI as "a royal saint . . .

weak in his saintliness . . . and possessed of the egoism of timid saintliness . . .," de Vere wrote:

> Several passages in your book gave me the impression that you hardly appreciate the degree in which, according to the Catholic Church, heroic strength enters into the idea of a Saint. No one who is soft or trivial in character can be a Saint. Faith itself is an act of spiritual daring, as well as of spiritual discernment, and without the gift of fortitude there can be no progress up the heights. . . .[6]

To this letter Dowden courteously replied:

> I have used the word "Saint" in a careless and vulgar way, and I feel this now myself, but I know partly, and I hope I shall know more and more, that the true conception of "saintliness" excludes all softness and selfish or weak scrupulosity. This is a part of Christian literature I should most like to submit my mind and heart to—the lives of noble Christian men and women—and though work prevents me from Catholic reading, I shall always try to make time for really good lives of Saints, if you will recommend me such books—such I mean as the autobiography and *Book of the Foundations* by St. Teresa, which I know, or the *Confessions of St. Augustine.*[7]

Dowden also acknowledged the justice of de Vere's disapproval of his treatment of Ophelia and Helena, and expressed his appreciation of de Vere's encouragement. He wrote:

> Your opinion of *Shakspere: His Mind and Art* and that of two or three other persons . . . have given me an authentic assurance that my attempt to interpret Shakespeare has been, up to a certain point, right and successful. . . .[8]

Writing to Dowden, de Vere made some original observations concerning Shakespeare and religion. He remarks that the great dramatist dimly outlines Christianity in his plays and treats it with reverence; when he writes in a Christian spirit at all, he is Catholic in tone. But de Vere agrees with Wordsworth, who stated that "in general the religious sentiment in Shakespeare's plays is less than that which may be called the average in actual life."[9] Shakespeare, de Vere believed, was Catholic in principle, but was perhaps too indifferent, or too much engrossed in business and pleasure, to take religion very seriously or to examine it very philosophically. He probably thought that the religious controversy of the time was but a repetition of former troubles between Church and State (as in the reigns of Henry I and Henry II). In all likelihood, de Vere thought, Shakespeare expected these disagreements to terminate in reconciliation, as former ones had ended.[10]

De Vere further encouraged Dowden by suggesting that he begin work on Wordsworth, who seemed to him more like Shakespeare than did any other poet: "As 'much will have more' I want you to undertake a kindred labor—as large a volume on Wordsworth";[11] and de Vere assured Dowden that he could make the work better, since, with details of Wordsworth's life before him, he could examine more closely Wordsworth's mind and art.

Seventeen years later Dowden informed de Vere that he already had finished seven volumes of his study of Wordsworth.[12] De Vere's suggestion, therefore, was carried out by Dowden, whom de Vere had once described as "a great Wordsworthian . . . with a minute knowledge of Wordsworth, as well as a comprehensive grasp of his greatness."[13] De Vere also praised Dowden's poetry for its elevation of thought, spontaneity and refinement.[14]

De Vere, moreover, encouraged his friend in his writings on Southey[15] and Shelley. In a letter to de Vere, Dowden acknowledged this debt. "I have a strong impression that my *Life of Shelley* must owe its origin to you."[16]

RICHARD HOLT HUTTON

As de Vere advised and encouraged Dowden, Richard Holt Hutton, the most influential critic of the last decades of the nineteenth century, evaluated the work of de Vere. And with him Hutton enjoyed a kinship of character and interests, as well as the companionship of mutual friends.

As co-editor of the *Spectator,* he was bound to merit de Vere's admiration for his able defense of Wordsworth when Ruskin called that revered poet third-rate.[1] Hutton was also a critic of Tennyson. And in the pages of the *Spectator* Hutton effectively praised Newman and his philosophy as illustrated in his *Apologia,* helping to make that work a remarkable success.

Although the friends resembled each other, they also differed. De Vere really enjoyed the society of others, whereas Hutton kept fairly aloof from it. While both were excellent conversationalists, Hutton was more critical, powerful and dominating than the genial and optimistic de Vere. They both shone in conversation during the small breakfasts at the Devonshire Club, of which Wilfrid Ward was a member. On these occasions de Vere was at his best, always more at ease among a small number of friends. At one such meeting he had to break up a spirited discussion on the great English poets, because of another appointment. After his departure Hutton remarked to Ward: "What a wonderful man this is; what simplicity and purity of character! I wish I were more like him."[2] At a later meeting, when the three were having breakfast at the old Saint George Club and Hutton was the first to leave, de Vere exclaimed: "What a wonderful man! How unworldly and single-hearted! How I wish I could be like him!"[3]

Hutton wrote an appreciative review of the Irish poet's *Saint Thomas of Canterbury* in the *Spectator,* the periodical in which he had also pronounced Sir Aubrey de Vere's *Mary Tudor* superior to Tennyson's *Queen Mary.* The publication of Hutton's review occasioned a letter which de Vere wrote to Sir Henry Taylor, July 6, 1876:

> Your being so much pleased with the critique in *The Spectator* (certainly a most friendly and useful one) only proves what I knew before . . . you are much more interested in the success of what I write than I am myself. . . . The first thing Tennyson said to me when we met was, "So I hear you have taken 'Becket' out of my hands." I told him that my work now being done, the sooner he wrote a better one, the better; but that I did not want the poetic mind of England to be in the first instance preoccupied by a drama setting forth what I regard as the natural prejudice on the subject, as contrasted with deeper and larger principles. . . .[4]

Although Hutton rated de Vere's *Alexander the Great* the finest drama of the day in conception, unity and restrained energy of diction, he maintained that de Vere's most effective and influential work lay in the field of literary criticism.[5] He based his judgment

on de Vere's remarkable keenness and correctness in his analysis
of poetic genius. As he encouraged his friend in criticism, he
frankly indicated the reasons for de Vere's lack of popularity,
especially regarding his poetry. He wrote:

> I do not think you ought to measure the chance of success
> of your essays by that of your poetry; though you are a true
> poet, you are a poet of that quiet and refined kind that, espe-
> cially writing as you do on religious subjects and in a Catho-
> lic sense, you can hardly expect a large public. Poetry to be
> really *popular* needs a very considerable volume of force.
> Yours is all qualitative. But the critical essays of a true poet
> on poets are always finer than any other critic can write. There
> are a touch and a feeling in them, which ordinary critics can-
> not emulate.[6]

Hutton stated further that de Vere had not won the popular
fancy because he went against the stream of tendency. In his review of de Vere's *Foray of Queen Meave,* he wrote:

> The only Irish writers of great beauty who have never re-
> ceived an adequate meed of admiration . . . are the two de
> Veres, father and son; and that we ascribe in no small degree
> at all to their being Irishmen, but [also] to their verse having
> an air of supreme and almost fastidious culture and dealing
> with themes so remote from popular imagination that it takes
> considerable effort . . . to enter heartily into the subjects of
> their verse . . .[7]

Later, in reviewing de Vere's *Poetical Works,* Hutton treated
the poems in detail. *The Search After Proserpine* he considered a
scholarly example of the author's taste; "Written under Delphi"
reveals the poet's nobility of sentiment, religious fervor and rare
good sense—"rare in an age of tortured phrase and doubtful
meaning." De Vere's epic and dramatic poetry lacks the "modern
air," as well as comic elements to relieve tragical and pathetic
scenes. In discussing de Vere's themes (man, conqueror and statesman; man, evangelist and saint; man, ruined by his own ambition
but still lord of fate), Hutton saw that they would naturally be
unpopular in a pessimistic age.

Hutton, whose judgment carried weight, did not place de Vere in the first rank of poets; but he keenly appreciated his friend's nobility of thought, wholesome outlook and lofty aim. He thus summarized the work of de Vere:

> No poet of our time . . . has struggled with nobler perse-verance to make his readers look up toward the fountains of poetry. If the air of those heights be somewhat cold and rare for modern lotus-eaters, we trust that some are yet able to bear its tonic purity: they will be rewarded by wider horizons and visions of nobler forms than have been presented to them by any other poet of our day, though it may be that one or two other poets have sung more beautifully of less worthy themes.[8]

Wilfrid Ward

Such men as Hutton, Tennyson, Manning and Ruskin pro-moted Wilfrid Ward, son of the noted W. G. Ward and author of de Vere's *Memoir*.[1] In 1875 on the occasion of de Vere's visit to his old friend, Bishop Herbert Vaughan, then a guest of the Wards, he became acquainted with Wilfrid. On this visit, too, de Vere inadvertently introduced Vaughan to Tennyson,[2] who was his companion at the time.

Later, at their "dining club,"[3] as well as at Ward's home in Hampstead, de Vere discussed the Irish problem and Irish litera-ture. Ward was impressed with his gentleness and refinement. He was struck by de Vere's ability to continue after the lapse of a year, "as though their former conversation had been broken off only half an hour previously."[4] In his *Memoir*, Ward presents de Vere in the last three decades of his life. His first impressions are vividly recorded:

> As a man of three score years he had still the simplicity, the unspoilt keenness of enjoyment, the buoyant hopefulness, the trustfulness, the reverence for all that was great and good, which belong to a youth as yet untouched by the world, whose brightness is undimmed by the disappointments and disillu-sions of life. In a letter written in middle age he declared that

he feels just as he did at eighteen. And at sixty he appeared
to his friends to be still unchanged. . . .[5]

De Vere's love for music, as well as his natural piety, also impressed Ward.

> Aubrey de Vere stayed . . . talking to Dr. Vaughan after
> the others had left, and I went into our chapel to play the
> organ. A little while later . . . I saw his slim figure in one of
> the benches rapt in devotion. I joined him and he begged me
> to play again the Andante from Beethoven's "Kreutzer Son-
> ata," which I had just finished. We walked to Farringford[6]
> together afterwards, talking on many things of common in-
> terest, and arranged to meet again.[7]

Other visits are recorded by Ward:

> I used also sometimes to go and talk with him at the
> Athenaeum, where year after year he appeared at the end of
> July, when the fashionable world was leaving London, and
> I well remember the tall, refined, rather aristocratic figure,
> dressed in velveteen coat, ascending the wide staircase. He
> talked much to me . . . of the friends and scenes of his early
> life, and of his favorite poets. His memory for poetry was
> extraordinary. . . .[8]

De Vere's love for old documents was manifested in his visit
at the Arundells' Wardour Castle, where Ward and he spent a
week together. To his companion he remarked:

> This is my ideal. A beautiful place, full of historic records
> of an ancient house with nothing of "smartness" or excessive
> wealth or display, which brings nearly always a touch of
> vulgarity.[9]

Ward liked to remember de Vere as a man of seventy-nine, an
excellent raconteur,[10] refined, dreamy, animated . . . telling the
old stories which had inspired his 'Inisfail' and his 'Legends of
Saint Patrick'."[11]

De Vere's letters to Ward contain keen and farsighted observations on the religious questions of his time—questions which

persist even today. Having been in Rome during the Vatican Council, he expressed his idea of papal infallibility, for example:

> My sojourn at Rome brought before me how utterly impossible (humanly speaking) it would have been for the Church to have done its work if it had not had a Central See, endowed with great power as well as dignity.[12]

The "Italian Question"—the temporal power of the Pope—upon which his "Saint Peter's Chains" has bearing, deeply interested de Vere. His opinion on the subject was modern. He argued that the Church, guided by the Holy See, is the only hope against growing agnosticism. Hence the Church must be free; papal independence he considered synonymous with religious freedom. He looked forward not to the return of the Papal States, but to a better solution of the problem, according to changed conditions.[13] No doubt the establishment of Vatican City would have constituted for him such a solution.

Writing to Ward of his "The Death of Copernicus," de Vere discussed the compatibility of theology and science, the theme of his poem. Again in advance of his time, he indicated the causes for apparent lack of harmony between the two, and he deplored this unnecessary misunderstanding. He wrote:

> Many of the apparent discrepancies between the Mind of the Church and what may be called the Mind of Science result from the fact that we are really very imperfectly acquainted with either of those two minds. Each extends a hand stored with truths, but each chooses to lift but a finger at a time; and this partial knowledge of truths, seen separately, and not in their wholeness and unity . . . must have also the effect of making Theology and Science sometimes at variance when they are in accord, or when one of the two is silent.[14]

Through his *Memoir,* Wilfrid Ward, who best understood the vital interests in de Vere's life, has made us better acquainted with "a devoted patriot, a true poet, a thinker of great imaginative insight—one whose personality is marked by spiritual beauty of the very highest order."[15]

11

AMERICAN

FRIENDSHIPS

I entirely expect to be in America before very long, though when I cannot say yet,"[1] wrote Aubrey de Vere to Charles Eliot Norton, in 1867. De Vere never realized his desire to visit the United States, but he always retained the keenest interest in America and in his American literary friends and correspondents. One of these correspondents found de Vere's letters "full of wisdom and truth, so warm with interest in all the questions relating to the condition of literature and education in America, and so tender in personal allusions that they are volumes in themselves, like his own presence, full of sunshine and happiness."[2]

De Vere admired Henry Wadsworth Longfellow and James Russell Lowell, and for more than forty years (1857-1898) he corresponded with Charles Eliot Norton, Harvard professor, translator of Dante's *Divine Comedy* and editor of *Carlyle's Correspondence*. In the last decade of his life he met and often corresponded with Walter George Smith, of the University of Pennsylvania, and his literary sister, Helen Grace Smith. Through George Edward Woodberry, Columbia University professor and writer, de Vere's work was published in America, and also through Woodberry de Vere became acquainted with Richard Watson Gilder, editor of the then famous *Century Magazine*. De Vere generously shared his knowledge of Wordsworth with the Wordsworthian scholars—Andrew J. George,[3] who met de Vere through Mrs. Wordsworth; Ellis Yarnall, author of *Wordsworth and the Coleridges;* and Henry Hope Reed, who introduced Wordsworth to the American public.[4]

De Vere's meeting in London with Henry James, in 1896, is mentioned in a letter the novelist wrote to his sister: "I breakfasted with the Nortons . . . and Mr. Aubrey de Vere, tu sais, the Catholic poet, a pleasant, honest old man [de Vere was but fifty-five at the time, and James was twenty-six!] and very much less high flown than his name. He tells good stories in a light, natural manner."[5]

Evidently de Vere early became interested in the work of Longfellow, for in 1848, a year after the publication of *Evangeline,* he sent a copy of the poem to Sara Coleridge. In 1853 he reviewed "The Golden Legend" and *The Poetical and Prose Works* of Longfellow in the *Dublin Review,*[6] thus bringing the American writer to the attention of the British public. De Vere did not consider Longfellow a poet of the first rank. He admired his "rich and varied imagination, deep appreciation of the beautiful both in matter and morals, and happy tact for the discernment and exhibition of character"; but he found the poems "defective in depth and simplicity." In "The Golden Legend," which de Vere considered Longfellow's best work, the American poet produced "a faithful poetic picture of the time" and handled the Catholic element well; but in the prose work *Kavanagh* de Vere noticed a lack of understanding of Catholicism.

De Vere, opposed to slavery, liked Longfellow's poems on that subject. He praised the clever and successful use of hexameter in *Evangeline.* However, on the whole, he found Longfellow's prose and poetry to "abound in promises rather than conclusions," for in his work there is lacking "a complete and consistent method of thought." Yet de Vere, five years later and after the publication of "The Song of Hiawatha" and "The Courtship of Miles Standish," wrote to Norton:

> Do not let Mr. Longfellow forget his kind intention of writing to me.—I am a great admirer of his poetry. I did my

"little possible," as the French say, to introduce it to my
countrymen, the Irish, (in England he is very popular) in
an article published some years since in the *Dublin Review*.
Some time or other I shall hope to make both his acquaintance
and Mrs. Longfellow's. . . .[7]

Ten years later, Longfellow arrived in London.[8] De Vere met
him and described the meetings to his cousin:

> I have seen a great deal of Longfellow, almost always be-
> tween twelve and one at night, after he returns from his
> parties, and while he is smoking his pipe before going to bed.
> —He is a very fine-looking man, a little like H. Taylor in face,
> though with not so much either of beauty or dignity. I have
> taken a great liking to him. . . . He has remained wholly un-
> affected by the great stir . . . made about him; but he is
> plainly a solidly good, upright, deep-hearted man, with a calm,
> grave conscientious way of thinking on all subjects, and I
> think he has wide sympathies. . . . His ways and bearing,
> though serious as well as gentle, are not depressed. He is en-
> tirely modest, and as simple as Wordsworth himself, of whom
> he speaks in very becoming terms of reverence and gratitude.[9]

The following year de Vere dedicated *Irish Odes and Other
Poems* to Longfellow. In his preface to the book de Vere expressed
his keen interest in Irish immigrants, "those Irish 'of dispersion,'
in that land that has extended to them its hospitality."[10] Longfellow's reaction to de Vere is implied in his message to D. F.
MacCarthy: "I am glad you dedicated one piece in the new volume
to Aubrey de Vere: a sweet and noble character, and a true poet,
who well merits recognition at your hand."[11]

Through Longfellow and Charles Eliot Norton, de Vere made
the acquaintance of James Russell Lowell, whom he considered
"a true poet as well as a delightful man."[12] He thought Lowell a
better poet than Longfellow and he admired his "singular genius
for letter-writing."[13] Lowell was a link between de Vere and
Richard Watson Gilder, to whom he wrote of de Vere:

> He is going to send you a poem (founded on an Irish
> legend) which is sure to be good—though whether good enough

I cannot say, for *I like him so much and have liked him so long*
that I can't tell . . . why or how he falls short. I told him I
feared the poem would be too long for you, etc., but the dear
old boy has a self-possession of hope that would be creditable
at ten years. He is naturally anxious about the manuscript,
and begs you to return it to Mr. Norton at Cambridge if you
shouldn't want it.[14]

But de Vere's relationship with his American friends was not
restricted to the exchange of letters alone. To those who visited
England he was a most charming host who went out of his way to
see that they met his own friends in society or saw the important
tourists' sights. He made Longfellow acquainted with Lady
Herbert and took him to visit her home at Wilton, "one of those
really grand old historical places . . . made of the monastic spoils."[15]
With Richard Watson Gilder he toured Westminster Abbey. Gilder
wrote to his friend George Edward Woodberry: "De Vere would
tell me what one illustrious man said to him kindly of the other
illustrious man: the two now cheek by jowl beneath the pavement
of Westminster. . . . We came upon the marble statue of Wordsworth. 'Did it look like?' I asked.—'Yes,' he said, 'It has his look
of contemplation.' "[16] De Vere probably introduced Lowell to
Henry Taylor, for he sent word to Norton that the Taylors were
expecting Lowell, who had been delayed in London, at their country
house at Bournemouth.[17] Both Woodberry and Norton visited
Bournemouth with de Vere, and de Vere also invited Walter George
Smith and his sister, whom he occasionally met in London, to his
home in Ireland. Mrs. Elizabeth Reed, wife of Henry Reed, wrote
about one of de Vere's visits to her: "Mr. de Vere is one of the
most fascinating men I ever met . . . I assure you it is very charming
to hear a man talk who was on intimate terms with Wordsworth,
Manning, Faber and Newman. . . ."[18]
Woodberry wrote from England to a friend:

Mr. de Vere is always with us after four o'clock and he is
very charming.—He's quite won my heart. Yesterday he gave
me one of the pleasures I have most wished for. He took me
out to call on Lady Shelley.[19]

In his correspondence with his American friends, de Vere discussed passing events, religion, literature and other mutual interests. He was interested in the Civil War and, in siding with the North, disagreed with some of his British friends. In a letter to George William Curtis, the noted litterateur and editor, Norton wrote early in the war:

> De Vere has taken from the beginning the most intelligent and sympathetic view of our great contest. I read you, I think, one of his letters about it; and in later letters he expressed his convictions still more fully and warmly. Nor is his volume *Antar and Zara*[20] without the marks of his hearty interest in our struggle.[21]

After the War, de Vere remarked that Mexico and Canada should be "left wholly to their own devices, for America would have a far nobler development if she consisted of several nations rather than one only."[22] The countries of North America united would (he continued) form not one nation, but one social company.

Regarding two pictures of Dante which Norton had sent him, de Vere replied: "In the younger face the Soul seems to be looking out on Beatrice . . . The aged face is that of one whom the warring elements have made reserved and retired. . . ."[23] As Norton was preparing his *Historical Studies of Church Building in the Middle Ages* (published in 1880), he and de Vere met on common ground. De Vere said that the cathedrals (for example, of Siena and of Bologna) fell short of what their builders intended them to be; but this fact was not to be lamented, for "it is better that man's aspirations should go beyond his powers of execution."[24]

With Miss Grace Norton, the sister of Charles Eliot Norton, de Vere exchanged opinions on Carlyle, and he sent her a copy of his brother Stephen's translations from Horace. Writing to her shortly before Christmas in 1895, he stated:

> We cannot always feel that blessings are blessings, but we can always know it, and act on that knowledge, clinging to God all the more closely as the tempest howls around us. It is in our saddest and most comfortless times, I believe, that we are making the greatest progress . . .[25]

In more than one letter de Vere recalled their meetings in the past, for example, "the pleasant walks and talks—pleasant indeed, though too few—in Oxford, among the green lanes of old England, and near beautiful Florence on that lovely little river, and amid the stately courts and grand gardens of Hampton Court. . . ."[26] (De Vere and the Nortons had met several times in Italy as well as in England.) About four years before his death, de Vere wrote to Miss Norton: "How I wish we were to meet this year at Windermere, and stand together beside Wordsworth's grave."[27]

De Vere's interest in Wordsworth's poetry and its spiritual influence never waned. Considering a certain passage in the *Excursion*, de Vere said to Norton that it "includes a distinct assertion of faith, hope, and charity as a means of communion with God, as the All-Holy Judge as well as the Universal Father . . ."[28] In another letter to Norton, four years later, he wrote:

> Faith . . ., as Wordsworth affirms (in his "Despondency Corrected"), is the one only support under the trials of life. I hope you admire that book of the "Excursion" as much as I do. It seems to me the finest piece of moral and religious philosophy ever put into poetry, and also the noblest assertion of theism—which in his later life the great bard saw completely to involve Christianity, implicitly if not explicitly. . . .[29]

And after another lapse of fourteen years, de Vere declared Wordsworth's "Ode on the Intimations of Immortality" the noblest affirmation of modern times, because of the ideas of truth, justice, beauty and goodness which it embodies.[30] De Vere also looked on Wordsworth's work as an antidote for the godless philosophy of John Stuart Mill and his French friend, Auguste Comte. De Vere expressed his own aim in writing:

> If anything that I have written should spiritualize the imagination of the reader . . ., I shall have reason to rejoice indeed; for I can say with sincerity that nearly all that I have written has been in the hope, or else with the desire, to sustain the cause of truth and justice, especially when assailed and misrepresented.[31]

Aubrey de Vere longed for an American publication of his work,[32] so that he might "enlarge his audience." As early as 1857

he wrote to Norton: "I should be delighted at the appearance of
an American edition of my poems, whether or not the profits come
to me."[33] He was also eager to publish his *Inisfail* at the small
price of one shilling so that persons of all classes might read it.[34]
But he was also deeply concerned over the prestige of his publishers. Hearing of a New York publisher[35] who expected to
publish a collection of Irish poets, he wrote:

> I do not know what his standard as a publisher may be.
> If it is a low one, my chance of a good circulation in America
> would probably be damaged by his bringing out my poems.
> And as much of our Irish poetry is wretched stuff written in
> bad English (to spite the "Sister Isle"), and smelling strongly
> of potatoes and whiskey, I do not much relish the idea of ap-
> pearing as part of this collection.[36]

Almost two decades later, George Edward Woodberry's article on de Vere appeared in the *Century Magazine;* it contained
the following passage:

> Several of de Vere's volumes deal with Ireland's legends,
> glories and aspirations with an amplitude and a loftiness not
> elsewhere to be found in our literature, and with a pure fervor
> such as characterized only the best of the "books of the
> spirit," that are so rare in the English tongue.[37]

And ten years later, in 1894, Woodberry edited two chapters of de
Vere's *Recollections,* also published in the *Century Magazine.*[38]
    The same year Woodberry saw to the publication by Mac-
millan of *Selections From the Poems of Aubrey de Vere.* The book,
with Woodberry's Preface,[39] pleased de Vere, who wrote to him in
gratitude:

> When I think of what America must be to the world, and
> what the influence of her literature must one day become on
> the enormous population which she must support, one cer-
> tainly cannot feel ashamed at being gratified by the prospect
> of one's works being read there[40]

In his Preface Woodberry said of de Vere's poetry:

> It takes wide range, but is predominantly either Bardic or
> Christian. The sympathy of the poet must have been fed with

patriotic fervor, akin to renewed inspiration, to enable him to
render the old lays of his country with such fidelity to their
native genius. Cuchullain once more becomes credible to fancy
—the imagination of a childhood world; and the songs of
Oiseen and Ethell strike with a music as of anvils.[41]

In all de Vere's poetry Woodberry found "one light and one breath
—the light of the spirit and the breath thereof."[42]

Woodberry thought de Vere's essays to be "worth more than
ordinary attention."[43] In his criticism, he thought, de Vere revealed
his own theory of poetry: that man is the only object of interest to
man, all else being subordinate. Woodberry also distinguished de
Vere's use of the word "passion" from the ordinary idea of the
word inasmuch as it was merely "a poetic glow, the exaltation of
feeling, the lyrical possession which attends the moment of creation
and passes into verse,"[44] and not an emotional passion.

Norton expressed his liking for de Vere's work to George
William Curtis, editor of *Harper's Magazine* and *Harper's
Weekly:*

> He has genuine poetic sensibility, and with age he gains
> power of expression and depth of thought. In everything he
> writes he shows the refinement of his taste, the delicacy of
> his feeling, and his strong religious sentiment. He is greatly
> pleased with any expression of appreciation from America.[45]

And in a letter from Rome to his mother, Norton tells of de Vere
himself:

> De Vere is sweet, refined and lovable as ever, and far more
> in his native element than in England. He came to us yester-
> day, bringing with him Father Hecker, Founder of the *Cath-
> olic World* and of the Paulist Community, who is a man of
> some consequence in Rome.[46]

De Vere brought to the attention of Europeans the quatrains
of American Father John Tabb. In a letter to the editor of the
Irish Monthly, he stated:

> I enclose a poem, which has been sent to me by an American
> lately received into the Church, and preparing for Holy
> Orders. He asks me (though I am not acquainted with him)

to get it published, if possible, in one of your periodicals; so I enclose it to you. It seems to me a very good poem. . . .[47]

Aubrey de Vere bridged a gap between the British Isles and the United States, serving as a link between the literary men of the two countries. In Europe he made known such American writers as Henry Wadsworth Longfellow and Father Tabb, and he also did his utmost, through the litterateurs of America, to extend the influence of Tennyson, Landor and Wordsworth. A cultured Anglo-Irish gentleman, de Vere merited the respect, admiration, and appreciation of many who at that time showed an inclination to look askance at Ireland and Catholicism. Without controversy and with the kindliest interest, de Vere was instrumental in broadening the outlook of the American intelligentsia of the last century.

12

AUBREY DE VERE,

HIS

LITERARY WORKS

Aubrey de Vere was more than a Victorian observer and friend of illustrious persons. He was an author in his own right—an author little known and appreciated today. During his long life, devoted almost exclusively to writing, de Vere produced six volumes of poetry, two poetical dramas, four volumes of essays, two of travel, many articles and reviews published in leading periodicals, his own *Recollections,* and a prolific correspondence. Through the medium of ode and sonnet, blank verse and prose, he painted classical and mythological characters, epic figures and pre-historic heroes, Irish and Saxon saints, and many eminent literary persons. His experiences in Greece and Turkey, Scotland and Switzerland were recorded in prose and sometimes verse. He touched on contemporary problems, literary criticism, and such religious doctrines as the Incarnation. He drew material from early epochs, delved into the pre-Christian past and the Middle Ages and took an active interest in people of his own day and age. All of de Vere's work reveals the aims of one "whose whole life was a happy blending of fidelities to his Church, his country and his muse, in an age which presented few examples of such conjunction."[1]

Moreover, de Vere's poems on traditional Irish themes did much to prepare the ground for the "Celtic Revival." In fact, "after Matthew Arnold's five lectures on Celtic literature, nothing perhaps did more to help the Celtic revival than Aubrey de Vere's insight into the Irish character and his reproductions of the early Irish epic poetry."[2] *The Foray of Queen Meave* (1882) affords a glimpse into the ages of paganism, and the Queen is quite a formidable character. Of her de Vere tells:

> In Cruachan, old Connacht's palace pile,
> Dwelt Meave, the queen, haughtiest of womankind,
> A warrioress untamed that made her will
> The measure of the world. The all-conquering years
> Conquered not her: the strength of endless prime
> Lived in her royal tread and breast and eye
> A life immortal. Queenly was her brow;
> Fulgent her eye; her countenance beauteous, save
> When wrath o'erflamed its beauty. With her dwelt
> Ailill her husband, trivial man and quaint,
> And early old. He had not chosen her:
> She chose a consort who should rule her not,
> And tossed him to her throne.[3]

The Foray of Queen Meave is founded on *Tain bo Cuailagné*, considered by many scholars the great Irish epic of ancient times. Cuchullain, the greatest of Irish legendary heroes and warriors, was called the Achilles of early Erin, but de Vere compared him with Hector because of his character; and, like Hector, Cuchullain defended the city in a spirit of patriotism rather than love of glory. In this epic he is victorious over Queen Meave, who has gone to war over a bull. Cuchullain's character is briefly indicated:

> Cuchullain loves his land o'er all!
> The man besides, though terrible to foes,
> Is tender to the weak.[4]

The Legends of Saint Patrick (1861) deals with the conversion of pagan Ireland to Christianity. The Apostle of Ireland speaks of his youth in "The Confession of Saint Patrick":

> A youth of sixteen or less
> With others of my land, by pirates seized,

Aubrey de Vere in Later Life

I stood on Erin's shore. Our bonds were just;
Our God we had forsaken, and His law,
And mocked His priests. Tending a stern man's swine
I trod those Dalaraida hills that look
Eastward to Elba.[5]

Inisfail (or *Ireland in the Olden Time*) covers Irish history
between the latter part of the twelfth century and the latter part
of the eighteenth—the six centuries between the Norman conquest
of Ireland and the repeal of the Penal Laws. That period "begins
with the evening twilight that succeeded a long and radiant, though
often stormy day; it keeps the watches of a tragic night; and it
ends with the happier omens of returning dawn."[6] This national
chronicle in three parts treats of the Norman invasion and gradual
amalgamation of Norman and Gael; the wars of religion which
completed the union of Norman and Gaelic races; the victories of
Cromwell and his confiscation of the land; and the Penal Laws.

The Bard Ethell, a thirteenth-century character, is firm in
his determination not to forgive those who have injured him; he
considered Saint Columba's admonition to forgive all wrongs "right
cruel and hard." He speaks:

I am Ethell, the son of Conn;
    Here I live at the foot of the hill;
I am clansman to Brian and servant to none;
    Whom I hated I hate, whom I loved love still.
Blind am I. On milk I live,
    And meat (God sends it) on each Saint's Day,
Though Donald Mac Art—may he never thrive—
    Last Shrovetide drove half my kine away! ...
... Sweet is the chase; but the battle is sweeter;
More healthful, more joyous, for true men meeter.[7]

And at the age of one hundred, in his pagan-Christian religion, he
ends his soliloquy (of fifteen stanzas) with characteristic inconsistency and unbroken will:

The men that were wicked to me and mine;—
    (Not quenching a wrong, nor in war nor wine),
I forgive and absolve them all, save three:—
May Christ in His mercy be kind to me![8]

Among the lyrics of *Inisfail* is the Celtic, mystical "Little Black Rose." In symbolic language de Vere expresses hope for the future of educationally starved Ireland:

> The little black rose shall be red at last;—
> What made it black but the March wind dry,
> And the tear of the widow that fell on it fast?—
> It shall redden the hills when June is nigh!
>
> The Silk of the Kine shall rest at last;—
> What drave her forth but the dragon-fly?
> In the golden vale she shall feed full fast
> With her mild gold horn, and her slow, dark eye.
>
> The wounded wood-dove lies dead at last!
> The pine long-bleeding, it shall not die!—
> This song is secret. Mine ear it passed
> In a wind o'er the stone plain of Athenry.[9]

Throughout Irish history, de Vere maintains, the lesson appears again and again: the vocation of Ireland is neither commercial nor artistic, but spiritual and apostolic. And realizing that his interpretation of Irish history did not meet the approval of English readers, he stated: "The book [*Inisfail*] was addressed not to the many but to the thoughtful and the few, and at least as much to English statesmen as to Irish patriots."[10]

In the same volume with *Inisfail* is a ten-stanza poem entitled "Chaucer," very different from the verse on Irish themes. With exhortations to read the work, de Vere says:

> . . . His song was a feast where thought and jest
> Like monk and franklin alike found place—
> Good will's Round Table! There sat as guest
> Shakespearean insight with Spenser's grace.
>
> His England lay laughing in Faith's bright Morn!
> Life in his eye looked as rosy and round
> As the cheek of the huntsman that blows on the horn
> When the stag leaps up, and loud bays the hound. . . .
>
> On lonely evenings in dull Novembers
> When streams run choked under skies of lead,
> And on forest-hearths the year's last embers,
> Wind-heaped and glowing, lie yellow and red.

Read Chaucer still! In his ivied beaker
  With knights and wood-gods and saints embossed,
Spring hides her head till the wintry breaker
  Thunders no more on the far-off coast.[11]

In his *Legends of the Saxon Saints,* written in 1879 at the
suggestions of Miss Fenwick, de Vere turns to England, and he
presents a picture of early British and Anglo-Saxon England in the
seventh century—the period when Augustine brought Christianity
and laid the foundation for British liberty and civilization. The
Venerable Bede, to whom de Vere dedicated the volume, served
as his guide:

> His [Bede's] records are, indeed, as rough as the crab-
> tree, but at the same time as fresh as its blossoms. Their chief
> touches reveal all the passions of the barbaric races; but the
> chief human affections, things far deeper than the passions,
> are yet more abundantly illustrated by them. It was a time
> when those conventions were not frozen by conventionality and
> forced to conceal themselves until they forgot to exist.[12]

In this book appear Augustine, Apostle of England; Sibert, the
King who built Westminster Abbey; Ceadmon, the cow-herd and
first English poet, and Bede himself.

Legends and Records of the Church and the Empire traces the
gradual fusion of the old Hebrew ideas of God (embodied in
Christianity) and Roman civilization. And *Mediaeval Records and
Sonnets* (1895) deals with a later period, when the Holy Roman
Empire was an accomplished fact. This volume, dedicated to
Kenelm Henry Digby, "who nobly asserted and proved the true
greatness of the Middle Ages, when recognized by few," afforded
de Vere an opportunity to rejoice in his beloved Middle Ages.
Since the author goes beyond the British Isles in his *Mediaeval
Records,* among the subjects of his blank verse are the Cid, Saint
Francis of Assisi, Joan of Arc, Copernicus and Hildebrand (Pope
Gregory VII). Towards Columbus de Vere takes a sympathetic
attitude. Considering some of the charges no doubt falsely connected with the name of the explorer, de Vere stated in his notes:
"It can hardly be supposed that Columbus, who though a wonder-
ful Christian hero, was a man and not an angel, never fell into any

error or inconsistency in the course of his long and stormy career. . . ."[13] The Preface of this volume, which also contains sonnets
on such persons as Dante's Beatrice, Father Damien, Edmund
Burke, Tennyson and Browning, makes worthwhile reading. De
Vere says in part:

> The Middle Ages still survive among us more than we know
> in their instincts of honor and affection. . . . They were
> eminently Christian ages. . . . Life to the earnest mediaeval
> Christian was both a light-hearted and a serious thing. It
> found a type in the vigil. The Believer watched and waited for
> a future both far off and near him—a future which moulded
> his present. That future rendered hope to him a great necessity
> and a great duty, as well as a constant support. . . .
>
> The Middle Ages were cheerful ages; and if their great
> Italian representative, Dante, was the most spiritual of poets,
> Chaucer, their great English representative, was the most
> mirthful and human-hearted.[14]

The Death of Copernicus (1889), a poem of about sixteen
pages, represents de Vere's attempt to "foreshadow the blending
of science with Christian faith," which he regarded as "the one hope
for the future of civilization; the cause of each being promoted in
such a spirit as not to interfere with the other. . . ."[15] In his belief
in the compatibility of religion and science, de Vere differed from
Ruskin and other contemporaries. *Saint Peter's Chains,* a series
of sonnets written through the years, touches on the Roman question; de Vere, like Manning, Brougham and statesmen of other
countries, believed that "the temporal power of the Pope, however
small the territory within which it is to be exercised, is necessary
for his independence, and his independence is an essential part of
Christian civilization and the well-being alike of all nations,
whether Catholic or Protestant."[16]

Antar and Zara, an "eastern romance," was composed in 1865,
when de Vere was traveling in the East, and when the horrible
persecutions of the Christians of Lebanon had not yet attracted any
permanent or effective attention from the Christian world. De Vere
calls the poem an experiment, in which the lover and the lady speak
alternately—she in the shorter tetrameter, he in pentameter. The

songs, as the poems really are, portray the typically eastern admiration for self-sacrifice. The poem begins:

> O wind of night! What doth she at this hour?
>   In those high towers half lost in rock and brake?
> Where is she? Sits she lonely in her bower?
>   If she sits pensive, is it for my sake?

De Vere's two poetical dramas (actually closet dramas), *Alexander the Great* (1874) and *Saint Thomas of Canterbury* (1876), follow a definite aim: they represent respectively the pagan and the Christian ideal of greatness. The Christian ideal, founded on humility, succeeds although it seems to fail; the pagan ideal, based on pride, fails in spite of apparent success. The Christian ideal, de Vere holds, advances whereas the pagan declines.[17]

De Vere did not think that Alexander was a "Macedonian madman," but one who combined the highest military genius with instinctive and unerring statesmanship and a comprehensive and technical intellect. "His aim," he says, "was to consolidate the whole world into a single empire, redeemed from barbarism, and irradiated with Greek science and art, an empire such that its citizens, from the mouths of the Ganges to the Pillars of Hercules, should be qualified to learn from Plato, and to take delight in Sophocles."[18] Of Thomas of Canterbury, the hero of de Vere's other drama, the author says: "Becket was, though a firm defender of the Church's rights when assailed, by no means a one-sided man. . . . In his estimate the State stood at a height immeasurably more exalted than that commonly claimed for it in our days; . . . and he believed also that the Christian religion which raises the nations, must ever itself remain, for their sake, as well as from inherent necessity, exempt from their control."[19]

May Carols, which was probably the result of a suggestion Pope Pius IX made to de Vere when they met in Rome, has for its theme the Incarnation. More than three thousand lines in separate poems build up a single poem dealing with the Mother of Christ, the link between God and man. The introduction runs:

> Upon Thy face, O Lord, Thy world
> Looks ever up in love and awe;

> Thy stars, in circles onward hurled,
>   Sustain the steady yoke of law.
>
> In alternating antiphons
>   Stream sings to stream and sea to sea;
> And moons that set and sinking suns
>   Obeisance make, O God, to Thee. . . .
>
> . . . The whirlwind, missioned with its wings
>   To drown the fleet or fell a tower,
> Obeys Thee as the bird that sings
>   Her love-chant in a fleeting shower.
>
> Amid an ordered universe
>   Man's spirit only dares rebel;
> With light, O God, its darkness pierce,
>   With love its raging chaos quell.

Of the *May Carols* de Vere wrote in his Preface: "This work must be regarded . . . as a single religious poem, dedicated to the honor of the Virgin Mother, and preserving ever a single aim—that of illustrating Christianity, at once as a theological truth and as a living power. . . ."[20] De Vere wrote of Mary:

> Tower of our hope! through thee we climb
>   Finite creation's topmost stair,
> Through thee from Sion's height sublime
>   Toward God we gaze through clearer air.[21]

Here and there in the volume are interludes—descriptions of nature. For example:

> Ripplings of sunlight from the wave
>   Ascend the white rock high and higher;
> Soft gurglings fill the satiate cave;
>   Soft airs amid the reeds expire.
> All round the lone and luminous mere
>   The dark world stretches, far and free;
> The skylark's song alone I hear,
>   That flashing wave alone I see.[22]

These stanzas suggest de Vere's other colorful lyrics, among which may be counted his sonnet "The Sun God":

> I saw the Master of the Sun. He stood
> High in his luminous car, himself more bright;

An archer of immeasurable might:
On his left shoulder hung his quivered load;
Spurned by his steeds the eastern mountain glowed;
Forward his eager eye, and brow of light
He bent; and, while both hands that arch embowed,
Shaft after shaft pursued the flying Night.
No wings profaned that godlike form: around
His neck high held an ever-moving crowd
Of locks hung glistening: while such perfect sound
Fell from his bowstring, that th'ethereal dome
Thrilled as a dewdrop; and each passing cloud
Expanded, whitening like the ocean foam.[23]

"The Ode to the Daffodil" is full of imagery

O Love-Star of the unbeloved March,
    When, cold and shrill,
Forth flows beneath a low, dim-lighted arch
    The wind that beats sharp crags and barren hill
And keeps unfilmed the lately torpid rill; . . .
. . . Herald and harbinger! With thee
Begins the year's great jubilee!
    Of her solemnities sublime
(A sacristan whose gusty taper
Flashes through earliest morning vapor),
    Thou ringest dark nocturns, and dim prime.
Birds that have yet no heart for song
    Gain strength with thee to twitter;
And warm at last, where hollies throng,
    The mirrored sunbeams glitter.
With silk the osier plumes her tendrils thin;
    Sweet blasts, though keen and sweet, the blue lake
        wrinkle;
And buds on leafless boughs begin
    Against gray skies to twinkle. . . .[24]

A further and deeper treatment of nature is apparent in the
"Autumnal Ode"; herein de Vere wished to express the idea that
nature does not truly satisfy, for man was made for eternity:

Minstrel and Genius, to whose songs or sighs
    The round earth modulates her changeful sphere,
That bendest in shadow from yon western skies,

And leanest, cloud-hid, along the woodlands sere,
Too deep thy notes—too pure—for mortal ear!
   Yet Nature hears them; without aid of thine
   How sad were her decline!
From thee she learns with just and soft gradation
Her dying hues in death to harmonize;
   Through thee, her obsequies
A glory wear that conquers desolation.

Through thee she singeth, "Faithless were the sighing
   Breathed o'er a beauty only born to fleet:
A holy thing and precious is the dying
   Of that whose life was innocent and sweet."
   From many a dim retreat
Lodged on high-bosomed, echoing mountain lawn,
   Or chiming convent 'mid dark vale withdrawn,
   From cloudy shrine or rapt oracular seat,
   Voices of loftier worlds that saintly strain repeat.[25]

In "Christmas, 1860," de Vere expresses reverence, as he seems to address his deceased father:

Alone, among thy books, once more I sit;
   No sound there stirs except the flapping fire;
Strange shadows of old times about me flit,
   As sinks the midnight lamp, or flickers higher.
I see thee pace the room; with eye thought-lit
   Back, back thou comest once more to my desire.
Low-toned thou readst once more the verse new-writ,
   Too deep, too pure for worldlings to admire.

That brow all honour, that all-gracious hand,
   That cordial smile, and clear voice musical,
That noble bearing, mien of high command,
   Yet void of pride!—Tonight I have them all.
Ah, phantoms vain of thought! The Christmas air
Is white with flying flakes.—Where are thou?—Where?[26]

De Vere's "Song" Swinburne considered "one lyrical poem . . . not written by Shelley, yet possible and even likely to be taken for Shelley's." It runs:

When I was young I said to Sorrow,
   "Come, and I will play with thee."—

He is near me now all day;
  And at night returns to say,
"I will come again tomorrow;
  I will come and stay with thee."

Through the woods we walk together;
  His soft footsteps rustle nigh me;
  To shield an unregarded head,
  He hath built a winter shed.
  And all night in rainy weather,
  I hear his gentle breathings by me.[27]

In de Vere's *The Search after Proserpine* appears evidence of his early love of Greek, his tour of Greece and his admiration for Walter Savage Landor, who commended the work. De Vere considered the myth of Proserpine and Ceres one of the most exquisite of Greek mythology; to the Greeks it meant "the restoration of Man, not of flowers—the victory over Death, not over Winter."[28] De Vere's last stanza expresses this idea:

Sullen skies today,
  Sunny skies tomorrow;
November steals from May,
  And May from her doth borrow;
Griefs—Joys—in Time's strange dance
Interchangeably advance;
The sweetest joys that come to us
  Come sweeter from past sorrow.

Very different is de Vere's prophetic strain as he realized the effect of increasing materialism and atheism in England:

The time may come
When rich as Carthage, great in arms as Rome,
Keen-eyed as Greece, this isle to sensuous gaze
A sun all gold, to angels may present
Aspect no nobler than a desert waste,
Some blind and blinding waste of sun-scorched sands
Trod by a race of pigmies—not of men—
Pigmies by passion ruled.[29]

The Household Poetry Book (An Anthology of English-Speaking Poets from Chaucer to Faber) and *Select Specimens of*

the Poets were edited by de Vere. They contain his own excellent
ideas on poetry in general, and splendid remarks on the poets.
Wilfrid Meynell thought the notes in the first collection most sane
and judicious. A few examples will substantiate the truth of Mr.
Meynell's judgment.

Of Chaucer, de Vere wrote:

> In the skill with which he delineates character he is an
> anticipation of Shakespeare. . . . Chaucer was to England what
> Dante was to Italy. . . . The Morning Star of English poetry,
> he was not less the Evening Star of the Middle Ages. . . .[30]

Of Spencer, he said:

> The religion and the chivalry of the Middle Ages were alike
> the inspirers of his song. . . . He was admirable in his apprecia-
> tion of classical mythology, as well as in his use of the chival-
> rous legend; and merits in a peculiar sense those epithets of
> "learned" and "sage". . . .[31]

And he said of Shakespeare:

> Without ceasing to be individual, his characters are generic
> also; and thus exhibit to us the universal moulds of nature,
> and an exposition of humanity as it exists in all places and
> ages. . . . Soundness of heart and cordial wisdom make them
> a mine of morality and of philosophy. . . . The religion of
> Shakespeare is not known. That he was a Christian no one
> that appreciates his poetry can doubt; in the whole series of
> his historical plays, in which he delineates ecclesiastical
> persons, and treads on tender ground, he never is betrayed
> into a sneer, or drops a hint of that polemical tradition which
> grew up in the courts of Elizabeth and James the First. . . .[32]

After praising Milton's majesty, his magnanimous spirit and sus-
tained solemnity, his massive structure, his austere yet sweet
Hebraic spirit, de Vere remarked that it was "impossible to defend
the mechanical details in the description of the war in heaven . . ."
He found Milton's "Arianism" evident in *Paradise Lost* and expressed surprise that the wonderful work should for so long a time
be ranked as a really Christian poem when Milton did not recognize
Christ as the Eternal Son of God.[33]

In his essays—*Essays Literary and Ethical* and *Essays Chiefly on Poetry* (two volumes)—de Vere treats of literary, governmental and religious subjects. Discerning criticism on Wordsworth and Landor, Shelley and Keats, Patmore and Taylor, Sir Samuel Ferguson and Archbishop Trench, along with consideration of such topics as "Church Property and Secularization," "A Few Notes on Modern Unbelief," "A Saint," "A Policy for Ireland" illustrate the nature and scope of de Vere's interests. A few of these essays, as well as "The Great Problems of the Nineteenth Century," and "The Plague of Controversy," were later published in a volume entitled *Religious Problems of the Nineteenth Century,* which proves de Vere's observation and awareness of contemporary problems.

Of Shelley he wrote:

> Great indeed is the bequest which Shelley has left us; and it is not without somewhat of remorseful sorrow that we remember what life gave him in return. . . . A sad career was his. He had his intellectual rapture and he had friends—few of them worthy of him; several of them deeply indebted to him; one of them fatal to him because the supplanter of his youthful faith—Godwin.[34]

And of Keats:

> The genius of Keats was Grecian to a far higher degree than that of Shelley. His sense of beauty was profounder still; and was accompanied by that in which Shelley's poetry was deficient—repose. . . . Beauty was the adornment of Shelley's poetry; it was the very essence of Keats'.[35]

Qualifying somewhat his opinion of Spenser in the *Household Poetry Book,* de Vere held that "except in his highest moods he seldom braced himself up to his best as Milton constantly did . . . and Shakespeare more often than is consistent with the fable that he 'never blotted a line.' "[36] De Vere considered Spenser's nature benign and sympathetic; but his political views were imbibed "from a ruthless time and reckless associates."[37] Spenser's most serious fault, de Vere explained, was a structural one. He contrasted Spenser with Chaucer:

In Chaucer . . . the stories are complete, each in itself; the narrative is easily followed; the interest, undivided; and the catastrophe conclusive. But in the *Faery Queen* the tales are interwoven; the same knights and ladies reappear successively in many of them; the story breaks off where the interest is at its crisis; and the reader is invited to follow again the fortunes of persons he has forgotten. . . .[38]

In his essay "A Saint" (really a review of *The Life of Saint Aloysius Gonzaga* by E. H. Thompson) de Vere makes statements of general interest. For example,

Sanctity is at once the simplest and the most "many-sided" of all things. . . . The Saints of God are divine works of art: they are the living monuments of supernatural grace, wrought out, touch by touch and line by line, by that Sanctifying Spirit who is *Digitus Paternae Dexterae*. . . . The Saints are mirrors of Christ. . . . In Christ we have the white light of sanctity; in the Saints, the colored beam of this or that virtue. . . .[39]

De Vere's correspondence, as has been shown, is, among other things, a valuable source of literary criticism. For example, in a letter to Taylor de Vere discussed one of his favorite topics— Shelley:

Shelley's character had (I think) two great natural defects: want of robustness, for it was cast too much in a feminine mould. This impaired his genius . . . taking from it solidity and self-possession, throwing his thought on wires, and making the emotional part of his nature proportionately too large in quantity, and too hysterical in quality. But the years were making him more of a man; and whatever he lacked in robust strength was made up to him by elasticity. Nothing could keep him down long.
Shelley's chief defect, however, seems to have been a lack of reverence, quite extraordinary in a man of his genius.[40]

An entirely different type of prose writing was that of de Vere's *English Misrule and Irish Misdeeds.* "Four Letters from Ireland Addressed to an English Member of Parliament" was a logical, courageous and indignant vindication of Ireland against

the uninterested and unjust government of England. Although de
Vere loved Egland and was opposed to all kinds of violent movements against government, he felt that Ireland was, in some
instances, not properly governed. The book aroused the hostile
criticism of some of de Vere's English friends, but it also merited
the praise of John Stuart Mill and Montalembert. De Vere suggested to the English two remedies: development of Irish agriculture and systematic emigration.

The *Recollections,* his longest prose work, de Vere began in
his eightieth year. In a letter to an American friend he charac-
teristically expressed his aim:

> I sent the chapters to three or four English publishers, but
> they do not think the work likely to be popular if published
> in a book. This is the more likely to be true as I had resolved
> from the first that the work should have nothing in common
> with those that apparently seek popularity by pandering to a
> vulgar, and too often an ill-natured, work of curiosity. On the
> contrary I had resolved that the work should contain nothing
> that could hurt the persons recorded, or could offend their
> friends—though much that might lead men to admire more
> wisely those whom they had admired before, and others also,
> of whom they had never heard. The book, however, interests
> me; and draws near to me again many once dear, who have
> long been snatched away, out of this life.[41]

As he had slightly lost grip at that advanced age, "many pithy
stories and memories of old times were lost."[42] He admitted he
found it difficult to begin the work and explained:

> Perhaps I could never have begun were it not that the
> Gladstonian Revolution going on here threatens that the roof-
> tree of every Irish gentleman's house will ere long fall on his
> head; and it leaves him in the meantime with little to live on,
> derived from Irish land. However, now that I have begun to
> warm to my task, fair scenes from the past rise like magnets
> before my eyes; and I seem to live my life again. It is a very
> pleasant work to me; it may cause my other works to be better
> known. (They were written in the hope that they might do
> good.)[43]

Despite the fact that de Vere wrote his reminiscences near the
end of his long life, the work affords an interesting insight into his
early years, perhaps typical of lives led by other young men of
his time and social standing. It furnishes a first-hand account of
the great Irish famine (1846-1850), during which de Vere revealed the practical side of his nature. It also affords a colorful
picture of travel, a century ago, in Switzerland, Italy and Scotland,
and, as has been indicated, the *Recollections* draws sincere, sympathetic portraits of such persons as Manning and Newman, Sir
Henry Taylor and Wordsworth, Sara and Hartley Coleridge. This
work, perhaps more than any other of his, presents tangible
evidence of his keen observation and discernment.

Picturesque Sketches of Greece and Turkey (two volumes),
published in 1850, still makes interesting reading. De Vere was no
doubt lured to Corfu by the fact that his brother, a Royal Engineer,
was stationed there. However, he made his journeys through Greece
and Turkey alone and thus gained a first-hand impression wherever
he went. Steering down the Adriatic, he found a delicious climate:
"the breeze instead of passing over the snows of the Apennines,
came to us warm from the Aegean, and mingled the softness of a
southern clime with the wild and exhilarating odors of the sea."[44]
Having arrived at Corfu, de Vere walked along the shore and
wondered just where Ulysses had met Nausicaa.[45] On his way to
Corinth he stopped at a small inn, where his supper consisted of a
handful of olives and a crust of bread—the usual meal of the
natives. His courier, an Albanian, told de Vere on the journey,
"You sleep tranquil at Athens tonight. You eat roast-beef—plenty.
You much comfortable. You see my fine clothes tomorrow."[46] The
clothes proved to be "the ordinary Greek costume . . . tricked out
in the most brilliant and harmonious colors, . . . as thick set with
silver and gold as Persian poetry is with metaphors."[47] Instead of
roast beef de Vere enjoyed at Athens Hymettus honey—pure,
fresh, fragrant—the essence of all flowers.

"The children, with their black, flashing eyes and muselike
foreheads, possess an extraordinary degree of loveliness; but among
the women of Athens beauty is not a frequent gift, although, where
met, it is beauty of the highest and most intellectual order. . . ."[48]

In Athens de Vere met a Mr. F., who had joined the Greek
cause, and had been intimately acquainted with Byron. For Lord
Byron, as a man of action and of business, Mr. F. had the greatest
respect. Whenever a quarrel arose between native chiefs, they went
to Byron, who acted as arbitrator, and manifested an admirable
temper and wisdom. De Vere regretted that Byron in England became "the child of the public whom he had spoiled"; otherwise
"what might he have accomplished!" De Vere visited Mr. F's
estate, which he described:

> It rises in some parts to an elevation of about 2000 feet,
> and is split into a labyrinth of picturesque defiles. . . . The
> rugged soil is richly sprinkled with magnificent oak-trees. . . .
> Between them stand . . . magnificent broad-headed pines with
> trunks twisted into fantastic shapes by many a storm. . . .
> The rocks glitter with the brilliant green leaves and white
> blossoms of the arbutus; and the ravines are so tangled with
> thickets of broom, lentiscus, holly, ivy, wild-pear, juniper,
> thyme, and dwarf evergreen oak that you are glad to follow a
> leader. . . .[49]

De Vere visited Delphi, Patras, and started for Constantinople; but on the way he and his fellow-travelers were "dropped"
at Syra, where they were placed in quarantine in a lazaretta, a by
no means comfortable place. De Vere tells of his inability to induce
the captain of a French vessel, stopping at Syra, to take him
aboard:

> I made one more desperate effort in an oration full of sub-
> limity and pathos, insisting on the laws of nations, the honor
> of the French flag, the insult to the English nation, and the
> rights of man. . . .[50]

But in the midst of it all the vessel steamed off, as captain and
officers removed their hats, shrugged their shoulders, lifted their
eyebrows and remarked, *"Pauvres diables!"*

When the time of quarantine was over, de Vere, through the
English consul, met the Secretary of the French packet office and
demanded the return of his money; the vessel, he explained, which
was to have taken him to Constantinople first brought him to plague-

stricken Alexandria and then dropped him at Syra. After a long argument in which the Frenchman indignantly refused de Vere's request and "snatched off and put on his spectacles a dozen times," de Vere's persistence triumphed and he received part of his money "out of politeness, not out of justice," as the secretary gave him to understand.[51]

De Vere enjoyed the bazaar at Smyrna—"as brilliant and as fascinating as a cavern of jewels described in a fairy tale—crimson and orange slippers, . . . Cashmere shawls and Persians carpets . . . jewelry, perfumery and sweetmeats." The mosques he found disappointing—of uninspired architecture—in keeping with "the flat and dreary rationalism" of the religion.[52]

Arriving at Constantinople, de Vere wrote:

> In all respects the external features of the city are founded on a Faith, and of a people gravely devoted to pleasure, and yet addicted also to meditation, and blindly submissive to fate.[53]

Of all the women he had seen de Vere considered the Armenian the most lovely. "Their eyes combine something of the Turkish languor with the 'lamping' irradiation of the Greek. Their hair curves in waves of glossiest black down their fair brows and their complexion has the freshness of the rosebud's inmost leaf."[54] Tall, stately and modest, they move with a suave, gentle grace. Their picturesque beauty is enhanced by crimson slippers, green or blue cloaks and long white veils.

To de Vere, a century ago, Constantinople seemed the heart of an empire visibly tottering to its fall—a sentenced city. So strong did he note the appeal to the senses at Constantinople that he remarked one "must either become wholly materialized, or take refuge in imagination and retrospection."[55]

Despite Aubrey de Vere's keen disappointment[56] in not reaching a large and appreciative audience and thus effecting the good he so ardently desired, he continued faithful to his vocation of writing[57] and refused to be diverted from it. He did not cater to popular taste but continued throughout his long life to express conscientiously his thoughts and ideals—the fruit of earnest study, observation and wide experience. His first volume, *The Waldenses,* appeared in 1842, but most of his works he published in the sixties and later.

Even a cursory survey of his output reveals, then, a wide scope and pleasing variety of prose and poetry—lyric, epic and dramatic. Lyrics, including his *May Carols;* delightful travelogues; sound criticism; informative recollections; and even dramas (one of which, *Saint Thomas of Canterbury,* equals, if not surpasses, Tennyson's later work on the same subject, *Thomas à Becket*): all these are worthy of study and appreciation. Moreover, in his vivid panorama of Ireland's heroic past, he was in a very real way a precursor of the Irish Renascence.

Even today, however, de Vere's contribution to literature is not entirely unrecognized. Hugh Walker in his *Literature of the Victorian Era* thought it worthwhile to quote de Vere's description of John Henry Newman,[58] as well as his remarks on Alfred Lord Tennyson.[59] Edmund Gosse repeated de Vere's statements on Wordsworth. And the contemporary biographer, Charles Tennyson, who knew Aubrey de Vere, graciously mentions him many times in his recent life of his famous grandfather. He affords glimpses of de Vere, and definitely indicates not only Tennyson's high regard for him, but also the obvious influence of "tall, gentle Aubrey de Vere . . . the cultured, chivalrous Irish poet."[60]

NOTES

BIBLIOGRAPHY

INDEX

NOTES

After his first citation in each chapter, Aubrey de Vere will
be designated simply de Vere. His father will always appear
as Sir Aubrey de Vere.

CHAPTER ONE

1. "Extracts and Memoranda," Sept. 31, 1831. Quoted in R. P. Graves, *Life of Sir William Rowan Hamilton*, I, 460.
2. At twelve Mary was drowned in the River Shannon, below her grandparents' home, Mount Trenchard. Catherine died in her fourteenth year, probably of fever.
3. Aubrey de Vere, "Memoir of Sir Aubrey de Vere," in *Sonnets* of Sir Aubrey de Vere.
4. De Vere, *Recollections*, p. 130.
5. Henry Peter Brougham (1778-1866)—one of the founders of the *Edinburgh Review;* a M.P. (1810) who helped to pass the Reform Bill (1831) and advocated the immediate abolition of slavery (1838).
6. William Conyngham Plunket (1764-1864)—Irish lawyer and judge who led the Whigs in the Irish Parliament; foremost champion of emancipation, although he opposed O'Connell's agitation.
7. George Canning (1770-1827)—British statesman and M.P. who contended for Catholic emancipation and laid the groundwork for the repeal of the Corn Laws.
8. Sir Robert Peel (1788-1850)—English statesman and M.P. who successfully combated advocates for Catholic emancipation and, as Prime Minister, removed the penal laws against Roman Catholics.
9. Published posthumously by William Pickering, through Aubrey.
10. *Sonnets*, p. 47.
11. *Ibid.*, p. 44.
12. *Ibid.*, p. 45.
13. De Vere, *Recollections*, p. 31.
14. Quoted in Wilfrid Ward, *Aubrey de Vere: a Memoir*, p. 6.

15. "Antigone" represents Sophocles in the act of conceiving his master-
piece:

> I saw the poet standing by himself
> Within a deep green wood; with long deep grass
> And weed and wild-flower thick about his feet,
> He pressed his forehead on a birch, one are
> Carelessly thrown around its silver stem.
> At last he moved; his head sunk slowly back,
> Until the invisible air upon his brow
> Rested serene: his eyelids faintly drooped
> 'til their black lashes met with gentlest touch;
> Thus he reclined like some clear sculptured form.
> Ere long a rapture thrilled him, and arose
> Upward with gradual motion 'til its power
> Increased upon his face with brightening gleam.
> Silent he mused a moment: then arose
> Bright as a god: around his temples wreathed
> A light of sun-fed locks:—silent he stood;—
> It was his hour of immortality!
> A glorious vision; from his own deep spirit
> Emerged, distinct and clear, a perfect Form—
> He saw—and cried aloud—"Antigone!"

16. "Did you hear of my Theological Discourse, which the University
Doctors gave a prize to?—a prize which in verity it did not deserve."
De Vere, letter to Hamilton. Quoted in Graves, *op. cit.*, II, 162.

17. "A church of England triumphant here below, pure as the earliest day-
dawn of the Faith, venerable as the sagest antiquity, cleansed of
mediaeval accretions, enriched by modern science . . . Such, ever since
my boyhood, had been my aspiration: how much more must it have
been his [Newman's] . . ." De Vere, *Recollections*, p. 261.

18. Lady Eleanor Shaw, Ms. letter to author, June 5, 1932.

19. Letter to Mrs. Villiers, Oct. 6, 1846. Quoted in Ward, *op. cit.*, p. 121.

20. *Recollections,* p. 117.

21. *Ibid.,* p. 97.

22. De Vere, letter to mother, Lent, 1839. Quoted in Ward, *op. cit.*, p. 36.

23. Letter to sister, June 25, 1841. Quoted in Ward, *op. cit.*, p. 66.

24. *Ibid.*

25. Freddy Elliot, "a delightful little boy of five or six, was taken charge
of by the Taylors during the absence of his father, Sir Charles Elliot,
then Governor of Bermuda." De Vere, *Recollections*, p. 146.
Sir Charles was one of Henry Taylor's chief friends.

26. *Picturesque Sketches of Greece and Turkey,* I, 10-11.

27. *Ibid.,* pp. 26-27.

28. *Ibid.,* II, 11-12.

29. De Vere, Diary, Oct. 31, 1845.
30. *Recollections,* p. 190.
31. Diary, Nov. 22, 1845.
32. *Ibid.,* Dec. 10, 1845.
33. *Ibid.,* Dec. 12, 1845.
34. *Ibid.*
35. The Ms. section of the Diary is headed "Diary of Aubrey de Vere," and was begun at Miss Fenwick's, October 31, 1845. The last date recorded is December 10, 1846. Wilfrid Ward evidently used this Diary when writing his *Aubrey de Vere: a Memoir.* However, he quoted entries prior to October 1845; and that section is missing from the author's copy of the Diary. The Diary itself is naturally more detailed than some of Ward's excerpts.
36. First Earl of Malmesbury (James Harris: 1746-1820)—English diplomat, ambassador to St. Petersburg (1777-1782), and minister at the Hague (1784).
37. Diary, June 1846.
38. July 9, 1846.
39. *Ibid.*
40. Quoted in Ward, *op. cit.,* p. 128.
41. Henry Taylor, letter to Miss Fenwick, July 1847, in *Correspondence of Henry Taylor,* p. 172.
42. Quoted in Ward, *op. cit.,* p. 136.
43. De Vere, Diary, Sept. 4, 1846.
44. Letter to de Vere, Feb. 19, 1848. Quoted in Ward, *op. cit.,* p. 138.
45. Letter to Mrs. Villiers, Sept. 1848. Quoted in Ward, *op. cit.,* p. 147.
46. Quoted in Ward, *op. cit.,* p. 152.
47. Letter, June 10, 1850. *Ibid.,* p. 156.
48. Letter to mother, June 1850. Quoted in Ward, *op. cit.,* p. 158.
49. Letter to Miss Fenwick, Aug. 29, 1851. Quoted in Ward, *op. cit.,* p. 171.
50. *Recollections,* p. 44.
51. Letter to sister, May 1838. Quoted in Ward, *op. cit.,* p. 40.
52. *See* p. 19-20.
53. Letter to Miss Fenwick, Dec. 1850. Quoted in Ward, *op. cit.,* p. 167.
54. Letter to Stephen Spring Rice, 1850. Quoted in Ward, *op. cit.,* p. 176.
55. Dr. John Jebb, Ms. letter to de Vere, Dec. 24, 1850.
56. Letter to Sara Coleridge, April 10, 1851. Quoted in Ward, *op. cit.,* pp. 168-170.
57. Ms. letter, Oct. 23, 1851.
58. Ms. letter, Oct. 29, 1851.
59. De Vere, letter to sister, May 15, 1851. Quoted in Ward, *op. cit.,* p. 170. The "three creeds" are the Apostles, Nicene, and Athanasian.
60. "The Gorham Judgment, which asserted so decisively the supremacy of the Privy Council over the Church of England in matters of doctrine,

made a great impression on Aubrey de Vere, as it did on Manning, Hope-Scott, Gladstone, and the T. W. Allies." Ward, *op. cit.*, p. 161.

61. Letter to Hamilton, Feb. 27, 1851. Quoted in Graves, *op. cit.*, I, 666.

62. Letter to Sara Coleridge, Feb. 2, 1851. Quoted in Ward, *op. cit.*, p. 184.

63. Letter to Sara Coleridge, April 10, 1851. Quoted in Ward, *op. cit.*, p. 169.

64. Letter to Miss Fenwick, Aug. 23, 1853. Quoted in Ward, *op. cit.*, pp. 218-219.

65. Mrs. Ellie Monsell, quoted in Ward, *op. cit.*, p. 376.

66. Lady Shaw, Ms. letter to author, June 5, 1932.

67. J. R. Monsell Ms. letter to author, undated (probably 1931).

68. D. R. O'Brien, Ms. letter to author, Oct. 13, 1936.

69. Ward, *op. cit.*, p. 316.

70. Helen Grace Smith, sister of George Walter Smith of the University of Pennsylvania. *Ibid.*, pp. 394-395.

71. Letter to Lady Taylor, 1873. Quoted in Ward, *op. cit.*, p. 319.

72. De Vere, in a letter to Charles Eliot Norton of Harvard, stated: "We have now another Arnold who informs the world, that what used to be worshipped as God is 'the tendency of all things to Righteousness'." Quoted in Ward, *op. cit.*, p. 321.

73. Quoted in Ward, *op. cit.*, p. 319.

74. De Vere, Diary, July 10, 1846.

CHAPTER TWO

1. Wordsworth acknowledged the receipt of the ode: "I sent you a message of thanks for . . . Mr. de Vere's ode. Assure him that I am duly sensible of the honour he has done me in his animated verses." William Wordsworth, letter to William Rowan Hamilton, Feb. 8, 1833. Quoted in R. P. Graves, *Life of Sir William Rowan Hamilton*, II, 38.

2. "The first visit which I paid on arriving in this country some ten days ago was as usual to the grave of Wordsworth." Aubrey de Vere, Ms. letter to Charles Eliot Norton from Ambleside, Aug. 24, 1898, when de Vere was eighty-four.

   Cf.: "I paid my usual pilgrimage to Wordsworth's grave in 1895 and 1896." De Vere, Ms. letter to Helen Grace Smith, Feb. 9, 1897.

   Cf.: ". . . revisiting the English lakes and . . . the chapel of Newman at Birmingham—things which I do annually." De Vere, Ms. letter to Norton, Oct. 1895.

3. "He [faithful James] told me many things of his old master that interested me much." De Vere, letter to Miss Fenwick, Sept. 1850. Quoted in Wilfrid Ward, *Aubrey de Vere: a Memoir*, p. 172.

   "I walked to the two Rydalian waterfalls . . . accompanied by his faithful James, who spoke all the time of his master." De Vere, letter to mother, Oct. 21, 1851. Quoted in Ward, *op. cit.*, p. 172.

4. Letter, in de Vere, *Recollections,* p. 199.

5. Letter to Henry Taylor, March 9, 1845, in *Correspondence of Henry Taylor,* I, 155-157.

6. Wordsworth, letter to Mr. Moxon, Nov. 5, 1841. Quoted in William Knight (ed.), *Poetical Works of William Wordsworth,* III, 405.

7. The article read in part:
   "He [Wordsworth] has exhibited only one limited, however lofty, region of life, and has made it far less his aim to represent what lies around him by means of self-transference into all his feelings, than to choose therefrom what suits his spirit of ethical meditation, and so compel mankind . . . into his own severe and stately school of thought. . . . We are compelled to listen to the bard, Wordsworth, as to a grave teacher of moral truth. . . . Even the shaping and inspired imagination itself is always subject to the considerate dominion of the moral idea. Emotion . . . is restrained in all his writings by the awful presence of self-centered will. . . ." (Issue of June-Sept. 1842, pp. 385-415.)— Knight (ed.), *Prose Writings of William Wordsworth,* p. 210.

8. Wordsworth, Ms. letter to Sir Aubrey de Vere, Sept. 30, 1842. This unpublished letter is apparently the only clue to the misunderstanding.

9. Wordsworth, letter to de Vere, Nov. 16, 1842, in de Vere, *Recollections,* pp. 126-128.

10. "It was only among his own mountains that Wordsworth could be understood." De Vere, "Recollections of Wordworth," *Essays Chiefly on Poetry,* II, 293.

11. Taylor alleged that Wordsworth and Scott did not appreciate each other; "but Scott would go perhaps nearer to a full appreciation of Wordsworth than Wordsworth of Scott." *Autobiography of Henry Taylor,* I, 148.

12. Letter to Hamilton, Jan. 10, 1843. Quoted in Graves, *op. cit.,* II, 402-403.

13. "Reading that memorable passage in the 'Excursion' again, I find that it includes a distinct assertion of Faith, Hope and Charity, as a means of Communion with God as the All-Holy Judge as well as the Universal Father. . . ." De Vere, Ms. letter to Norton, Jan. 24, 1874.

14. "The Wisdom and Truth of Wordsworth's Poetry," *Essays on Poetry,* I, 258-259.

15. De Vere, Ms. letter to Knight, Nov. 4, 1887.

16. In "Recollections of Wordsworth," *Essays on Poetry,* II, 285-286.

17. To Dr. Park of St. Andrews he said:
    "A man may write very good verses, but if there is nothing in them to refine and elevate and purify, he had better keep them locked up in his desk. I write as I live. I have ever endeavoured to live in the light

of my own conscience, and to regard whatever powers I had as trusts for use, not for pleasure only. . . . I am every day receiving letters . . . expressive of gratitude for moral benefit derived from what I have produced. Benefit to young and old, to children as well as grown men." Quoted in John Eglinton, "Wordsworth at Rydal Mount," *Fortnightly Review,* DLXV (Jan. 1914), 335.

18. "Aubrey de Vere," Ceylon *Catholic Messenger,* Sept. 23, 1881.

19. De Vere, "Recollections of Wordsworth," *Essays on Poetry,* II, 282-283.

20. "From about 1806, Coleridge . . . ceased to be a direct formative influence in Wordsworth's life and thought." H. W. Garrod, *Wordsworth —Lectures and Essays,* p. 77.

"The beginning of the change from the naturalism and sensationalism of his early poetry to a more definitely orthodox attitude dates from the death of his brother in 1805." Ernest de Selincourt, *The Prelude,* quoted in Garrod, *loc. cit.*

"When sorrow and bereavement came to William and Dorothy Wordsworth . . . they learned that in nature alone was nothing which in the end they could abide by." J. C. Shairp (ed.), *Recollections of a Tour Made in Scotland,* p. xi.

21. "A man of large and catholic nature is not necessarily guilty of egotism even when the chief subject of his poetry is himself, since it is not of himself . . . that he writes, but rather of those deep thoughts and great main feelings which concern him as a human being, and which therefore possess a universal application to all human beings. . . ." De Vere, letter to Hamilton, Jan. 10, 1843. Quoted in Graves, *op. cit.,* II, 403.

22. De Vere, *Recollections,* p. 124.

23. Diary, March 9, 1845.

24. De Vere, Ms. letter to Knight, undated (probably 1887).

25. "The Genius and Passion of Wordsworth's Poetry," *Essays on Poetry,* I, 128.

26. "We are sometimes told that, in our days, Poetry which does not affect the 'sensational' must not hope to be popular. The 'sensational' includes several schools, the worst of which is . . . sensual as well as sensational. The fanatics of this school declaim about Passion: but they mean by the word little more than appetite intellectualized." De Vere, *Irish Odes and Other Poems,* p. xi.

27. "Every great poet is a teacher; I wish either to be considered as a teacher or as nothing." Wordsworth, letter to Beaumont. Quoted in Knight (ed.), *Prose Writings of Wordsworth,* p. 61.

28. "Genius and Passion of Wordsworth," *Essays on Poetry,* I, 135.

29. *See:* William Allingham, *A Diary,* pp. 293-296.

30. To Charles Mackey, Wordsworth said:

"I never read anybody's poetry but my own. . . . It is not vanity

that makes me say this. I am an old man and little time is left to me
. . . I use that little . . . to revise all my poems carefully, and make
them as perfect as I can. . . ." Quoted in Eglinton, *loc. cit.*

31. Ms. letter to Knight, June 10, 1890.
32. *Ibid.*
33. Ms. letter, Nov. 4, 1893.
34. De Vere, Ms. letter to Knight, Nov. 12, 1893.
35. Wordsworth compared his poems to a Gothic church, with ante-chapel,
    oratories, recesses, etc. The place of honor, the "high altar," was the
    end of his volume. De Vere believed the "Ode on the Intimations of
    Immortality" deserved that place.
36. Ms. letter, Nov. 12, 1893.

CHAPTER THREE

1. "Reception of the Early Poems," *Essays Chiefly on Poetry,* I, 503.
2. "Reminiscences of Tennyson" in Hallam Tennyson, *Alfred Lord
   Tennyson: a Memoir,* I, 207.
3. Diary, April 18, 1846. Quoted in Wilfrid Ward, *Aubrey de Vere: a
   Memoir,* pp. 71-72.
4. Aubrey de Vere, "Reminiscences," in H. Tennyson, *op. cit.,* II, 109.
5. Letter to Miss Fenwick. Quoted in Una Taylor, *Guests and Memories,*
   pp. 164-165.
6. Letter to Henry Reed. Quoted in H. Tennyson, *op. cit.,* I, 210.
7. William Allingham, *A Diary* (ed. H. Allingham and D. Radford),
   pp. 292-296.
8. Letter to Mrs. Edward Villiers, 1845. Quoted in Ward, *op. cit.,* p. 76.
9. De Vere, Diary, July 16, 1845.
10. De Vere, letter to Miss Fenwick, Oct. 14, 1850. Quoted in Ward,
    op. cit., pp. 158-160.
11. De Vere, letter to Mrs. Villiers, undated. Quoted in Ward, *op. cit.,*
    p. 146.
12. Letter to Miss Fenwick, *See* note 9.
13. These quotations, from the same letter, may be compared to Alling-
    ham's reports of dinner conversations at the Tennysons', in his *Diary,*
    p. 186.
14. Allingham, *loc. cit.*
15. Quoted in de Vere, *Essays on Poetry,* I, 507.
16. Ms. letter to Alice Thompson (Meynell), Oct. 7, 1876.
17. Letter to Coventry Patmore, Jan. 16, 1863. Quoted in Ward, *op. cit.,*
    p. 264.
18. *Edinburgh Review,* XC (Oct. 1849), 388-433.
19. Quoted in H. Tennyson, *op. cit.,* I, 260-261.
20. *Ibid.,* p. 281.

21. Allingham, *op. cit.,* p. 186 (Sept. 3, 1868).

22. De Vere, "Reminiscences" in H. Tennyson, *op. cit.,* I, 211.

23. Quoted in Charles Tennyson, *Alfred Tennyson,* p. 236.

24. Letter to H. Tennyson. Quoted in H. Tennyson, *op. cit.,* I, 189.

25. *Essays on Poetry,* I. 503.

26. Ward, "Tennyson, W. G. Ward, and Other Farringford Friends" in H. Tennyson (ed.), *Tennyson and his Friends,* p. 231.

27. Ward, *Aubrey de Vere: a Memoir,* pp. 312-313.

28. Cf.: "His [Tennyson's] friendship with Simeon, Ward, and Aubrey de Vere had given him a warm admiration for their single-minded faith and devotion to their Church, while the mystical side of his nature found much that was congenial in the Catholic communion, and he strongly resented the expulsion of the religious orders from France." Charles Tennyson, *op. cit.,* pp. 413-414.

29. De Vere, *Mediaeval Records and Sonnets,* p. 258.

CHAPTER FOUR

1. Letter to Ellis Yarnall, April 25, 1900. Quoted in Wilfrid Ward, *Aubrey de Vere: a Memoir,* p. 406.

2. Ward, *op. cit.,* pp. 11-12.

3. Letter to Sara Coleridge, Oct. 1845, in Aubrey de Vere, *Recollections,* pp. 199-200.

4. De Vere, *Recollections,* p. 315.

5. Ward, *op. cit.,* p. 176.

6. Sara Coleridge, letter to Henry Reed, May 19, 1851. Quoted in L. N. Broughton (ed.), *Sara Coleridge and Henry Reed,* p. 66.

7. De Vere, Diary, Oct. 4 and 10, 1846. Quoted in Ward, *op. cit.,* pp. 93-94.

8. Letter to de Vere, Sept. 1845. Quoted in Edith Coleridge, *Memoir and Letters of Sara Coleridge,* p. 236.

9. Letter to de Vere, 1846. Quoted in E. Coleridge, *op. cit.,* p. 263.

10. De Vere, Diary, Sept. 12, 1846. Quoted in Ward, *op. cit.,* p. 93.

11. Letter to de Vere, Jan.-July, 1851. Quoted in E. Coleridge, *op. cit.,* p. 349.

12. Letter to de Vere, Nov. 4, 1849. Quoted in E. Coleridge, *op. cit.,* p. 407.

13. "The Two Chief Schools of English Poetry. Poetic Versatility, Shelley and Keats," *Essays Chiefly on Poetry,* II, 128-133.

14. Letter to Sara Coleridge, April 10, 1851. Quoted in E. Coleridge, *op. cit.,* pp. 168-169.

15. Letter to Sara Coleridge, Nov. 9, 1851. Quoted in E. Coleridge, *op. cit..* p. 197.

16. Letter to Sara Coleridge, Nov. 15, 1851. Quoted in E. Coleridge, *op. cit..* p. 199.

17. Quoted in E. L. Griggs, *Coleridge Fille,* p. 220.

18. Sara Coleridge, quoting de Vere. Quoted in E. Coleridge, *op. cit.*, pp. 338-339.
19. Griggs, *op. cit.*, p. 181.
20. *Ibid.*, p. 219.
21. Quoted in Ward, *op. cit.*, p. 88.
22. Letter to de Vere, July 11, 1849. Quoted in E. Coleridge, *op. cit.*, p. 369.
23. *Recollections*, p. 133.
24. The death of her husband, also her cousin, Henry Nelson Coleridge.
25. Quoted in Ward, *op. cit.*, p. 96.
26. "Poems by Hartley Coleridge" (Critique) and "Essays and Marginalia" (Review), *Edinburgh Review*, XCIV (July 1851), 68-97.
27. Hugh Walker, *Literature of the Victorian Era*, p. 255.
28. P. 36.
29. *Recollections*, p. 135.
30. Griggs, *op. cit.*, p. 91.
31. De Vere, letter to Henry Taylor, 1845 or 1846, in *Recollections*, p. 132.
32. Letter to Reed. Quoted in E. Coleridge, *op. cit.*, p. 378.
33. Letter to Yarnall. *See* note 1.
34. *Recollections*, pp. 196-199.

CHAPTER FIVE

1. Taylor, speaking of de Vere in 1840, said: "My wife had no other very intimate friend, but that one was worth a thousand . . . I am afraid to speak of him as he deserves." *Autobiography of Henry Taylor*, I, 253.
   On April 8, 1886, de Vere wrote to Mrs. Edward Villiers: "Taylor was by many degrees the chief friend that I have ever had . . . the most constant of friends, as well as the one most helpful for good." Quoted in Wilfrid Ward, *Aubrey de Vere: a Memoir*, pp. 361-364.
2. Taylor, *Autobiography*, I, 99.
3. She was the daughter of de Vere's uncle, Thomas Spring Rice, later Lord Monteagle. Two of her brothers were Sir Charles Spring Rice and Stephen Spring Rice, de Vere's close friend. One of Charles' sons, Sir Cecil Arthur Spring Rice, was British ambassador to the United States from 1913 to 1918.
4. *Correspondence of Henry Taylor* (ed. Edward Dowden).
5. Taylor, *Autobiography*, I, 41.
6. *Ibid.*, pp. 39-40.
7. Taylor, *Correspondence*, pp. 1-3.
8. *Ibid.*, p. 220.
9. *Ibid.*, p. 265.
10. Aubrey de Vere, "Philip van Artevelde," *Essays Chiefly on Poetry*, I, 292.

11. Hugh Walker, *Literature of the Victorian Era*, p. 269.

12. Taylor, *Autobiography*, I, 166.

13. Cf. William Rowan Hamilton, letter to de Vere, Aug. 29, 1834. Quoted in R. P. Graves (ed.), *Life of Sir William Rowan Hamilton*, II, 105.

14. Ward, *op. cit.*, p. 32.

15. Letter to Taylor, 1847 or 1848, in Taylor, *Autobiography*, II, 24.

16. Letter to Taylor, Oct. 30, 1868. Quoted in Ward, *op. cit.*, p. 267.

17. De Vere's disapproval of Dryden displeased Gerard Manley Hopkins. Writing to Robert Bridges, he stated: "I was asked to my friends at Howth, to meet Aubrey de Vere. However, he was called away to London and when I came was gone. I was disappointed till it was mentioned that he did not think Dryden a poet. Then I thought, and perhaps said, I had not missed much. And yet you share this opinion or something like it with him . . ." *Letters of Gerard Manley Hopkins to Robert Bridges* (ed. C. C. Abbott), p. 280.

18. De Vere, letter to Taylor. *See* note 16.

19. These letters had been given to Taylor by Wordsworth's friend, Miss Fenwick. (The second volume of *Essays Chiefly on Poetry* de Vere dedicated to the memory of Scott and Southey, "in whose poetry Imagination ever walked side by side with Virtue and Honor.")

20. Letter to Taylor, Nov. 24, 1865. Quoted in Ward, *op. cit.*, p. 270.

21. Cf. de Vere, letter to Taylor, Nov. 18, 1893, in Taylor, *Correspondence*, p. 283.

22. In *Essays on Poetry*, II, 1-99.

23. *Ibid.*, p. 28.

24. Taylor, *Correspondence*, pp. 206-207.

25. Letter to de Vere, Nov. 28, 1862. *Ibid.*, p. 251.

     Taylor stated the same idea to a friend: "Aubrey de Vere's book is full of thought and genius that could not fail to be felt if he would but conceive his audience . . . But his life has been a soliloquy, and he has talked so long to himself in solitudes and wildernesses of thought, that he often seems as if he understood no other audience. Still . . . many of these poems . . . must make themselves heard." Letter to the Countess of Minto, Oct. 4, 1861, in Taylor, *Correspondence*, p. 230.

26. Taylor, letter to Lord Blachford, Aug. 21, 1882, in Taylor, *Correspondence*, p. 406.

27. Letter to Hamilton, Feb. 1, 1856, in Taylor, *Autobiography*, II, 143.

28. *Ibid.*, p. 146.

29. Letter to Taylor, March 3, 1868, in Taylor, *Correspondence*, p. 280.

30. De Vere, letter to Taylor, Nov. 18, 1893, in Taylor, *Correspondence*, pp. 323-324.

31. *Autobiography*, II, 8.

32. *Ibid.*, p. 116.

33. Walker, *op. cit.*, p. 270, considers it admirable in plot and characterization.
34. Ms. letter to G. E. Woodberry, March 29, 1900.
35. Ms. letter to Charles Eliot Norton, June 15, 1885.
36. Ms. letter to William Knight, May 1, 1882.

CHAPTER SIX

1. Basil Champneys, *Memoirs and Correspondence of Coventry Patmore,* I, 96.
2. Cooke and Stevenson, *English Literature of the Victorian Period,* pp. 172-174.
3. Champneys, *loc. cit.*
4. Cf. Derek Patmore, *Portrait of my Family,* p. 125.
5. Champneys, *loc. cit.*
6. Quoted in Edmund Gosse, *Coventry Patmore,* p. 168.
7. Quoted in D. Patmore, *op. cit.*, p. 114.
8. Cooke and Stevenson *loc. cit.*
9. Quoted in Gosse, *op. cit.*, p. 53.
10. *Ibid.*, p. 55.
11. Letter to Mrs. Gummer, in D. Patmore, *op. cit.*, p. 93.
12. *Ibid.*, p. 95.
13. "The Poetry of Coventry Patmore," *Essays Literary and Ethical,* pp. 127-128.
14. Hugh Walker, *Literature of the Victorian Era,* p. 526.
15. Aubrey de Vere, *op. cit.*, p. 149.
16. Quoted in Herbert Read, "Coventry Patmore," in H. J. and Hugh Massingham (eds.), *The Great Victorians,* p. 365.
17. *Op. cit.*, p. 138.
18. Letter to C. Patmore, Jan. 16, 1863. Quoted in Wilfrid Ward, *Aubrey de Vere: a Memoir,* p. 265.
19. Read, *op. cit.*, p. 358.
20. *Essays Literary,* pp. 128-150.
21. Read, *op. cit.*, p. 360.
22. Quoted in Calvert Alexander, S. J., *The Catholic Literary Revival,* p. 63.
23. Quoted in Champneys, *op. cit.*, II, 242.
24. *Ibid.*, I, 142.
25. *Ibid.*, p. 198.
26. Quoted in D. Patmore, *op. cit.*, pp. 125-126.
27. *Ibid.*, p. 129.
28. Quoted in Champneys, *op. cit.*, II, 122.
29. Quoted in D. Patmore, *op. cit.*, p. 124.
30. Quoted in Champneys, *op. cit.*, II, 54.

31. *Ibid.,* p. 213.
32. Quoted in D. Patmore, *op. cit.,* p. 139.
33. Quoted in Gosse, *op. cit.,* p. 103.
34. De Vere, *Essays Literary,* pp. 139-142. The entire article, pp. 126-150, contains the critique which was in the *Edinburgh Review.*
35. *Ibid.,* p. 150.
36. Quoted in Champneys, *op. cit.,* II, 326.
37. D. Patmore, *op. cit.,* p. 167.
38. Ms. letter to Charles Eliot Norton, Aug. 12, 1868.
39. De Vere, letter to Rev. Matthew Russell, S.J., April 2, 1877. Quoted in the *Irish Monthly,* XXIX (1911), 425.
40. Ms. letter to John Dennis, April 24, 1897.
41. Ms. letter to John Dennis, Aug. 24, 1899.
42. Quoted in C. C. Abbott (ed.), *Correspondence of Gerard Manley Hopkins and Richard Watson Dixon,* p. 112.
43. Ms. letter to John Dennis, Jan. 8, 1899.

CHAPTER SEVEN

1. Hugh Walker, *Literature of the Victorian Era,* p. 47.
2. Henry Taylor, *Autobiography,* I, 256.
3. Lord Brougham was the power behind the Edinburgh University appointments, one of which Carlyle was eager to obtain. (Lawrence and Elizabeth Hanson, *Necessary Evil: the Life of Jane Welsh Carlyle,* p. 120.)
4. Quoted in Wilfrid Ward, *Aubrey de Vere: a Memoir,* p. 79.
5. "Carlyle had a command of vivid words and telling phrases. . . . He repeatedly succumbs to temptation, studying effect more than truth, and sometimes ruining effect through exaggeration. . . ." Walker, *op. cit.,* p. 34.
6. Letter to Mrs. Edward Villiers, 1845. Quoted in Ward, *op. cit.,* pp. 79-80.
7. *Ibid.*
8. *Ibid.*
9. Letter to Jeannie Welsh, Sept. 28, 1848, in Jane Welsh Carlyle, *Letters to her Family* (ed. Leonard Huxley), p. 311.
10. "Necessary Evil" was one of Carlyle's nick-names for his wife.
11. Letter to Carlyle, July 7, 1849, in Alexander Carlyle (ed.), *New Letters and Memorials of Jane Welsh Carlyle,* I, 257.
12. Thomas Carlyle, letter to Sir Charles Gavan Duffy, May 29, 1849. Quoted in Duffy, *Conversations with Carlyle,* p. 36.
13. In a letter to de Vere, Feb. 19, 1848. Quoted in Ward, *op. cit.,* pp. 134-136.

Stephen, a friend of Taylor in the Colonial Office, did excellent work against slavery.

14. Carlyle, letter to de Vere, Feb. 5, 1848. Quoted in Ward, *op. cit.*, p. 133.
15. Carlyle, letter to de Vere, 1849. Quoted in Ward, *op. cit.*, p. 134 (note).
16. Letter to Lady Taylor, Sept. 19, 1848, in Taylor, *Correspondence*, p. 185.
17. Letter to Miss Fenwick, Nov. 1850. Quoted in Ward, *op. cit.*, p. 166.
18. De Vere, letter to Taylor, June 6, 1881. Quoted in Ward, *op. cit.*, p. 330.
19. Related in Ward, *loc. cit.*
20. William Knight, "Thomas Carlyle," *Retrospects*, p. 20.
21. Letter to Sara Coleridge, Feb. 20, 1852. Quoted in Ward, *op. cit.*, p. 204.
22. Letter to Taylor, Oct. 5, 1877, in Taylor, *Correspondence*, pp. 375-376.
23. Letter to Taylor, May 21, 1880. Quoted in Ward, *op. cit.*, pp. 341-342.
24. Quoted in Ward, *op. cit.*, p. 323.
25. Ms. letter to Walter George Smith, April 21, 1900.
26. Letter to Taylor, June 6, 1881. Quoted in Ward, *op. cit.*, p. 328.
27. Ms. letter to Charles Eliot Norton, June 1, 1883.
28. Ms. letter to Norton, June 23, 1889.
29. *Ibid.*
30. Quoted in Maisie Ward, *The Wilfrid Wards and the Transition*, p. 223.
31. De Vere, letter to Miss Norton, June 14, 1889. Quoted in W. Ward, *op. cit.*, pp. 380-381.

CHAPTER EIGHT

1. Elizabeth Thompson, later Lady Butler, was a painter of war scenes.
2. Viola Meynell, *Alice Meynell: a Memoir*, p. 48.
3. *Ibid.*
4. Ms. letter to Alice Thompson, July 2, 1874.
5. Wilfrid Meynell, Ms. letter to author, July 19, 1934.
6. W. Meynell, Ms. letter to author, Sept. 10, 1934.
7. The dates of the letters are: July 2, Aug. 12, 1874; Feb. 25, 1875; Aug. 9 and 12, Oct. 7 and 27, Nov. 15 and 22, Dec. 4, 1876; Jan. 5, 1877.
8. This Ms., written by de Vere, was probably enclosed in one of the letters.
9. W. Meynell, in a letter to the author (*see* note 6), stated that this Ms. was "in Alice's handwriting."
10. Ms. letter, Dec. 4, 1876.
    Cf.: "Alfred Tennyson used when reading me his *In Memoriam* poems in Ms. to discourse much and well on the 'shape,' as he called it, of poems, and sometimes cancelled the most striking stanzas of a poem ... to prevent its being 'long-backed' or otherwise unshapely ..." Ms. letter, Oct. 7, 1876.
11. Ms. letter, July 12, 1874.

12. Ms. letter, Oct. 27, 1876.

13. Ms. letter, Feb. 25, 1875.

14. Ms. letter, Jan. 5, 1877.

15. The poems reviewed are: "To the Beloved," "An Unmarked Festival," "Song of the Spring to the Summer" (now "The Spring to the Summer"), "Song of the Day to the Night" ("The Day to the Night"), "The Cradle Song" ("The Cradle Song at Twilight"), "Sonnet to ————" ("A Poet of One Mood"), "Parted," "Builders of Ruins," "To the Beloved Dead," and "In March." The last two poems do not appear in Alice Meynell's *Poems* (Scribner, 1925). It is possible that "In March" became "In Early Spring" or "In February": the criticisms of de Vere may be applied to either.

   "To the Beloved Dead" may have been omitted because Mrs. Meynell "expunged what she thought most crude in the Preludes." V. Meynell, *op. cit.*, pp. 77-78.

16. Ms. commentary on poems.

17. Alice Meynell, *Poems,* pp. 18-19.

18. Ms. commentary.

19. Alice Thompson in Ms. notes on conversation with de Vere.

20. *Ibid.* Further remarks on Shelley will be found in Chapter XII.

21. *Ibid.*

22. *Ibid.*

23. De Vere, quoted in V. Meynell, *op. cit.,* p. 51.

24. Ms. letter, Aug. 22, 1874.

25. Letter to Lady Taylor, 1877. Quoted in V. Meynell, *op. cit.,* p. 61.

26. V. Meynell, *loc. cit.* Among these writers were Francis Thompson, of course, and Coventry Patmore, George Meredith, Chesterton and Belloc, Joyce Kilmer, Aubrey Beardsley, William Watson, Oscar Wilde, Lionel Johnson, Katherine Tynan, W. B. Yeats and the Irish revivalists. Even young Theodore Maynard often "dropped in" on Sundays.

27. W. Meynell, Ms. letter to author, March 16, 1934.

28. Alice Meynell, Ceylon *Catholic Messenger,* Sept. 23, 1881.

CHAPTER NINE

1. Aubrey de Vere, letter to Sara Coleridge, Feb. 2, 1846. Quoted in Wilfrid Ward, *Aubrey de Vere: a Memoir,* p. 103.

2. De Vere, letter to Mrs. Edward Villiers, 1845. Quoted in Ward, *op. cit.,* p. 75.

NEWMAN

3. "Wordsworth and Newman: they were the two for whom my love has been most like idolatry." De Vere, interview with Edmund Gosse, 1896. Quoted in Ward, *op. cit.,* p. 392.

Through Wordsworth de Vere also became interested in Frederick
William Faber, for some time Anglican clergyman at Ambleside, and
after his conversion to Catholicism, Superior of the London Oratory.

4. Richard Monckton Milnes, letter to de Vere, 1838. Quoted in Ward,
   op. cit., p. 30.
5. Letter to sister, Dec. 25, 1838. Quoted in Ward, *op. cit.,* p. 31.
6. *Ibid.*
7. Quoted in Edmund Gosse, "Aubrey de Vere," *Portraits and Sketches,*
   pp. 119-125; and in Ward, *op. cit.,* p. 392.
8. *Ibid.*
9. Julian Abernethy, *English Literature,* p. 502.
10. De Vere, letter to Sara Coleridge, Feb. 12, 1846. Quoted in Ward, *op.
    cit.,* p. 104.
11. De Vere, *Recollections,* p. 263.
12. Letter to Sara Coleridge, Nov. 11, 1850. Quoted in Ward, *op. cit.,* p. 182.
13. Quoted in Matthew Russell, S.J., "Poets I Have Known," *Donahoe's
    Magazine,* XLVI (1901), 555-570.
14. *Recollections,* p. 266.
15. *Ibid.,* p. 268.
16. Letter to Charles Spring Rice, July 11, 1868. Quoted in Ward, *op. cit.,*
    pp. 274-275.
17. Letter to de Vere, July 6, 1864. Quoted in Ward, *op. cit.,* pp. 306-307.
18. Letter to de Vere, Aug. 31, 1870. Quoted in Ward, *op. cit.,* pp. 307-308.
19. Quoted in *Recollections,* p. 282.
20. *Ibid.,* p. 278.
21. *Ibid.*
22. *Ibid.,* p. 279.
23. Hugh Walker, *Literature of the Victorian Era,* p. 115.
24. "Lines suggested by a Volume of Cardinal Newman's Poetry," in
    Recollections, p. 287:

> Hid in each cord there winds one central strand;
> Hid in each breast a panting heart doth lie;
> Hid in the lines that map the Infant's hand
> There lurks, some say, a life-long destiny;
> Through the dropt leaf, 'gainst wintry sunset scanned
> Shines that fine web whose firm geometry
> Sustained the nascent frame and each new dye
> Fed by spring dews, by autumn breezes fanned.
> Stamped on this book what note we? One decree
> Writ by God's finger on a destined soul,
> That each new thought an act, and, leaving free
> The spirit, shaped the life into a whole:
> What was that great behest? that mastering vow?
> England, God's work completed, answer thou!

25. Letter to Grace Norton, 1891. Quoted in Ward, *op. cit.*, p. 382.
26. *Selections from the Poems of Aubrey de Vere* (ed. G. E. Woodberry), p. 306.
27. *Recollections,* p. 286.

MANNING

1. *Recollections,* pp. 298-306.
2. J. Lewis May, *Cardinal Newman,* p. 16.
3. Cf.: "Dr. Manning is here, a wily and soft dialectician . . ." Charles Eliot Norton, letter from Rome to his mother, March 1, 1857, in Sara Norton and M. A. de Wolfe Howe (eds.), *Letters of Charles Eliot Norton,* I, 166.
4. *Recollections,* p. 288.
5. Letter to mother, Aug. 14, 1850. Quoted in Wilfrid Ward, *Aubrey de Vere: a Memoir,* pp. 161-162.
6. De Vere, *Recollections,* p. 289.
7. *Ibid.,* p. 288.
8. *Ibid.,* p. 306.
9. *Ibid.,* p. 299.
10. Letter to de Vere, 1847, in de Vere, *Recollections,* p. 300.
11. *Ibid.*
12. *Recollections,* p. 289.
13. *Ibid.,* p. 290.
14. *Ibid.,* pp. 290-291.
15. *Ibid.*

Cf.: "15th November 1851—On Wednesday at St. Esprit, or by the road, lost my bag with writing-case, money, letters and journals. A sharp vexation. The letters and journals especially valuable. But from this loss I desire to learn:

1. To mortify selfishness, and too great sensitiveness in matters which touch myself.
2. To learn sympathy with others in their losses. I should care little what they lost, so that I lost nothing [*sic.*].
3. To learn detachment and love of poverty.

I have lost:

1. Money
2. Journals
3. Letters

For the first, I ought to trust. For the second, to be less contemplative. For the third, to be dead to earthly and natural affection." Henry Manning, Diary. Quoted in E. S. Purcell, *Life of Cardinal Manning,* I, 640.

16. De Vere, *Recollections,* pp. 291-292.
17. Cf. Purcell, *op. cit.,* pp. 727-729, 799, 800.

18. De Vere, *Recollections,* pp. 293-294.
19. *Ibid.,* pp. 294-295. Cf. Manning's evidently sincere statements in his Diary, 1851-1854, quoted in Purcell, *op. cit.,* 11, 17.
20. Purcell, *op. cit.,* II, 685-686.
21. Journal, Feb. 17, 1889. Quoted in Purcell, *op. cit.,* II, 687-688.

　　Cf.: "Purcell's picture of Manning as an intriguer for his own advancement always seemed to me as untrue as it was unkind." Wilfrid Ward, quoted in Maisie Ward, *The Wilfrid Wards and the Transition,* p. 219.

　　Of Purcell's biography of Manning, de Vere wrote: "That life . . . which had such an immense circulation and was expected to damage his reputation has not, I believe, done it any harm. No one of sense can believe that ambition could have been the cause of his leaving the Church of England, the highest dignities of which lay at his feet, for the Catholic Church, where he expected to be a nobody. Gladstone, who read that book with intense interest, said in a letter to me immediately afterwards, that all who admired him before reading that book would admire the Cardinal more after they had read it . . ." Ms. letter to Helen Grace Smith, Feb. 9, 1895.

22. Quoted in de Vere, *Recollections,* p. 295.
23. *Ibid.*
24. *Ibid.,* p. 296.
25. *Ibid.,* p. 302.
26. Letter to de Vere, Feb. 6, 1885. Quoted in Ward, *op. cit.,* pp. 349-350.
27. Hugh Walker, *Literature of the Victorian Era,* p. 130.
28. Letter to de Vere, Christmas, 1889, in de Vere, *Recollections,* p. 303.
29. De Vere, "Reminiscences of Cardinal Manning," *Recollections,* p. 304.
30. *Ibid.,* p. 305.
31. *Ibid.*

VAUGHAN

1. Wilfrid Ward, *Aubrey de Vere: a Memoir,* p. 205.
2. *Ibid.*
3. Letter to mother, Feb. 28, 1852. *Ibid.,* p. 208.
4. Sir Vere de Vere (Aubrey's eldest brother) and his wife were received into the Catholic Church by Henry Edward Manning.
5. Letter to Miss Fenwick, Aug. 23, 1852. Quoted in Ward, *op. cit.,* pp. 218-219.
6. J. G. Snead-Cox, *Life of Cardinal Vaughan,* p. 38.

　　Cf: "From the first he intended to do 'something intense' and 'something heroic' for God and Church." Snead-Cox, *op. cit.,* p. 205.

7. "The family of Vere, from Ver near Bayeux, France, . . . was founded in England by Aubrey (Albericus) de Vere, who obtained vast estates from the Conqueror." *Dictionary of National Biography,* XX, 219.

CHAPTER TEN

MILNES

1. Diary, April 5, 1845. Quoted in Wilfrid Ward, *Aubrey de Vere: a Memoir*, p. 71.
2. "Reminiscences of Richard Monckton Milnes" in T. Wemyss Reid, *Life, Letters, and Friendships of Richard Monckton Milnes*, I, 116-117.
3. R. M. Milnes, letter to de Vere, May 25, 1836. Quoted in Reid, *op. cit.*, pp. 195-196.
   Milnes humorously advised de Vere to buy the book if he had 11s/6d.
4. Letter to de Vere, March 28, 1837. Quoted in Reid, *op. cit.*, p. 194.
5. Milnes, letter to de Vere. *See* note 3.
6. *Ibid.*
7. Letter to de Vere, 1838. Quoted in Ward, *op. cit.*, pp. 29-30.
8. Aubrey de Vere, "Reminiscences of Milnes" in Reid, *op. cit.*, p. 115.
9. Milnes, letter to de Vere. *See* note 4.
10. "I was recommending Milnes once to publish a compact edition of his best poems, when he replied that he would be too glad to do so when possible; but he feared they were too nearly on the same level to make such discrimination possible . . ." De Vere, letter to Coventry Patmore, Jan. 16, 1863. Quoted in Ward, *op. cit.*, pp. 264-265.
11. Reid, *op. cit.*, pp. 113-120.
12. Quoted in de Vere, "Reminiscences of Milnes" in Reid, *op. cit.*, p. 116.
13. Vol. II, p. 565.

LANDOR

1. Aubrey de Vere, "Reminiscences of Richard Monckton Milnes" in T. Wemyss Reid, *Life, Letters and Friendships of Richard Monckton Milnes*, I, 113-120.
2. *Ibid.*, pp. 116-117.
3. Letter to William Rowan Hamilton, Oct. 6, 1832. Quoted in R. P. Graves, *Life of Sir William Rowan Hamilton*, I, 617.
   This criticism agrees with that of George Saintsbury, *Cambridge History of English Literature*, XIII, 215: "Landor is Hellenic generally, but not definitely pagan."
4. Letter to Hamilton, Sept. 10, 1835. Quoted in Graves, *op. cit.*, II, 163.
5. Sara Coleridge, letter to de Vere, Aug. 31, 1846, in Edith Coleridge, *Memoir and Letters of Sara Coleridge*, p. 286.
6. Quoted in Una Taylor, *Guests and Memories*, p. 57.
7. De Vere, *Recollections*, p. 301.
8. The two anthologies are *The Household Poetry Book* (no date) and *Select Specimens of the Poets* (1860). The contents of the volumes are similar, except that the former contains about twenty more poems at the end.

9. In *Essays Chiefly on Poetry*, II, 142-188.

10. *Ibid.*, p. 156.

11. *Ibid.*, p. 157.

12. *Ibid.*, p. 158.

13. *Ibid.*, pp. 159-160.

14. *Ibid.*, p. 161.

15. *Ibid.*, pp. 167-168.

16. Ms. letter to G. E. Woodberry, March 29, 1900.

17. Saintsbury, *op. cit.*, XIII, 209.

18. See p. 126. Verses addressed to de Vere appear also in Landor, *Works*, VIII, 244, 256.

19. Henry Taylor, *Autobiography*, I, 255.

20. Letter to Mrs. Paynter, June 1847, in Stephen Wheeler (ed.), *Letters of Walter Savage Landor, Private and Public*, p. 159.

21. Letter to John Forster, Oct. 23, 1848, in John Forster (ed.), *Walter Savage Landor: Works and Life*, p. 497.

22. Quoted in Wilfrid Ward, *Aubrey de Vere: a Memoir*, p. 256.

23. *Ibid.*

24. The book is inscribed: "W. S. Landor, Esq., with the author's respects." In a different hand is the following inscription: "Given to Kate Field by Mr. Landor. Florence, Italy, 1861."

   Mr. J. E. Woodhead of Chicago purchased the book and corresponded with de Vere, who informed him that years had intervened between his sending the book to Landor and the latter's acknowledging it. (G. E. Wall, "Stray Words from Walter Savage Landor," *The Critic*, March, 1901, pp. 238-240.)

25. Quoted in Wall, *op. cit.*, p. 239.

26. *Ibid.*

27. Ward, *op. cit.*, p. 136.

28. *Letters Private and Public*, p. 159.

29. Quoted in H. Taylor, *Autobiography*, I, 254-255.

RUSKIN

1. Henry Taylor had recommended this book to de Vere. (E. T. Cook, *Life of Ruskin*, I, 145.)

2. Aubrey de Vere, quoted in Cook, *op. cit.*, p. 54.

3. De Vere, Diary, July 2, 1845. Quoted in Wilfrid Ward, *Aubrey de Vere: a Memoir*, p. 85.

4. *Ibid.*, July 4, 1845.

5. De Vere was a member of the Church of England at this time.

6. D. A. Wilson, *Carlyle at his Zenith*, p. 454.

7. Letter to Mrs. Hewitt, Sept. 13, 1862. Quoted in Cook, *op. cit.*, II, 51.

8. R. H. Wilenski, "John Ruskin" in H. J. and Hugh Massingham (eds.) *The Great Victorians*, p. 415.

9. "Till recently Ruskin's writing on social economics was generally regarded as Utopian literature . . . ," but "he has been shown right not only in general lines, but in a great many details." Wilenski, *op. cit.,* pp. 419-421.

10. De Vere, Ms. letter to Charles Eliot Norton, Nov. 16, 1873.

11. "When Ruskin was fifty-nine, his brain gave way, and he had periodic mental breakdowns for the remainder of his life." Wilenski, *op. cit.,* p. 419.

12. Ms. letter to Norton, Jan. 24, 1874.

13. Ruskin, diary notes, Sept. 13 and 16, 1877, in Cook, *op. cit.,* p. 395.

14. Norton's influence over Ruskin was remarkable. Of him Ruskin wrote: "Norton saw all my weaknesses, measured all my narrownesses, and from the first took serenely . . . a right of guidance; . . . though the younger of the two, he never allowed me the slightest violation of the laws either of good writing or social prudence without instant blame or warning . . ." *Praeterita,* p. 423.

15. De Vere, letter to Norton, Dec. 8, 1878. Quoted in Ward, *op. cit.,* pp. 323-324.

16. *Modern Painters,* III, 252.

17. De Vere, Ms. letter to Norton, Dec. 21, 1881.

THE BROWNINGS

1. Letter to Sara Coleridge, Feb. 12, 1846. Quoted in Wilfrid Ward, *Aubrey de Vere: a Memoir,* pp. 102-103.

2. Letter to William Rowan Hamilton, "St. John's Day," 1846. Quoted in R. P. Graves, *Life of Sir William Rowan Hamilton,* III, 544.

3. Letter to Edward Dowden, Dec. 27, 1874, in *Letters of Edward Dowden and his Correspondents,* p. 71.

4. For de Vere's further criticism of Browning see Chapter VIII.

5. Ms. letter to Alice Meynell, Dec. 4, 1876.

6. Letter to William Allingham, Sept. 29, 1865. Quoted in H. Allingham and E. Baumer Williams (eds.), *Letters of William Allingham,* p. 174.

7. Hugh Walker, *Literature of the Victorian Era,* pp. 367-368.
   Such critics as C. T. Winchester, Sir Henry Jones, Lascelles Abercrombie, Oliver Elton, Edmund Gosse and Louis Cazamian have since expressed judgments similar to de Vere's.

8. Walker, *op. cit.,* pp. 442-443.

9. Sunshine seems symbolic of de Vere's natural enthusiasm and optimism. As he was at that time fired with the zeal of a recent convert, he probably impressed Browning with that aspect of his character.
   Cf.: "Everything that belongs to the old days wears for me a magical brightness, and a colouring like that of mountains a little before sunrise." De Vere, letter to Henry Taylor, March 3, 1868, in *Correspondence of Henry Taylor,* p. 280.

10. Robert Browning, letter to de Vere, probably April, 1852. Quoted in Ward, *op. cit.*, p. 216.
11. Letter to Ward, 1889. Quoted in Ward, *op. cit.*, p. 373.
12. "Robert Browning," *Macmillan's Magazine*, LXI, 258.

MACAULAY

1. Hartley Coleridge wrote of the "bravado of Macaulay and such like spouting-club heroes." Letter to Denvent Coleridge, 1836. Quoted in E. L. Griggs, *Letters of Hartley Coleridge*, p. 93.
2. Cf.: "Half the pleasure we take in Macaulay's writing arises from the author's sincere and convinced satisfaction with himself." Edmund Gosse, *History of English Literature*, IV, 259.
3. Cf.:"What he [Macaulay] lacks is . . . depth of reflection." Hugh Walker, *Literature of the Victorian Era*, p. 835.
4. Cf.: "He is without vision of unseen things; he has no message to the heart; the waters of the soul are never troubled by his copious and admirable flow of sound information." Walker, *loc. cit.*
5. Aubrey de Vere, letter to Mrs. Edward Villiers, undated. Quoted in Wilfrid Ward, *Aubrey de Vere: a Memoir*, pp. 74-75.
6. Cf.: "He [Macaulay] has a deeper and more fundamental notion of order than of truth . . . His main concern is by no means the anxious search after the exact shade, nor . . . a scrupulous reverence of facts, nor even the care of documentation." Cazamian, *History of English Literature*, p. 1137.
7. Letter to Rev. Matthew J. Russell, S. J., May 24, 1887. Quoted in M. J. Russell, S. J., "Unpublished Letters of Aubrey de Vere," *Irish Monthly*, XL, 103.

DOWDEN

1. Edward Dowden of Trinity College, Dublin, edited *Correspondence of Henry Taylor*.
2. Dowden, letter to de Vere, Aug. 22, 1874, in *Letters of Edward Dowden and his Correspondents*, p. 66.
   In this letter he stated: "I want to put my hand on Shakespeare's shoulder for a moment only, and find it difficult. He eludes me . . . There ought to be methods by which one could force a dramatic poet to discover himself and announce his name, and tell you his secret."
3. Aubrey de Vere wrote: "I looked on each of his plays as a huge Alp in an Alpine range—and to climb a mountain is so much more difficult than to walk in a valley (though also a thing that rewards labour more). I have often turned from Shakespeare, I am ashamed to say, in order to read what I admired far less . . ." Letter to Dowden, Dec. 27, 1874, in Dowden, *Letters*, p. 71.
4. Letter to Dowden, March 17, 1875, in Dowden, *Letters*, p. 73.

5. Cf.:

"Henry VI is a royal saint, weak in his saintliness . . .

"Shakespeare . . . says that this saint of a feeble type upon the throne of England was a curse to the land and to the time . . . He is yet possessed of egoism, the egoism of timid saintliness. His virtue is negative because there is no vigorous basis of manhood within him out of which heroic saintliness might develop itself. For fear of what is wrong, he shrinks from what is right . . . Henry knows nothing of zeal; and he is amiable, not charitable . . .

"The feeble saint, . . . cast down upon the occurrence of a piece of brutal knavery, can himself abandon to butchers the noblest life in England . . . Humoring his timorous, irritable conscience, Henry is incapable of action, and allows things to take their course. . . .

"In prison Henry at last is really happy; now he is responsible for nothing . . . His latter days he will spend, to the rebuke of sin and the praise of his Creator, in devotion . . ." *Shakspere: His Mind and Art,* pp. 168-179.

6. Letter to Dowden, March 17, 1875, in Dowden, *Letters,* p. 73.

7. Letter to de Vere, April 7, 1875, in Dowden, *Letters,* pp. 78-79.

8. *Ibid.*

9. De Vere, letter to Dowden. *See* note 6.

10. *Ibid.,* p. 75.

11. *Ibid.*

12. Letter to de Vere, May 30, 1892, in Dowden, *Letters,* p. 258.

13. Ms. letter to William Knight, Aug. 1, 1883.

14. Letter to Dowden, Dec. 24, 1876, in Dowden, *Letters,* p. 102.

De Vere's estimate of Dowden's poetry coincides with that of Oliver Elton, *A Survey of English Literature,* III, 297: "Dowden's taste and skill are remarkable; and he has left a little intimate poetry, delicate in execution."

15. Dowden, letter to Todhunter, Feb. 11, 1879, in Dowden, *Letters,* p. 132. He wrote: "Aubrey de Vere urges Southey strongly, and Sir Henry Taylor has offered me the use of hundreds of Southey's letters."

16. Letter to de Vere, in Dowden, *Letters,* p. 223.

HUTTON

1. Cf.: "If Ruskin had taken the trouble to read Mr. Aubrey de Vere's fine essays in the *Month,* on the Genius and Passion of Wordsworth, I do not think he would have ventured to write this rather flippant and very obtuse criticism." Richard Holt Hutton, *Contemporary Thought and Thinkers,* II, 107.

2. Quoted in Wilfrid Ward, *Aubrey de Vere: a Memoir,* p. 314.

3. *Ibid.,* pp. 314-315.

4. *Ibid.,* p. 302.

5. De Vere's essays on Wordsworth, Keats, Shelley and others seem to justify Hutton's opinion of de Vere's critical ability.
6. Quoted in Ward, *op. cit.,* p. 257.
7. In *The Spectator,* LV (Aug. 5, 1882), 1023.
8. "The Poetical Works of Aubrey de Vere," *The Spectator,* LVIII (Oct. 25, 1884), pp. 1407 ff.

WARD

1. Cf.: "Mr. Aubrey de Vere's will names as his literary executors: Mr. Wilfrid Ward, Mr. Wilfrid Meynell, Mrs. Towle (daughter of Sir Henry Taylor and the Hon. Lady Taylor, who was Mr. de Vere's cousin), and Miss Agnes Lambert . . . £50 is to be given to the first one who, in the order here given, will undertake the task of editing some correspondence he docketed before his death as 'to be published'; and this task has now virtually been undertaken by Mr. Ward." *The Athenaeum,* April 5, 1902.
2. The meeting of Tennyson and Vaughan is related in Chapter III. Cf.: Wilfrid Ward, *Aubrey de Vere: a Memoir,* pp. 312-313.
3. "In 1887 we formed a dining club, of which Lord Emly was president, and I was secretary, for the purpose of discussing the Irish problem, then of such interest to all Catholics . . . " Ward, *op. cit.,* p. 315.
4. *Ibid.*
5. *Ibid.,* p. 3.
6. Tennyson's home, where de Vere was then a guest.
7. Ward, *op. cit.,* p. 313.
8. *Ibid.,* p. 315.
9. *Ibid.,* p. 316.
10. Cf.: "He [de Vere] was a delightful raconteur . . ." Lady Shaw, Ms. letter to author, June 5, 1932.
11. Ward, *op. cit.,* p. 375.
12. Letter to Ward, Oct. 9, 1891. Quoted in Ward, *op. cit.,* p. 371.
13. Ward, *op. cit.,* pp. 364-365.
14. Letter to Ward, Oct. 17, 1889. *Ibid.,* p. 369.
15. P. v.

CHAPTER ELEVEN

1. Ms. letter, April 17, 1867.
2. Andrew J. George, "Aubrey de Vere," *Atlantic Monthly,* LXXXIX (June 1902), 829.
3. George edited *The Complete Poetical Works of William Wordsworth.*
4. In a letter to Ellis Yarnall, April 25, 1900, de Vere wrote: "I have lately been reading again that beautiful book on English literature by Professor Reed, which was so much appreciated by Wordsworth, and

the influence of which in America must have enabled Wordsworth's
poetry to do so great a work in the way of spiritualizing the American
as well as the English mind." Quoted in Wilfrid Ward, *Aubrey de Vere:
a Memoir,* p. 407.

5. Henry James, letter to sister, March 10, 1869, in Percy Lubbock (ed.),
   Letters of Henry James, I, 17.
6. March—June, 1853, pp. 359-407.
7. Ms. letter to Charles Eliot Norton, May 24, 1858.
8. "Arrived in London on June 26, 1868; Mr. Longfellow and his party
   took rooms in Langham Hotel. Immediately a flood of hospitality
   flowed in upon him . . . Received midnight calls from Bulwer and
   Aubrey de Vere." Samuel Longfellow, *Life of Henry Wadsworth
   Longfellow,* I, 113.
9. Letter to Charles Spring Rice, July 11, 1868. Quoted in Ward, *op. cit.,*
   pp. 275-276.
10. *Irish Odes and Other Poems,* p. vi.
11. Letter to D. F. MacCarthy, undated. Quoted in Matthew J. Russell,
    S. J., "Poets I Have Known," *Donahoe's Magazine,* XLVI (1901),
    555-570. MacCarthy was an Irish poet and translator of the dramas of
    Calderón. His first volume (1850) was entitled *Ballads, Poems and
    Lyrics.*
12. Ms. letter to Norton, May 1, 1892.
13. Ms. letter to Norton, Aug. 8, 1894.
14. Letter to Richard Watson Gilder, Sept. 12, 1881, in C. E. Norton (ed.),
    Letters of James Russell Lowell, p. 258.
15. Aubrey de Vere, Ms. letter to Norton, Aug. 24, 1869.
16. Letter to G. E. Woodberry, Aug. 24, 1895, in Rosamond Gilder (ed.),
    Letters of Richard Watson Gilder, pp. 283-284.
17. De Vere, Ms. letter to Norton, Dec. 21, 1881.
18. Mrs. Elizabeth Reed, letter to her children, June 10, 1873. Quoted in
    L. N. Broughton, *Wordsworth and Reed,* p. 277.
19. Letter to Caroline Bournemouth, Aug. 16, 1891, in *Selected Letters of
    George Edward Woodberry,* pp. 12-13.

    Cf. the following from a letter by de Vere two days after Wood-
    berry's letter: "We — that is, Sir Henry Taylor's daughters and I —
    have been seeing a great deal of your friend, Woodberry, to whom
    they took a great liking at Bournemouth. We brought him to see many
    relics of Shelley at his [Shelley's] daughter-in-law's . . ." Ms. letter
    to Norton, Dec. 23, 1895.
20. Two sonnets in de Vere's *Antar and Zara* are entitled "The American
    Struggle."
21. Letter to G. W. Curtis, Oct. 2, 1861, in Sara Norton and M. A.
    de Wolfe Howe (eds.), *Letters of Charles Eliot Norton,* I, 159.
22. Ms. letter to Norton, Feb. 2, 1868.

23. Letter to Norton, Sept. 25, 1865. Quoted in Ward, *op. cit.*, p. 266.

24. Letter to Norton, Feb. 1, 1881. Quoted in Ward, *op. cit.*, p. 325.

25. Letter to Grace Norton, Dec. 23, 1895. Quoted in Ward, *op. cit.*, p. 386.

26. Letter to Grace Norton, Aug. 10, 1891. Quoted in Ward, *op. cit.*, p. 383.

27. Letter to Grace Norton, Jan. 4, 1898. Quoted in Ward, *op. cit.*, p. 388.

28. Ms. letter to Norton, Jan. 24, 1874.

29. Letter to Norton, Dec. 8, 1878. Quoted in Ward, *op. cit.*, p. 324.

30. Ms. letter to Norton, Nov. 1, 1892.

31. Ms. letter to Woodberry, Oct. 11, 1894.

32. De Vere, Ms. letter to Woodberry, Sept. 27, 1894.

33. Ms. letter to Norton, Aug. 29, 1857.

34. Inexpensive editions of de Vere's work were evidently printed, for the author received from Wilfrid Meynell a paper-covered copy of de Vere's *Legends of Saint Patrick.*

35. Farrell & Sons, 107 Fulton Street, New York.

36. Ms. letter to Norton, Oct. 14, 1867.

37. "Aubrey de Vere," *Century Magazine,* Oct. 1884.

38. A Ms. memorandum, evidently written by Gilder and dated January 10, 1894, affords the information that de Vere received four guineas a page for two articles, of about 7500 words each. Another note states that there were seventeen pages; therefore, de Vere received approximately $350 for the chapters on Newman and Manning, later incorporated in the *Recollections.*

39. This Preface, under the title "Aubrey de Vere: Poet and Critic," is one of the essays in Woodberry's *Studies of a Litterateur.*

40. Ms. letter to Woodberry. *See* note 31.

41. *Studies of a Litterateur,* p. 159.

42. *Ibid.,* pp. 166-167.

43. *Ibid.,* p. 168.

44. *Ibid.,* pp. 168-175.

45. Letter to G. W. Curtis. *See* note 21.

46. Letter to mother, April 18, 1870, in S. Norton and Howe (eds.), *op. cit.,* I, 379.

47. Quoted in M. J. Russell, S. J., "Unpublished Letters of Aubrey de Vere," *Irish Monthly,* XXXIX (July 1911), 564.

CHAPTER TWELVE

1. Rev. Ignatius Ryder (Newman's successor at the Oratory), in the dedication of his poems to Aubrey de Vere. Quoted in Matthew J. Russell, S. J., "Poets I Have Known," *Donahoe's Magazine,* XLVI (1901), 569-570.

2. "Aubrey de Vere," *Encyclopedia Britannica* (14th ed.), VII, 283.

3. *The Foray of Queen Meave,* pp. 119-120.

4. *Ibid.,* p. 144.

5. *Legends of Saint Patrick,* p. 148.

6. *The Sisters* and *Inisfail,* p. 6.

7. *Ibid.,* pp. 139-140.

8. *Ibid.,* p. 151.

9. *Ibid.,* p. 297.

10. Aubrey de Vere, *Recollections,* pp. 354-355.

11. *The Sisters,* pp. 64-65.

12. *Legends of the Saxon Saints,* Preface, p. xlvii.

13. "If Columbus erred, . . . his greatness can well afford the admission of that error by his most ardent admirers. But the act in question was one which we cannot now judge." De Vere, *Mediaeval Records and Sonnets,* pp. 269-270 (note).

14. Preface, pp. ix, xiii.

15. Quoted in Wilfrid Ward, *Aubrey de Vere: a Memoir,* p. 368.

16. De Vere, *Recollections,* pp. 296-297.

17. "In it [*Alexander the Great*] I have endeavored to delineate the old Pagan type of heroism, of which Alexander was perhaps the chief example, and at the same time to illustrate some of the moral relations in which the chief races stood to each other, and in which the great Successive Empires stood . . . to that later Christian Civilization . . . which was one day to exalt humanity." De Vere, Ms. letter to James Russell Lowell, June 16, 1874.

18. *Alexander the Great,* Preface, pp vii-viii.

19. *Saint Thomas of Canterbury,* Preface, p. xxix.

20. *May Carols,* Preface, p. ix.

21. *Ibid.,* p. 104.

22. *Ibid.,* p. 127.

23. *The Search after Proserpine and Other Poems,* p. 67.

24. *The Sisters,* p. 42.

25. *Irish Odes and Other Poems,* p. 282.

26. *Selections from the Poems of Aubrey de Vere* (ed. G. E. Woodberry), p. 299.

27. *Ibid.,* p. 216.

28. *Proserpine,* Introduction, p. 4.

29. *Saxon Saints,* p. 26.

30. *Household Poetry Book,* p. 12.

31. *Ibid.,* p. 21.

32. *Ibid.,* p. 42.

33. *Ibid.,* p. 112.

34. *Religious Problems of the Nineteenth Century,* p. 43.

35. *Essays Chiefly on Poetry,* II, 133-134.

36. *Ibid.,* I, 36.

37. *Ibid.,* p. 14.

38. *Ibid.,* p. 37.

39. *Ibid.*, pp. 229, 232.
40. Ward, *op. cit.*, p. 333.
41. Ms. letter to Charles Eliot Norton, Oct. 1895.
42. J. R. Monsell, Ms. letter to author, 1931.
43. Letter to Norton. *See* note 41.
44. *Picturesque Sketches of Greece and Turkey,* I, 2.
45. *Ibid.*, p. 20.   .
46. *Ibid.*, p. 63.
47. *Ibid.*, p. 117.
48. *Ibid.*, p. 144.
49. *Ibid.*, p. 175.
50. *Ibid.*, II, 77.
51. *Ibid.*, p. 83.
52. *Ibid.*, pp. 97-100.
53. *Ibid.*, p. 123.
54. *Ibid.*, p. 161.
55. *Ibid.*, p. 282.
56. "Literary labor, with the hope of a result, must be a very animating thing! For a great many years I have never written anything in prose or verse without the knowledge that, on account of jealousies and animosities, either political or polemical, what I wrote was but a letter to some few friends, known and unknown . . ." De Vere, letter to Norton. Quoted in Ward, *op. cit.*, p. 256.
57. "As I have failed to interest the public by my own poetry, which (besides its demerits) had, as I well knew when writing it, the disadvantage of unpopular themes (though themes well worthy of song, and too long neglected), I became the more desirous to benefit the cause of Poetry . . . by directing the attention of the young to some of the best poets we have had." De Vere, letter to Henry Taylor. Quoted in Ward, *op. cit.*, pp. 257-258.
58. Pp. 126-127.
59. P. 304.
60. *Alfred Tennyson,* pp. 503, 200.

Published Works of Aubrey de Vere

POETRY

Alexander the Great. London: King, 1874.
Antar and Zara: An Eastern Romance. London: King, 1877.
The Foray of Queen Meave. London: Kegan, Paul, Trench, 1882.
Irish Odes and other Poems. New York: Catholic Publication Society, 1869.
Legends and Records of the Church and the Empire. London: Kegan, Paul, 1887.
Legends of St. Patrick. London: Cassell, 1889; Macmillan, 1892.
Legends of the Saxon Saints. London: Kegan, Paul, 1879.
May Carols. London: Richardson, 1870; Burns & Oates, 1881.
Mediaeval Records and Sonnets. London: Macmillan, 1893.
Poems from the Works of Aubrey de Vere (edited by Lady Margaret Domvile). London: Catholic Truth Society, 1904.
Saint Thomas of Canterbury. London: King, 1876.
The Search after Proserpine and other Poems. London: Kegan, Paul, 1884.
Selections from the Poems of Aubrey de Vere (edited by George Edward Woodberry). New York: Macmillan, 1894.
The Sisters and Inisfail. London: Longmans, 1867.

PROSE

Constitutional and Unconstitutional Political Action. Limerick: McKern, 1881.
English Misrule and Irish Misdeeds. London: Murray, 1848.
Essays, Chiefly on Poetry, 2 vols. London: Macmillan, 1887.
Essays, Literary and Ethical. London: Macmillan, 1889.
Ireland and Proportionate Representation. Dublin: Hodges & Figgis, 1885.
Ireland's Church Question. London: Longmans, 1868.
Picturesque Sketches of Greece and Turkey, 2 vols. London: Bentley, 1850.
Recollections. New York: Arnold, 1897.
Religious Problems of the Nineteenth Century. London: St. Anselm's Society, 1893.

Miscellaneous Articles

Household Poetry Book (edited with biographical and critical notes, by Aubrey de Vere). London: Burns & Oates, 1886.

"Ireland's Sins and Ireland's Hopes," *Fraser's Magazine*, September 1850.

"Irish Colonization," *Edinburgh Review*, XCIII, 1850.

"Irish National Education," *Dublin Review*, February 1860.

"Literature in Its Relation with Religion," *The Month* (England), IV, 1866.

"The Plague of Controversy," *Dublin Review*, June 1854.

Preface to *Heroines of Charity*. New York: Sadlier, 1855.

Select Specimens of the Poets (edited with biographical notes by Aubrey de Vere). London: Burns & Lambert, 1860.

"Thoughts on Saint Gertrude," *The Month*, III, 1865; *Catholic World*, II, 1865.

Reviews

Hartley Coleridge, *Works (Edinburgh Review*, XCIV, July 1851).

Mrs. Jameson, *Legends of the Madonna (Dublin Review*, March 1853).

Henry Wadsworth Longfellow, *Poems (Dublin Review*, February 1860).

Coventry Patmore, *The Angel in the House (Edinburgh Review*, January 1858).

J. Endell Taylor, *Principles of Christian Worship (Dublin Review*, March 1853).

Alfred Tennyson, *The Princess (Edinburgh Review*, XC, October 1849).

Unpublished Writings of Aubrey de Vere

Diary, October 31, 1845—December 10, 1846.

Notes on Alice Meynell's early poems, undated, probably enclosed in de Vere's letters to her, July 2, 1874—January 5, 1877.

Manuscript letters.

Manuscripts relating to Aubrey de Vere
(in possession of author)

Letters to him.

Letters between his friends.

Letters to the author.

Secondary Works: General and Special

Abernethy, Julian. *English Literature*. New York: Merrill, 1916.

Alexander, Calvert, S. J. *The Catholic Literary Revival*. Milwaukee: Bruce, 1935.

Allingham, William. *A Diary* (edited by H. Allingham and D. Radford). London: Macmillan, 1907.

————. *Letters* (edited by H. Allingham and E. Baumer Williams). London: Longmans, 1911.

Bald, Robert Cecil. *Literary Friendships in the Age of Wordsworth*. Cambridge: University Press, 1932.

Batho, Edith. *The Later Wordsworth*. New York: Macmillan, 1933.

Beatty, Frederika. *William Wordsworth of Rydal Mount*. New York: E. P. Dutton, 1939.

Benson, Arthur Christopher. *Alfred Tennyson*. New York: E. P. Dutton, 1907.

Bishop, Maria Catherine. *A Memoir of Mrs. Augustus Craven* (Pauline de la Ferronnays), 2 vols. London: Bentley, 1894.

Blunden, Edmund. *Leigh Hunt and His Circle*. New York: Harpers, 1930.

Bregy, Katherine. *Poets' Chantry*. St. Louis: B. Herder, 1912.

Brooke, Stopford A. *Tennyson: His Art and Relation to Modern Life*. New York: Putnam, 1894.

————, and Rolleston, T. W. *A Treasury of Irish Poetry*. New York: Macmillan, 1923.

Brookfield, Charles and Frances. *Mrs. Brookfield and Her Circle*, 2 vols. New York: Scribners, 1905.

Broughton, Leslie Nathan (ed.). *Sara Coleridge and Henry Reed*. Ithaca: Cornell University Press, 1937.

———— (ed.). *Wordsworth and Reed*. Ithaca: Cornell University Press, 1933.

Burdett, Osbert. *The Idea of Coventry Patmore*. London: Oxford University Press, 1921.

Cambridge History of English Literature. New York: Macmillan, 1932. Vols. XI-XIII.

Carlyle, Jane Welsh. *Letters to Her Family* (edited by Leonard Huxley), London: Murray, 1924.

————. *New Letters and Memorials* (edited by Alexander Carlyle). New York: John Lane, 1903.

Champreys, Basil. *Coventry Patmore*, 2 vols. London: Bell, 1900.

Chesterton, Gilbert Keith. *Saint Francis of Assisi*. New York: George H. Doran, 1924.

————. *The Victorian Age in Literature*. New York: Henry Holt, 1913.

Coleridge, Edith. *Memoir and Letters of Sara Coleridge* (edited by Her Daughter). New York: Harpers, 1874.

Coleridge, Ernest Hartley. *Life and Correspondence of John Duke Lord Coleridge,* 2 vols. New York: Appleton, 1904.

Colvin, Sir Sidney. *Memories and Notes.* London: Arnold, 1921.

Cook, E. T. *Life of Ruskin,* 2 vols. London: George Allen, 1911.

Cooke, John D., and Stevenson, Lionel. *English Literature of the Victorian Period.* New York: Appleton-Century-Crofts, 1949.

Deering, Arthur. *Sir Samuel Ferguson, Poet and Antiquarian.* Philadelphia: University of Pennsylvania, 1931. (Dissertation).

De Selincourt, Ernest. *The Prelude.* London: Oxford University Press, 1926.

De Vere, Sir Aubrey. *Sonnets.* London: Pickering, 1875.

Dowden, Edward. *Letters of Edward Dowden and His Correspondents.* New York: E. P. Dutton, 1914.

————. *Shakspere: His Mind and Art* (10th ed.). London: Paul, Trench, Trubner, 1892.

Duffy, Sir Gavan. *Conversations with Carlyle.* New York: Scribners, 1892.

Dunn, Stanley Gerald. "A Note on Wordsworth's Metaphysical System," *Essays and Studies by Members of the English Association,* Vol. XVIII. London: Oxford University Press, 1933.

Elton, Oliver. *A Survey of English Literature* (1780-1880), 4 vols. New York: Macmillan, 1924.

Emerson, Ralph Waldo. *Journals* (edited by Edward Waldo Emerson), 10 vols. Boston: Houghton Mifflin, 1909. Vol. VII.

Fausset, Hugh L'Anson. *Tennyson: A Modern Portrait.* New York: Appleton, 1923.

Ferguson, Lady Mary Catherine. *Sir Samuel Ferguson in the Ireland of His Day,* 2 vols. Edinburgh: Blackwood, 1896.

Fields, Annie. *Authors and Friends.* Boston: Houghton Mifflin, 1897.

Forster, John. *Walter Savage Landor: A Biography,* Vol. I; *Works and Life,* Vol. II. London: Chapman and Hall, 1874.

Fox, Caroline. *Journals and Letters* (edited by Horace N. Pym). Philadelphia: Lippincott, 1882.

Froude, James Anthony. *Thomas Carlyle: A History of His Life in London,* 2 vols. New York: Harpers, 1884.

Garnett, Richard, and Gosse, Edmund. *An Illustrated History of English Literature,* 4 vols. London: Macmillan, 1931.

Garrod, Heathcote William. *Wordsworth: Lectures and Essays.* Oxford: Clarendon Press, 1927.

Gilder, Richard Watson. *Letters* (edited by Rosamond Gilder). Boston: Houghton Mifflin, 1916.

Gosse, Edmund. *Coventry Patmore.* New York: Scribners, 1905.

————. "Aubrey de Vere," *Portraits and Sketches.* London: Heinemann, 1912.

Graves, Alfred Perceval. *The Book of Irish Poetry.* London: Fisher, n.d.

_____. *Irish Literature and Musical Studies.* London: Mathews, 1913.

_____. *To Return to All That.* London: Jonathan Cape, 1930.

Graves, Robert Perceval. *Life of Sir William Rowan Hamilton,* 3 vols. Dublin: Hodges & Figgis, 1882.

Griggs, Earl Leslie. *Coleridge Fille.* London: Oxford University Press, 1940.

_____. *Hartley Coleridge: His Life and Work.* London: University of London Press, 1929.

Gunning, John P. *Aubrey de Vere: A Memoir.* Limerick: Guy, 1902.

Hall-Patch, W. *Father Faber.* New York: Kenedy, 1914.

Hanson, Lawrence and Elizabeth. *Necessary Evil: The Life of Jane Welsh Carlyle.* New York: Macmillan, 1952.

Harper, George McLean. *William Wordsworth: His Life, Works and Influence,* 2 vols. London: Murray, 1929.

Higginson, Thomas W. *Henry Wadsworth Longfellow.* Boston: Houghton Mifflin, 1902.

Holland, Bernard Henry. *Memoir of Kenelm Henry Digby.* London: Longmans, 1919.

Hopkins, Gerard Manley. *Letters of Gerard Manley Hopkins to Robert Bridges* (edited by Claude Colleer Abbott). London: Oxford University Press, 1935.

_____. *The Correspondence of Gerard Manley Hopkins and Richard Watson Dixon* (edited by Claude Colleer Abbott). London: Oxford University Press, 1935.

Horton, Robert F. *Alfred Tennyson: A Saintly Life.* London: Dent, 1900.

Hudson, Henry N. *Studies in Wordsworth.* Boston: Little Brown, 1884.

Hunt, Leigh. *Autobiography* (edited by Roger Ingpen), 2 vols. New York: E. P. Dutton, 1850.

Hutton, Richard Holt. *Cardinal Newman.* London: Methuen, 1905.

_____. *Contemporary Thought and Thinkers,* 2 vols. London: Macmillan, 1894. Vol. II.

James, Henry. *Letters* (edited by Percy Lubbock), 2 vols. London: Scribners, 1920.

Knight, William (ed.) *Letters to the Wordsworth Family,* 3 vols. Boston: Ginn, 1907.

_____. *Retrospects,* 1st series. London: Smith Elder, 1904.

_____ (ed.). *Wordsworthiana.* London: Macmillan, 1889.

Landor, Walter Savage. *Letters, Private and Public* (edited by Stephen Wheeler). London: Duckworth, 1899.

Legouis, Emile, and Cazamian, Louis. *History of English Literature.* New York: Macmillan, 1930.

Legouis, Emile. *Wordsworth in a New Light.* Boston: Harvard University Press, 1923.

Leslie, Shane. *Henry Edward Manning: His Life and Labors.* London: Burns, Oates and Washburne, 1921.

Longfellow, Ernest W. *Random Memories.* Boston: Houghton Mifflin, 1922.

Longfellow, Samuel L. *Life of Henry Wadsworth Longfellow,* 3 vols. Boston: Houghton Mifflin, 1891.

Lousbury, Thomas R. *The Life and Times of Tennyson.* New Haven: Yale University Press, 1915.

Lowell, James Russell. *Letters* (edited by Charles Eliot Norton). New York: Harpers, 1894.

Massingham, H. J., and Hugh (eds.). *The Great Victorians..* New York: Doubleday Doran, 1932.

Maurice, Frederick. *The Life of Frederick Denison Maurice.* New York: Scribners, 1884.

May, Lewis J. *Cardinal Newman.* New York: Lincoln MacVeagh, 1930.

Meynell, Alice. *Poems.* New York: Scribners, 1925.

Meynell, Viola. *Alice Meynell: A Memoir.* New York: Scribners, 1929.

Miles, Alfred H. *Poets and Poetry of the Nineteenth Century.* London: Routledge, 1891.

Minchin, Harry C. *Last Days, Letters and Conversations of Walter Savage Landor.* London: Methuen, 1928.

Moulton, Charles W. (ed.). *Library of Literary Criticism,* 8 vols. Buffalo: Moulton Publishing Company, 1908. Vol VIII.

Navarro, Mary Anderson de. *A Few Memories.* London: Osgood McIlvaine, 1896.

_____. *A Few More Memories.* London: Hutchinson, 1936.

Nicoll, W. Robertson, and Wise, Thomas J. *Literary Anecdotes of the Nineteenth Century.* London: Hodder and Stoughton, 1896.

Nicolson, Harold. *Tennyson.* Boston: Houghton Mifflin, 1925.

Norton, Charles Eliot. *Letters* (edited by Sara Norton and M. A. de Wolfe Howe). Boston: Houghton Mifflin, 1913.

Noyes, Alfred. "Tennyson and Some Recent Critics," *Some Aspects of Modern Poetry.* New York: Stokes, 1924.

O'Neill, George, S. J. "Catholic Activity in English," *Representative Catholic Essays* (edited by G. Carver and E. Geyer). New York: Macmillan, 1927.

_____. *Essays on Poetry.* Dublin: The Talbot Press, 1919.

Patmore, Coventry. *Poems.* With Introduction by Basil Champneys. London: Bell, 1906.

Patmore, Derek. *Portrait of My Family.* New York: Harpers, 1935.

Paul, Herbert. *Men and Letters.* London: John Lane, 1901.

Purcell, Edmund Sheridan. *Life of Cardinal Manning,* 2 vols. London: Macmillan, 1896.

Rannie, David Watson. *Wordsworth and His Circle*. London: Methuen, 1907.

Read, Herbert. *Wordsworth—The Clark Lectures*. New York: Jonathan Cape and Harrison, 1931.

Reid, T. Wemyss. *Life, Letters and Friendships of Richard Monckton Milnes,* 2 vols. New York: Cassell, 1891.

Robinson, Henry Crabb. *Correspondence with the Wordsworth Circle* (edited by Edith J. Morley), 2 vols. Oxford: Clarendon Press, 1927.

————. *Diary, Reminiscences, and Correspondence* (edited by Thomas Sadler), 2 vols. London: Macmillan, 1872.

Robinson, Lennox (ed.). *Golden Treasury of Irish Verse*. New York: Macmillan, 1932.

Ruskin, John. *Letters* (edited by Charles Eliot Norton), 2 vols. Boston: Houghton Mifflin, 1904.

————. *Modern Painters,* 5 vols. New York: Wiley, n.d. Vol. III.

————. *Praeterita*. Boston: Dana Estes, 1885.

Shairp, J. C., *Recollections of a Tour in Scotland* (3rd ed.). Edinburgh: Douglas, 1894.

Sharp, Elizabeth A. *William Sharp* (Fiona MacLeoad): *A Memoir*. New York: Duffield, 1910.

————, and Sharp, Mathay J. *Lyra Celtica*. Edinburgh: John Grant, 1924.

Sheehan, Canon Patrick. *Early Essays and Lectures*. London: Longmans Green, 1906.

Shuster, George A. *The Catholic Spirit in Modern English Literature*. New York: Macmillan, 1922.

Smith, Thomas F. A. *Life and Literary Works of Mrs. Augustus Craven*. Nürnberg: Nister, 1910.

Snead-Cox, J. G. *Life of Cardinal Vaughan,* 2 vols. London: Herbert and Daniel, 1910.

Spring-Rice, Sir Cecil. *The Letters and Friendships* (edited by Stephen Gwynn), 2 vols. Boston: Houghton Mifflin, 1929.

Squire, T. C. *Cambridge Book of Lesser Poets*. New York: Macmillan, 1927.

Stedman, Edmund Clarence. *Victorian Poets*. Boston: Houghton Mifflin, 1903.

Taylor, Henry. *Autobiography,* 2 vols. New York: Harpers, 1885.

————. *Correspondence* (edited by Edward Dowden). London: Longmans, 1888.

————. *Notes from Books* (2nd ed.). London: Murray, 1849.

Taylor, Una. *Guests and Memories*. London: Oxford University Press, 1924.

Tennyson, Charles. *Alfred Tennyson*. New York: Macmillan, 1949.

Tennyson, Hallam Lord. *Alfred Lord Tennyson: A Memoir,* 2 vols. London: Macmillan, 1897.

_____. *Tennyson and His Friends*. New York: Macmillan, 1911.

Thompson, Francis. *A Renegade Poet and Other Essays*. Boston: Ball Publishing Company, 1910.

Tuell, Anne Kimball. *Mrs. Meynell and Her Literary Generation*. New York: E. P. Dutton, 1925.

Tynan, Katharine. *The Middle Years*. London: Constable, 1916.

_____. *Twenty Five Years Reminiscences*. New York: Devin-Adair, 1913.

Walker, Hugh. *The Literature of the Victorian Era*. London: Cambridge University Press, 1931.

Ward, Maisie. *The Wilfrid Wards and the Transition*. New York: Sheed and Ward, 1934.

Ward, Wilfrid. *Aubrey de Vere: A Memoir*. London: Longmans, 1904.

_____. *Men and Matters*. New York: Longmans, 1914.

_____. *Ten Personal Studies*. London: Longmans, 1908.

_____. *Life of John Henry Cardinal Newman*, 2 vols. London: Longmans Green, 1927.

Warren, Herbert T. *The Centenary of Tennyson*. London: Oxford University Press, 1909.

Watson, William. *Poems,* 2 vols. London: John Lane, 1905. Vol. II.

Watts, M. S. *George Frederic Watts: The Annals of An Artist's Life,* 2 vols. New York: George H. Doran, 1913.

Wilson, David Alec. *Carlyle at His Zenith*. London: Kegan Paul, Trench, Trubner, 1927.

_____. *Carlyle on Cromwell and Others*. London: Kegan Paul, Trench, Trubner, 1925.

Winchester, Caleb. *An Old Castle and Other Essays*. New York: Macmillan, 1922.

Woodberry, George Edward. *Literary Memoirs of the Nineteenth Century*. New York: Harcourt Brace, 1921.

_____. "Aubrey de Vere," *Makers of Literature*. New York: Macmillan, 1900.

_____. *Studies of a Litterateur*. New York: Harcourt Brace, 1921.

Wordsworth, Christopher. *Memoirs of William Wordsworth*. Boston: Ticknor, Reed and Fields, 1851.

Wordsworth, Dorothy. *Journals* (edited by William Knight). London: Macmillan, 1924.

Wordsworth, Willam. *Complete Poetical Works* (edited by Andrew J. George). Boston: Houghton Mifflin, 1904.

_____. *Poems,* 2 vols. London: W. Kent, 1880.

_____. *Poetical Works* (edited, with Memoir, by Edward Dowden), 7 vols. London: Bell, 1893.

_____. *Poetical Works,* Vols. I-IX; *Life,* Vols. X-XII (edited by William Knight). Edinburgh: Paterson, 1899.

_____. *Poetical Works* (edited by Henry Reed). Philadelphia: James Kay, 1837.

_____. *Prose Works* (edited by Alexander B. Grosart), 3 vols. London: Moxon, 1876.

_____. *Prose Works* (edited by William Knight). London: Macmillan, 1896.

Yarnall, Ellis. *Wordsworth and the Coleridges.* New York: Macmillan, 1899.

Secondary Materials: Periodicals

"Aubrey de Vere," *The Catholic World,* LXXIV (October 1901), 567.

"Aubrey de Vere, Poet," *Edinburgh Review,* CCI (1905), 27-54.

"Aubrey de Vere: His Personality and Friendships," *The Literary Digest,* XXIX (July—December 1904), 597-598.

"Aubrey de Vere," *The New Era,* August 26, 1899.

"Aubrey de Vere," *The Saturday Review* (England), XCIX (January 1905), 85.

"Aubrey de Vere" (obituary notices), *The Tablet,* January 24, 1902; *The Weekly Register,* January 24, 1902.

Barnes, John. "Hands Across St. George's Channel," *The Catholic World,* CXI (April—September 1920), 649-658.

Barrington, Michael. "The Philosophy of Aubrey de Vere," *Temple Bar,* CXXXI (January—June 1905), 664-680.

"Cardinal Manning as Recollected by Aubrey de Vere," *The Weekly Register,* September 4, 1897.

Cunningham, Rev. Francis A. "Father Faber," *Donahoe's Magazine,* XLV (January—June 1901), 540-557.

Dennis, John. Letter to Editor, *The Spectator,* LXXXVIII (1902), 174-175.

Eglinton, John. "Wordsworth at Rydal Mount," *Fortnightly Review,* XCV: New Series (February 1914), 345-356.

George, Andrew J. "Aubrey de Vere," *Atlantic Monthly,* LXXXIX (June 1902), 829-835.

Gosse, Edmund. "Aubrey de Vere" (poem), *Fortnightly Review,* LXXI: New Series (February 1902), 342.

Hutton, Richard Holt. "Poetical Works of Aubrey de Vere," *The Spectator,* LVII (1884), 1407-1409.

Meynell, Alice. "Aubrey de Vere," Ceylon *Catholic Messenger,* September 23, 1881.

_____. "Father Tabb," *The Catholic World,* XC (October 1909—March 1910), 577.

_____. "Tennyson," *Dublin Review,* CXLVI (January—April 1910), 62-71.

Meynell, Wilfrid. "Et Cetera," *The Tablet,* January 25, 1902.

————. "Thomas à Becket and St. Thomas of Canterbury," *The World,* September 3, 1879.

Myers, Ernest. Letter to Editor, *The Spectator,* LXXXVIII (1902), 213.

O'Connor, R. F. "A Notable Convert" (Aubrey de Vere), *American Catholic Quarterly Review* (Philadelphia), XXXIX (1914), 215-231.

O'Neill, George, S.J. "A Centenary of Aubrey de Vere," *Irish Monthly,* XLII (1914), 237-244.

"The Poems by Alfred Tennyson," *The Quarterly Review,* LXX (1842), 385-416.

Russell, Matthew J., S.J. "Poets I Have Known," *Donahoe's Magazine,* XLVI (July—December 1901), 555-570.

————. "Unpublished Letters of Aubrey de Vere," *Irish Monthly,* XXXIX (1911); XL (1912); XLII (1914); XLIII (1915).

Smith, Helen Grace. "Aubrey de Vere," *Irish Monthly,* XXVII (1899), 64-71.

————. "Talks with Aubrey de Vere," *Weekly Register,* February 11, 1899.

Smith, Walter George. "Aubrey de Vere," *Alumni Register* (University of Pennsylvania), VII (May 1902), 381-392.

Taylor, I. A. "Recollections of Aubrey de Vere," *The Catholic World,* LXVI (October 1897—March 1898), 621-633.

Towle, E. A. "Aubrey de Vere: A Portrait," *The Month* (England), C (September 1902), 232-243.

————. "Recollections of Aubrey de Vere," *Sewanee Review,* VII (July 1899), 271-286.

Wall, G. E. "Stray Words from Walter Savage Landor," *The Critic,* XXXVIII (March 1901), 238-240.

Will of Aubrey de Vere, *The Athenaeum,* April 5, 1902.

"Wordsworth, Mrs. Hemans and R. P. Graves," *The London Mercury,* VI (May—October 1922), 395.

INDEX

NIHIL OBSTAT:

GUSTAVUS DUMAS, S.J. *Censor Deputatus*

IMPRIMATUR:

EDUARDUS P. HOAR, LL.D., P.A. *Vicarius Generalis*

Brooklyni, die XXVIII Martii 1953.